# Launder and Gilliat

MANCHESTER
UNIVERSITY PRESS

**BRIAN MCFARLANE, NEIL SINYARD** *series editors*

ALLEN EYLES, PHILIP FRENCH, SUE HARPER,
TIM PULLEINE, JEFFREY RICHARDS, TOM RYALL
*series advisers*

# Launder and Gilliat

BRUCE BABINGTON

**Manchester University Press**

MANCHESTER AND NEW YORK

distributed exclusively in the USA by Palgrave

*Published by* Manchester University Press
Oxford Road, Manchester M13 9NR, UK
*and* Room 400, 175 Fifth Avenue, New York, NY 10010, USA
www.manchesteruniversitypress.co.uk

*Distributed exclusively in the USA by*
Palgrave, 175 Fifth Avenue, New York,
NY 10010, USA

*Distributed exclusively in Canada by*
UBC Press, University of British Columbia, 2029 West Mall,
Vancouver, BC, Canada V6T 1Z2

*British Library Cataloguing-in-Publication Data*
A catalogue record for this book is available from the British Library

*Library of Congress Cataloging-in-Publication Data applied for*

ISBN 0 7190 5667 5 *hardback*
      0 7190 5668 3 *paperback*

First published 2002

10  09  08  07  06  05  04  03  02          10  9  8  7  6  5  4  3  2  1

Typeset in Scala with Meta display
by Koinonia, Manchester
Printed in Great Britain
by Bookcraft (Bath) Ltd, Midsomer Norton

To the Civic, St James, Odeon, Plaza, Regent, Embassy, Oxford, Roxy, Tivoli, Rialto (Newmarket), Victory (Green Lane), Crystal Palace (Mount Eden), Berkeley (Mission Bay), Tudor (Remuera), and all the other sites of a 1950s filmgoing childhood.

# Contents

LIST OF PLATES                                                    *page* viii
SERIES EDITORS' FOREWORD                                                  ix
ACKNOWLEDGEMENTS                                                           x

1   Introduction: Produced, written and directed by Frank
    Launder and Sidney Gilliat                                            1

2   Keeping the home fires burning: the home front trilogy
    – *Millions like Us, Two Thousand Women, Waterloo Road*              44

3   Very individual pictures: *The Rake's Progress, I See a
    Dark Stranger*                                                       94

4   'Happy days': *The Blue Lagoon, The Happiest Days of
    Your Life, The Belles of St Trinian's*, etc.                        134

5   Authors and genres: thrillers and comedies                         175

6   Last words                                                          207

FILMOGRAPHY                                                             210
SELECT BIBLIOGRAPHY                                                     238
INDEX                                                                   241

# List of plates

1  *The Story of Gilbert and Sullivan*                           *page* 37

2  *Millions Like Us* 1                                               38

3  *Millions Like Us* 2                                               38

4  Frank Launder and Sidney Gilliat                                   39

5  *2000 Women*                                                       40

6  *Waterloo Road*                                                    40

7  *The Rake's Progress*                                              41

8  *I See a Dark Stranger*                                            41

9  *The Blue Lagoon*                                                  42

10  *The Happiest Days of Your Life*                                  43

All illustrations reproduced courtesy of BFI films: Stills, Posters and Designs. Every effort has been made to obtain permission to reproduce the illustrations in this book. If any proper acknowledgement has not been made, copyright-holders are invited to contact the publisher.

# Series editors' foreword

The aim of this series is to present in lively, authoritative volumes a guide to those film-makers who have made British cinema a rewarding but still under-researched branch of world cinema. The intention is to provide books which are up-to-date in terms of information and critical approach, but not bound to any one theoretical methodology. Though all books in the series will have certain elements in common – comprehensive filmographies, annotated bibliographies, appropriate illustration – the actual critical tools employed will be the responsibility of the individual authors.

Nevertheless, an important recurring element will be a concern for how the oeuvre of each film-maker does or does not fit certain critical and industrial contexts, as well as for the wider social contexts, which helped to shape not just that particular film-maker but the course of British cinema at large.

Although the series is director-orientated, the editors believe that a variety of stances and contexts referred to is more likely to reconceptualize and reappraise the phenomenon of British cinema as a complex, shifting field of production. All the texts in the series will engage in detailed discussion of major works of the film-makers involved, but they all consider as well the importance of other key collaborators, of studio organisation, of audience reception, of recurring themes and structures: all those other aspects which go towards the construction of a national cinema.

The series will explore and chart a field which is more than ripe for serious excavation. The acknowledged leaders of the field will be reappraised; just as important, though, will be the bringing to light of those who have not so far received any serious attention. They are all part of the very rich texture of British cinema, and it will be the work of this series to give them all their due.

# Acknowledgements

Thanks to the following: Andrew Higson, Charles Barr, Neil Sinyard and Allan Kibble for help with finding copies of films; Andrew Moor, John Saunders and Ron Guariento for insightful conversations about British film; Peter Evans – note the passage on p. 8 on Launder and Gilliat's working methods which so pleasantly calls to mind our own more modest but equally unruffled years of collaboration; Desmond Graham for conversations about World War II; my British Film 1 classes at Newcastle University for their insights about Launder and Gilliat; the Department of English Literary and Linguistic Studies at Newcastle University for research grants spent on viewing films and microfiches; Neil Sinyard for offering and encouraging the project. As a later writer on Launder and Gilliat I owe a debt to Geoff Brown's *Launder and Gilliat* (1977), a major piece of scholarship not only on the pair but on the British film industry. Thanks too to Helen Tuton and Hermann Moisl for word-processing expertise that kept the text from disappearing, and to Khun Jiab for insisting that I put more jokes in and tolerating all my disappearances between dinner and *Frasier*.

# Introduction
# Produced, written and directed
# by Frank Launder and Sidney Gilliat

> Genius, Arthur, isn't the delicate plant Grace thinks it is, oh no,
> no, no. It's as hardy as a Jerusalem artichoke. (Grace's Father
> (Wilfred Hyde-White) in *The Story of Gilbert and Sullivan* (1953))

## Signs and symbols

It is one of the most familiar trademark signatures in British film,
along with Gainsborough's lady, the Archers' arrowstruck target,
Rank's muscular gong beater and London Films' Houses of
Parliament. The basic pattern (varied slightly over Launder and
Gilliat's long partnership) is a medium long shot of the interior of
a film studio, the foreground dominated by the silhouettes of two
canvas chairs. In the background technical staff move around
setting the film stage for a shot. The camera closes in on the two
chairs, the backs of which are lit to reveal that one is labelled
FRANK LAUNDER and the other SIDNEY GILLIAT. Other graphics are
then added to construct over the scene the notation A FRANK
LAUNDER AND SIDNEY GILLIAT PRODUCTION.

Over the years this brief prelude collects many pleasurable
associations from the films it introduces, some of which will be
explored in this book devoted to one of the great partnerships of
British film. Beginnings, as Monescu remarks in Lubitsch's
*Trouble in Paradise* (1932), are always difficult, but one solution is
to attend briefly to this beginning of almost every Launder and
Gilliat film from 1945 on, and to inspect the vignette through

which Launder and Gilliat constantly announced themselves. Their logo is not overtly metaphoric in the way that Gainsborough's elegant female portrait, the Archers' patriotic conflation of Agincourt, the RAF and a touch of the outlaw, Korda's assertion of the centrality of Britain or Rank's of the exoticism of Empire are. Launder and Gilliat made some of their most significant films under Rank's patronage and drew attention to that sheltering sign, just after they ceased working with Rank, in *The Happiest Days of Your Life* (1950). Here, instructed to sound the school gong, Miss Gossage (Joyce Grenfell) whacks it so enthusiastically that Miss Whitchurch (Margaret Rutherford) admonishes her by saying, 'A tap, Gossage, I said a tap. You're not introducing a film' – a moment that takes on nostalgic intertextual resonance when in sound-track quotation it forms the beginning of Terence Davies's *The Long Day Closes* (1993), where it functions, *primus inter pares*, as a synecdoche for the enchantments of 1940s and 1950s cinema.

Launder and Gilliat's joke, with its self-consciousness about opening signs and proprietory symbols, licenses a reading of their sign along the following lines. Theirs is basically a realistic working scene, as befits two film-makers who spent long lifetimes working on films at almost every non-technological stage of preproduction, production and postproduction, with the exception of editing. Yet, though it plays down metaphor, it is also not without a certain glamour, an understated touch of the romance of technology, and, for all its modesty, more than a hint of self-assertion in the forward movement of the camera and the sudden lighting of the names on the chairs. Projecting themselves in their Press Director Iris De Cartier's Individual Films publicity as 'one of the most businesslike partnerships in British film',[1] constantly working craftsmen rather than self-proclaimed auteurs they might have been, but they cared enough about their films and their dual name to bring a court case over an NBC (American) television screening of *The Constant Husband* (1953) so broken up by advertisements that they considered their reputations compromised.[2]

Equally, the signature scene emphasizes, in the details that make up the background work on the set – someone striding across stage carrying a script or log book, staff shifting furniture, a lighting technician attending to lamps, etc. – the everyday processes of film-making in a way that the other logos do not, pointing to the labour associated with film-making and the multiple contributions necessary to the making of any feature film. All this coexists with, rather than cancels out, the not unpowerful foregrounding of the producers' names and the auteurist force of the announcement that completes the title sequence of all their films, some version of WRITTEN AND DIRECTED BY FRANK LAUNDER AND SIDNEY GILLIAT. (The ideal case as with *Millions Like Us* (1943), later breaking up into variants where one or both wrote, and one directed, but both produced.)

## Short view of a long haul: Launder and Gilliat 1928–42

As the twin-chair logo suggests, Launder and Gilliat are names that now belong together as inevitably as the Hobbs and Sutcliffe that Charters and Caldicott (Basil Radford's and Naunton Wayne's serial comic characters in *The Lady Vanishes* (1939) *Night Train to Munich* (1940), and *Millions Like Us*) would have suggested, the Gilbert and Sullivan they made a biopic about, or their younger film-making contemporaries, the identical twins, the Boulting Brothers, Roy and John. Initially used in *I See a Dark Stranger* (1946), the second film Launder and Gilliat co-produced for their company Individual Pictures (in a basic prototype, with the chairs but without camera movement and lighting up of the names, and with no technical staff in the background), some version of it continued to appear to the end of their careers, whatever the variations of writing and directorial credits on their films and after they metamorphosed Individual Pictures into Launder-Gilliat Productions Ltd. in 1950, and then worked with London Films, and, in the later part of their career, predominantly with British Lion Films.

Yet, of course, Launder and Gilliat weren't born in a Siamese-twin-like entanglement and they pursued independent, though almost chronologically identical careers, in the late 1920s and early and mid-1930s British film industry. Gilliat, a year younger (born in 1908 to Launder's 1907), made the marginally faster beginning. After reading History and English at London University he followed his father into journalism, where he made a transition to the film industry when W. C. Mycroft, the film critic of the *Standard*, became scenario chief at the new British International Pictures and hired the 21-year-old hopeful book critic, who almost immediately was marginally involved with major projects, writing titles for a Jack Buchanan vehicle, *Toni* (Arthur Maude, made in 1928) and for Hitchcock's *Champagne* (1928), and doing research work, again for a Hitchcock film, *The Manxman* (also made in 1928). Launder, while a young civil servant in the Office of Bank-ruptcies (a period remembered in the comedy of bureaucracy in *The Happiest Days of Your Life* and the *St Trinian's* cycle), had ambitions both as an actor with the Brighton Repertory Company and as a playwright. Also beginning his film career at Elstree Studios with British International Pictures, Launder's first major opportunity was as joint scenarist on a version of Hardy's *Under the Greenwood Tree* (1929). In fact the future partnership was teasingly prefigured with this film by Gilliat's working on it as an uncredited literary advisor.[3]

From these beginnings both young writers worked at full pelt over the next ten years on an almost unbelievable number of films. If this apprenticeship, in a firmly commercial industry with infrequent pretensions to art, produced only a few substantial works, it clearly was full of practical lessons in film-making under tight constraints and stringent financial and temporal pressures that stood Launder and Gilliat in good stead in their later careers. The capacities and influences that turned them into more than ordinary film-makers, touched with genius in perhaps half a dozen films and with more than common abilities in many others, are harder to trace than those that gave them their energetic general competence. But this competence is important, and in both men's early careers the variety of tasks that they undertook, based around their dominant scriptwriting interests, grounded them in the pragmatic realities of film-making. Thus both men wrote titles for silent films. Both frequently worked in screenwriting partner-ships with other writers. Both vetted the work of other scenarists

(Launder doing substantial work as a script editor) and also were brought in many times to patch up other writers' scripts. Both wrote story outlines for other writers. Both adapted novels and plays. Both also experienced the peculiar restraints of creating vehicles for well-known comedians, a discipline which helped them when writing for comic actors like Alastair Sim and Margaret Rutherford in *The Happiest Days of Your Life*. (Launder worked with Max Miller, Will Hay and The Crazy Gang, while Gilliat worked with the Hulberts, Jack and Claude.) Gilliat also worked on MGM's British-based production of the glossy, pseudo-English but enormously effective *A Yank at Oxford* (Jack Conway, 1938), which though it may have been traumatic for the writer, unused to Hollywood assembly-line writing, must have impressed with its high Hollywood production values, much greater than those of most English films of the period. Gilliat, in particular, had early experience as an assistant director on a couple of Walter Forde's films in 1929 and was an uncredited associate producer to Edward Black at Gainsborough in 1935–36, prefiguring the executive and producing role the pair later took up with British Lion Films from 1958 on, which occupied (too) much of their time in later life.[4] Apart and together they must have picked up many hints from the more talented directors they worked with, Walter Forde, Victor Saville, Robert Stevenson, Jack Conway and, of course, Hitchcock and Carol Reed. Gilliat in fact had close relations both with Jack Conway, the director of *A Yank at Oxford*, who was interested in taking him to America, and with Hitchcock, who invited him to Hollywood to work on *Rebecca*, an offer he declined. There is no doubt that this varied training aided the ability to work creatively under pressure which their busy partnership exhibited.

By the late 1930s both Launder and Gilliat were well known individually as writers. In 1936 they had their first joint screen-writing collaboration, on de Courville's *Seven Sinners*, an engaging thriller with railway elements that were to feature in several famous films which they scripted, most notably Hitchcock's *The Lady Vanishes* and Reed's *Night Train to Munich,* elements which Gilliat had prefigured in his 1932 script for Walter Forde's *Rome*

*Express*. Besides being a virtuosic piece of plotting, *Seven Sinners* illustrates the pair's adaptability, for part of its appeal was based on the American actors Constance Cummings and Edmund Lowe whose comic-antagonistic romance echoes romantic comedy Screwball couples like William Powell and Myrna Loye and Clark Gable and Claudette Colbert. Launder and Gilliat's script exhibits a delighted mastery of the mode, to which they were able, with the development of front-line British players in Margaret Lockwood and Michael Redgrave, to give an English accent in *The Lady Vanishes* a couple of years later. This demonstration of mastery of the Hollywood Screwball mode may have been connected to hopes of working in America, but it is also a good example of their knowledge of the cinema around them.

In retrospect the first of two turning points of their joint career was their third collaboration, the screenplay for *The Lady Vanishes*, not actually written for its director, Alfred Hitchcock, but picked up by him when the original project with another director (Roy William Neill) fell through. Hitchcock usually developed his scripts with his writers, so his taking over a completed scenario, and using it largely intact (a revised beginning and extended end rewritten by the duo under Hitchcock's direction were the most important changes), suggests what expert screenwriters the pair had become.[5] Not only did they thus write for Hitchcock (Gilliat, who had much earlier had a very minor role on *The Manxman*, in 1928, was also the joint scenarist for Hitchcock's last British film, *Jamaica Inn*, 1939) but they also wrote separately and together for another emerging major director, Carol Reed, Launder on *A Girl Must Live* (1939), Gilliat on *Girl in the News* (1940) and *Kipps* (1941), and back together again on the screenplay which cemented their reputation as a partnership, *Night Train to Munich*, followed by the scenario for Reed's historical war film *The Young Mr Pitt* (1942).

*The Lady Vanishes*, an instant classic that established the pair as more formidable together than apart, led within three years (via the two wartime Reed films and a variety of work on Ministry of Information propaganda shorts such as *Partners in Crime* (1942)), to the second turning point – the offer of writing and directing a feature-length home front documentary for the Ministry of

Information. This project metamorphosed into the fictional but documentary-influenced *Millions Like Us* (approved of, though not sponsored by the MOI, and produced at Gainsborough), Launder and Gilliat's first large-scale writing–directing collaboration. Their partnership would shortly be extended in one more direction by their assumption of the roles of joint producers in 1944. *Millions Like Us*, seen in its own time and later as a key text of British war-time cinema, and even of a national cinema beyond the exigencies of war, launched Launder and Gilliat on a long new inflection of their careers.

## One live as two, two live as one

Immediately following *Millions Like Us*, converted to the idea of directing their own scripts, both Launder and Gilliat then followed separate projects as singly credited writer-directors at Gainsborough, Launder making *Two Thousand Women* and Gilliat *Waterloo Road* during 1944, though Gilliat in his comments makes it clear that Launder made important suggestions for *Waterloo Road*,[6] and it is likely that Gilliat had some input into *Two Thousand Women*. When they came back together as producers as well as directors and writers in 1945, they continued to direct singly even in projects where there was a double credit for the script. Their explanation for giving up joint direction was that while it had benefits for the directors, it tended to confuse the actors.[7] This practice of joint production and single direction instituted the pattern of the rest of their careers – on the one hand, films which both wrote and co-produced while one directed (as in their next two, *The Rake's Progress* (1945), directed by Gilliat, and *I See a Dark Stranger* (1946), directed by Launder), and on the other, films which both produced but one wrote (occasionally with another co-writer) and directed, as with the two following, *Green for Danger* (1947, written and directed by Gilliat) and *Captain Boycott* (1947, written and directed by Launder), with assisting writers, Claude Gurney and Wolfgang Wilhelm respectively, on both scripts. Only seven out of the remaining nineteen films had a double writing credit, though there were a few exceptional cases where a single external scriptwriter was used, e.g. Bryan Forbes on Gilliat's *Only Two Can Play* (1962), or a script was written for another director, e.g. Launder's script for *Ring of Spies,* directed by Robert Tronson, 1963).[8] However, in all the cases of single Launder or Gilliat credits we should assume that the co-producer's role involved considerable input. Gilliat's comments on Launder's advice on *Waterloo Road* have already been cited, while Launder's on *The Story of Gilbert and Sullivan* (though it was 'more Sidney's cup of tea than mine') reveal that he made important structural comments on the script of that film,[9] and we should assume the same with Gilliat's role as producer of Launder's work. In Kevin MacDonald's interview with Gilliat there is a description of the pair's working methods on their most bonded projects which shows the closeness of their partnership:

> We always talked the story over first. If we wanted to do a full treatment and it was a bulky affair, we would take it away in sections. We'd do an outline to roughly block out the story and then divide it up. 'I'll do the full treatment from A to B and you take B to C.' Then we'd pass them back to each other for revision. Once we'd started actual scripting we'd pass each sequence backwards and forwards and make the style uniform – which makes it pretty unreasonable when people say: 'Oh, that's where Sidney started and Frank left off'. Of course, there were characteristic phrases which he used, and others no doubt which I used, but by eliminating them you could make it reasonably uniform.[10]

Yet we are dealing with Launder *and* Gilliat, a remarkable partnership of two individuals, not a single composite animal, however close they were. (And Gilliat in the same interview notes that they had at least one serious quarrel when they disagreed about the length of the beginning section of *Millions Like Us*.[11]) A range of collaborative modes obviously suited them, allowing the closest association on the projects they were most in tune with as a partnership, but also necessary flexibility for both partners over the long run of their collaboration, enabling either man to follow particular interests, to take the primary role in projects to which he was especially committed and the secondary, advisory one in others that he might not have chosen for himself. Looking across their films, one becomes aware of differences which were occasionally the subject of their usually dual-focused advertising, e.g. the Individual Films publicity piece which proceeds

> Yet some attempt must be made (for biographical purposes) in tribute to their marked originality and values as individuals ... Launder and Gilliat, thirty-eight and thirty-seven respectively, the one: dark, agile and purposeful; the other: a little fairer, sleepy and purposeful.[12]

Gilliat described himself as 'bookish', which he noted Launder definitely was not, so that we might from one perspective see their mutual interaction as crossing Gilliat's originally novelistic interests with Launder's theatrical ones, resulting in a happy screenwriting combination, strong both on dramatic structure and novelistic detail. Gilliat had a passion for opera and wrote two performed libretti, one based on a Saki story *The Open Window* (music by Malcolm Arnold, 1956), and one based on *Our Man in Havana* (music by Malcolm Williamson, 1963). In comedy his taste ran to sophisticated sexual subjects, with *The Constant Husband* and *Only Two Can Play* dominantly his projects, while the theatre-influenced, actor-friendly Launder inclined to farce. Also Gilliat's input into the later thrillers was greater, something Raymond Durgnat pointed to when suggesting that Gilliat faintly recalled 'Hitchcock's feeling for the shabby genteel ... and thrillers ... though without Hitch's sado-pessimistic depth',[13] and Geoff Brown adds his passion for detail, citing the Vosnian language invented for *State Secret* (1950).[14]

On the other hand, Launder, though capable of the almost Chestertonian poetry of the precise London locations of *Ring of Spies*, was taken by the Celtic Fringe, directing all four of the Scottish/Irish films, with Gilliat only credited on the scripts of *I See a Dark Stranger* and *Geordie* (1955). Launder also seems to have been more possessed by one of the pair's great thematics, the female group (first presented in *Millions Like Us*, then inflected in *Two Thousand Women* and *The Happiest Days of Your Life,* and finally reworked in the *St Trinian's* cycle), which was as much Launder's enthusiasm as *The Story of Gilbert and Sullivan* was Gilliat's.[15] The evidence of Gilliat's late *Endless Night* (1972), and Launder's commitment to the *St Trinian's* cycle, is that Gilliat was more responsive to post-1950s cinema, and was the more analytical personality, the latter being reflected in the more frequent reference to his statements than to Launder's in this book. However, this should not be taken as an implicit secondarization of Launder, whose skills were vital to the partnership, and who was the primary creative figure in three of the absolutely central films made by the pair, *Two Thousand Women*, *I See a Dark Stranger* and *The Happiest Days of Your Life*. Where the kind of differences noted here are particularly relevant they will be investigated, but what follows, without collapsing two individuals into one, takes the co-producing credit seriously and sees the films as fundamentally enabled by the partnership, even where contributions were unequal. Thus this book is centred on the products of the partnership rather than their deconstruction into individual shares, and does not aim at being an exercise in textual detective work separating Beaumont from Fletcher or Roeg from Cammell.

### 'Too many films and not enough words to go round'

Launder and Gilliat's prolific output is a problem for any study of them. Separately and then together, credited or uncredited, in major or minor roles, from 1928 up to *Millions Like Us* in 1942 they worked on over 100 completed projects, according to Brown's authoritative filmography. With the twenty-five post *Millions Like Us* films (and disregarding their work as producers for others later in their careers), that adds up to 130 or so texts, an enormous output which it is impossible to discuss except in the most general fashion. The decision taken here is to limit analysis to the period from *Millions Like Us* on, to the writing-directing (and then producing) partnership, the only exceptions being the joint screenwriting that immediately led to the later films, and a few other co-written or singly written works that reflect directly on the later ones, e.g. *Rome Express* (de Courville, 1932) and *Seven Sinners* (Forde, 1936).

Rather than try to cover everything in the same detail, I have made choices of emphasis based on my belief that most of Launder and Gilliat's most significant films cluster in the period 1943 to 1953, and that *Millions Like Us*, *Two Thousand Women*, *Waterloo Road*, *The Rake's Progress*, *I See a Dark Stranger*, *The Blue Lagoon* (1949), *The Happiest Days of Your Life* and *The Story of Gilbert and Sullivan* constitute the centre of their work and demand the bulk of analysis, getting on for two thirds of the book. A final, generically oriented, chapter covers the later comedies and thrillers, and also allows a backward look at the formative comedy–thriller–romance screenplays. However, this policy certainly short changes certain films. *The Constant Husband*, *Only Two Can Play*, *Green for Danger*, *The Green Man* (1956) and *Endless Night* are works that, as I have written this book, I have come to see as especially victimized by my choices, along with *The Story of Gilbert and Sullivan* which tends to slip through dominant generic categories simply because it is the only musical Launder and Gilliat made after the 1930s, though both were involved with musicals in their earlier days (for instance, Gilliat with the once famous *Chu-Chin Chow* (Forde, 1934) and *My Heart is Calling* (Gallone, 1934); Launder with Marcel Varnel's *O-Kay for Sound* (1937)).

Aware of such inevitable marginalizations, I have made an at least slightly extended reading of one of these films, *The Story of Gilbert and Sullivan*, at the end of this chapter. Elsewhere I hope that omissions are more than balanced by what my schema allows in the way of deeper analysis. Another consequence of concentrating on readings of a limited number of films is a lack of attention to Launder and Gilliat's more frequent and/or more distinguished collaborators, such as the co-screenwriter Val Valentine, the editor Thelma Myers (later Thelma Connell), the photographer Wilkie Cooper, the composers and musical directors Louis Levy (in the Gainsborough films), William Alwyn, Malcolm Arnold and Muir Mathieson, and, on the production side, Sidney Gilliat's brother, Leslie. Additionally there are major figures whose contribution was restricted to a very small number of films, or even a single one, like the photographers Jack Cox and Arthur Crabtree (at Gainsborough), Bernard Herrmann who composed the score of *Endless Night*, and, in costume and design, Elizabeth Haffenden and Vincent Korda. Given Launder and Gilliat's generosity in acknowledging their colleagues' contributions (and their own obvious feelings about Hitchcock's lack of acknowledgement of their work on *The Lady Vanishes*)[16] it is right to direct the reader's attention to where their and others' contributions are recorded in the filmography at the end of this volume.

## Conversations with Launder and Gilliat

At many points this book refers to statements made by Launder and Gilliat, first to Geoffrey Brown in his annotated filmography (1977), and second by Gilliat to Kevin MacDonald in a late interview (1993). Any critical-interpretative work should approach such material cautiously, grateful for light it sheds, especially on the kind of details only known by those intimately concerned with production, but also aware of the problematics of authorial statements and the intentionalist fallacy ('trust the tale and not the teller'). These autobiographical sources have various differences. The first covers the whole of the pair's careers apart and together; the second concentrates only on certain periods. The first alternates statements by Launder and by Gilliat; the second interviews only Gilliat and concentrates on his role in the partnership and films in which he was the primary mover. There is also an important difference of approach, with Brown choosing a self-effacing role, not attempting to guide the film-makers in what they say, and MacDonald questioning more directly. Though MacDonald's approach yields certain benefits, especially in the more textually focused remarks he elicits from Gilliat about *The Rake's Progress* (see Chapter 3), the manifold virtues of the duo's commentaries on their films seldom touch on the textually analytical. These virtues include almost total recall of places, persons and circumstances, a generosity to colleagues, many shrewdly revealing anecdotes and intimate details of personnel and production, a huge interest in the multifarious and confusing world of earlier British film production, but little comment on the texts (though MacDonald's strategy pays off again when Gilliat makes interesting remarks about narrative and visual senses in his film-making, and reveals more of his interest in European cinema than one gleans from his comments to Brown). More often, though, they tend to say things like 'It didn't really come off, not for me' (Gilliat on *London Belongs to Me* (1948) or 'The mixture [of satire and comedy] was not 100% satisfactory' (Launder on *Lady Godiva Rides Again* (1952)), or simply assert that 'neither Maurice Evans nor Robert Morley were exactly right for their parts' in *The Story of Gilbert and Sullivan* (Gilliat).[17] Such analytical reticence – more pronounced in Launder than Gilliat, whose temperament, as revealed in the late interview and the interstices of the earlier, was certainly more contemplative – reflects the way most film-makers outside of the art cinema (of which, except for the documentary movement, Britain notoriously had none) discussed things.

Take a representative instance: Launder's discussion of *The Blue Lagoon* in Brown, where the kind of question they don't approach in their discussions of their films can be seen. *The Blue Lagoon*, both then (mid-1970s) and now, was probably the least seen and commented on of the post *Millions Like Us* films, even though it was, as Launder notes, the most economically successful of all their films and the second most successful of Rank's (after *The Red Shoes* (1948)).[18] Some of these questions that later directors, in tune with different critical discourses, might have addressed, are: Why the choice of Stacpoole's novel, when it seems so different from Launder and Gilliat's other films? Why were particular narrative changes made? Were the makers conscious of importing into the film class and social themes not in the novel? What problems did the narrative's overt sexual interests cause the makers? Was the film's ending deliberately constructed to be ambivalent? Such questions and answers are never articulated. Instead Launder's commentary focuses on very pragmatic elements: the problems of shooting in Fiji, the false economics of returning to Pinewood for studio filming, the rigidity of Rank's exhibition network in dealing with the film's popularity, and Launder and Gilliat's dislike of the 'Independent Frame' movement at Pinewood. Such discourse is far from empty, much of its detail is fascinating information with various kinds of value, but it tends to avoid explanation of, or speculation about, matters of meaning, whether the meanings intended by the makers or those read by audiences and critics, moving away from the text to practical matters of production (though sometimes a remark which is only tangential to the text can be suddenly revealing, as when Gilliat tells MacDonald apropos of *Millions Like Us* that two of the women working on the film (Terry Randall/Annie Earnshaw) had husbands or fiancés killed during its making).[19] All this being so, the analyst interested in what and how the films mean, has to accept Launder and Gilliat's witty and constantly interesting commentary for the informational value it has, which is, however, often of a different order than what this book tries to say.

As distinct from their contemporaries the Boulting Brothers, never slow to engage in controversy or to project themselves as spokesmen for the British film industry, Launder and Gilliat were more reticent film-makers, who, apart from the usual publicity routines (getting *Picture Post* coverage of location shooting in the Dolomites for *State Secret*, or publicizing Launder's real-life source for *Two Thousand Women*),[20] didn't much intervene in or create debates as the Boultings did. The Boultings' frequent articulation of principles and aims not only was to their advantage as practising film-makers, but has also helped to stimulate later discussion of them, their programmatic aspect making them seem more central to British film than the quieter pair.[21] Launder and Gilliat's difference may make them seem both more amorphous and marginal, lesser and more difficult to grasp. From early on, though recognized, they tended to gain a certain limited kind of praise, the basic pattern of which can be seen in the reviews for *Green for Danger*. The *Manchester Guardian*'s critic (8 February 1947), after beginning 'It is difficult to find the right level of praise' for their films, goes on to find it by saying 'They do not pretend to greatness: they cannot be compared with the ambitious things done nowadays in some British studios'. The *Mail*'s critic (7 February 1947) does something related in an elaborate school hierarchy image: 'They don't quite get into the Sixth Form with those distinguished scholars Carol Reed ("Odd Man Out") and David Lean ("Great Expectations") and that distinguished but erratic pixie Michael Powell ("A Matter of Life and Death"). But they are out on their own at the head of the Upper Fifth.' The problem with such judgements, whatever their degree of truth, is that they lead to superficial readings, with terms like 'unambitious', 'unpretentious' and 'light entertainment' inhibiting serious attention.

Trying to get beyond this, yet at the same time recognize the points that underlie such terminology, involves delicate negotiations between approaches that see the films as belonging to transpersonal ideologies and aesthetic practices shared with other British films of the period, and others that wish to assert undoubted degrees of authorial difference. Antonia Lant's phrase (apropos of *I See a Dark Stranger*), that the pair were 'canny readers of the national barometer',[22] is useful, because while crediting the film-makers' intelligence and intentions, it leaves space for the unconscious, which any authorially oriented account of their output needs to invoke, given the gap between the way they usually talk about the films and the complex effects the films register, let alone the sense that they, like other cultural producers, are sites through which the transpersonal discourses of the society are more or less personally inflected. It is also useful in suggesting them as *responders* rather than *initiators*, makers of brilliant entertainment films who, because of their ability to respond to the ideological weather around them, do much more than produce merely efficiently pleasant films. (Lant's insight partly parallels Durgnat's in *A Mirror for England* when he writes of 'their relaxed romping in and out of the system's little loopholes and byeways'.[23]) In this they are different from *initiators* like the Boulting Brothers, a number of whose best films spring directly from articulatable political attitudes, whether coherent or incoherent, which impel their texts, but whose less personally driven entertainment films show little of the ability of their more committed films (such as *Heavens Above* (1963) and *I'm All Right, Jack* (1959)) to reflect the weather significantly. Conversely, exciting though those ideas that Launder and Gilliat toyed with for making films about Karl Marx (*Red Prophet*) and the Industrial Revolution

(*Sleeping Sword*) may seem[24] – and when I began this book I imagined that those 'lost' projects would be central to what I would write, might provide a definitive centrepoint that would ideologically underpin and clarify the rest of their work – sober reassessment makes one feel that it isn't strange they came to nothing. With the half exception of *Millions Like Us*, one might almost propose a law that the significance of Launder and Gilliat's films tends to be in inverse relation to the degree to which they announce a thesis (at any rate one more detailed than, say, the necessity of winning the war and the importance of the home front, or 'the fate of the mobile woman', or representing the under-represented working class). *The Happiest Days of Your Life* might stand as a paradigm of their art, a film without apparent serious content whose ability to be serious is paradoxically guaranteed by its apparent unseriousness. By contrast, a film like *Left Right and Centre* (1959), which announces intentions of political satire, compares feebly with a work like the Boultings' *I'm All Right, Jack* (released in the same year).

Lant's metaphor is also useful in suggesting reasons for the gradual relative falling away in quality in Launder and Gilliat's output. 'Canny readers of the national barometer', dependent on the weather, their creative highpoint coincided with an exceptionally optimistic period of British film-making, the war and immediate postwar years. Where the Boulting Brothers were able to remake themselves in the mid to late 1950s, and a figure like Lean could detach himself from general trends, Launder and Gilliat seemed more directly affected by the often negative British cinema environment of the 1950s, a soil which even hardy Jerusalem artichokes found unnutritious. The kinds of films they were associated with were not at the centre of the new movements in British cinema in the early 1960s, and though Gilliat made an interesting late film (*Endless Night*, 1972) and Launder produced a notable script for *Ring of Spies* (1963), in both of which, as well as in Gilliat's fine *Only Two Can Play* (1961), there are many indications of the film-makers' ability to adapt to new times had conditions been more propitious, 'canny readers' seem to have become 'cautious readers', prone to repetition, especially in the

overextended *St Trinian's* cycle which bears only negative comparison with the Boultings' state-of-the-nation satires at the point
where the 1950s met the 1960s. Both film-makers spent a
growing amount of time in their later working life running British
Lion at the expense of their own films, but the choice itself may
have been influenced by senses of ebbing creative energies and
displacement from the creative mainstream of British cinema.

## Authors and styles

Launder and Gilliat, like all their British contemporaries except
Hitchcock and Powell and Pressburger, operated wholly within
the conventional formal systems of the British commercial cinema.
This book does not lay out a *Système L et G* which might separate
them formally from their contemporaries (let's say the Boulting
Brothers, Asquith, Lean) in terms of spatial systems, length of
shots or other formal markers of auteurism. Perhaps even to
suggest this in the British context is quixotic. The research
required to detect minute differences would be prohibitively great
for results destined to be unrevealing. In his chapter 'The Bounds
of Difference' in *The Classical Hollywood Cinema*, David Bordwell
argues that Hollywood auteurship is not marked by radical breaks
with ruling paradigms,[25] and this must be even more true of the
British cinema. Bordwell's point about the Hollywood cinema is
that where either formal or thematic markers of auteurism exist,
these operate within the boundaries of a group style.[26] His
statement that 'even auteurs ... spend a lot of time obeying the
rules'[27] is true even of those British film-makers of the period who
most subvert the paradigmatic style, e.g. Hitchcock and Powell
and Pressburger. In this they are like Sirk in Bordwell's Hollywood example, where, whatever meaningful differences operate,
they are not at the level of the building blocks of the dominant
style: 'no auteur critic has in practice shown that, say, the shot/
reverse shot patterns, or the usage of light across all of Sirk's films
constitute a distinct handling of the classical paradigm.'[28] If
Hitchcock and Powell and Pressburger cannot be said to operate

more than sometimes in tension with the group style, how much more must this be the case with Launder and Gilliat.

Where one might find evidence of stylistic inclinations at this basic level, such as a preference in some films for the use of the dissolve where other directors might use a cut (observable both in *The Rake's Progress* and *I See a Dark Stranger*), the tendency is not ubiquitous and is difficult to relate to either thematics or an overall aesthetic philosophy. Equally one might be struck by the sophistication of Launder and Gilliat's montage in oneiric sequences such as Bridie's remarkable dream in *I See a Dark Stranger* or Percy's under sentence of death in *London Belongs to Me*. But brilliant though these are, there is no way that Launder and Gilliat's deployment of them is more pervasive than or radically different from that of their contemporaries. They are used where the narrative demands them and not outside of the traditional loci. (Another form of montage is foreshortening of the narrative, as in, for example, *The Rake's Progress*, where we see Vivian fulfilling his role as 1930s playboy, or Geordie's progress through Samson's bodybuilding exercises to his twenty-first birthday, or the long virtuosic sequence in *The Story of Gilbert and Sullivan* where the duo's music spreads through London discussed on p. 30.) The montage passages in *Millions Like Us*, which arguably significantly inflect the classical fiction style for periods near the beginning of the film, are a part exception, but they have no real parallels in other Launder and Gilliat films and therefore need to be read as stemming from the demands of that particular project, a proof of Launder and Gilliat's virtuosity and adaptability, but not of any deeprooted tendencies. One last instance. When at the beginning of the flashback in *State Secret* Gilliat constructs an extended subjective sequence as Marlowe (Douglas Fairbanks Jr) breakfasts, receives the letter inviting him to Vosnia, and goes to work and then to his club, the sequence is undoubtedly modelled on the narrative-long use of the device in Robert Montgomery's *The Lady in the Lake* (1946), which, though a conventional film in other respects, is in this one certainly a rupturing of the classical paradigm. In identical style Gilliat relates all the events from Marlowe's point of view, i.e. without anchoring shots showing

Marlowe. However, the trope is only sustained for the single sequence and nothing like it occurs elsewhere in the film. It is as if Gilliat were curious about Montgomery's method, or eager to show his ability to play with it (and, of course, he and Launder were well acquainted with Hitchcock's liking for point-of-view shots), but nothing more than the isolated sequence is built around the technique and there are no analogous examples in any of the other films.

Feelings, then, about the individuality of the authors and their films rest on a more diffuse set of factors, pointing to a second level at which difference is constituted, not by systematic formal departures from the norm, but what is defined by Leonard Meyer as less systematic individual manipulation of group conventions: 'For any specific style there is a finite number of rules, but there is an indefinite number of possibilities for realizing or instantiating such rules.'[29] Within the classical British cinema we should expect outstanding differences to be located in the areas of (i) choice and development of subject matter, (ii) script and narrative structure, (iii) actors and acting, and (iv) mise en scène, and for stylistic choices to be closely linked to the generic or other demands of particular projects rather than radically adapting the projects to favoured stylistic options.

We might note then (i) *Choice of projects.* There are, for instance, other war films than Launder and Gilliat's which eschew the combat zone, e.g. *The Bells Go Down* (Dearden, 1943), *The Lamp Still Burns* (Elvey, 1943), *The Gentle Sex* (Howard, 1943), but in their war trilogy Launder and Gilliat do it more consistently than anyone else. The same may be said of their – particularly Launder's – penchant for the female-centred film (either with solo female heroines or the female group) in *Two Thousand Women, I See a Dark Stranger,* the *St Trinian's Cycle* and comedies such as *Lady Godiva Rides Again* and *Folly to be Wise* (1953). Films with female protagonists are comparatively common, but the female group film is rare. Again one may cite as parallels *The Lamp Still Burns* and *The Gentle Sex,* but the interest (particularly in a comic inflection) is distinctive. Another distinctiveness might be seen in Launder and Gilliat's attraction to 'Celtic Fringe' subjects, both melodramatic and comic, in which again they are not unique but are arguably more committed than other contemporaries, with two films set in Ireland, *I See a Dark Stranger* and *Captain Boycott* (1947), two comedies in Scotland, *Geordie* and *The Bridal Path* (1959), and one in Wales, *Only Two Can Play*, and with another, *The Constant Husband*, having some pronounced references to Wales.

(ii) *The 'quality' and qualities of their screenplays.* Classical British film-making was based on the finished screenplay, not on improvisation from a deliberately less completed base. Brown rightly underlines Launder and Gilliat's beginnings in, and continuing commitment to, scriptwriting, and their move to direction in no way altered their attitutude to what they saw as the basis of good cinema. Indeed one of the factors that probably pushed them towards direction of their own writing was the dispute they had with the director, Carol Reed, and the star, Robert Donat, during the making of *The Young Mr Pitt* (1942), over what they saw as the sometimes too lifelessly hagiographic direction which the director and star imposed on their script.[30] Brown also quotes a number of his subjects' verbal felicities to suggest something of the writer-directors' particular tone, including this from *The Green Man*:

> 'But it can't be!' says the heroine after George Cole's vacuum salesman has found blood on the piano stool – 'Not here – not in Turnham Green!' She is engaged to a BBC radio announcer, one Reginald Willoughby Pratt (Colin Gordon), ineffably pompous and ridiculous: 'By heaven', he says to Cole, incensed, 'I'd thrash the life out of you – if I didn't have to read the nine o'clock news!' – a line (and a character), one feels, which only Launder and Gilliat could have produced.[31]

The idiosyncrasies also suggest the importance of Launder and Gilliat's predilection for the comic, a leaning that constantly tips their work in the second of the genres that dominate their output, the thriller, over into the comedy–thriller–romance. Here again they are not alone since their inclinations were shared not just by Hitchcock but by Forde, de Courville and others, but since Launder and Gilliat wrote for these directors they were themselves partly constitutive of a genre which Gilliat traced back to UFA cinema.

If emphasis on the screenplay turns us back to Launder and Gilliat's writing rather than visual craft, it is important to qualify this in two ways: (i) with an insistence that witty dialogue is not a sign of pejorative theatricality, even if the latter is a fault of which British cinema has often, sometimes justifiably, been accused; and (ii) with a reminder that the screenwriter's art is narrative and structural as well as verbal, and built around the ability to imagine cinematic, as distinct from theatrical or novelistic, scenes. Launder twice in his earlier career had the misfortune to be the scenarist for versions of Shaw plays, *How He Lied to Her Husband* (Lewis, 1930) and *Arms and the Man* (Lewis, 1932), which were made under a Shavian fiat of no alterations to the stage version except for cuts. This experience of pejoratively theatrical film-making was so traumatic that later in their careers the two risked alienating Alexander Korda by refusing his pet project to remake *Arms and the Man*.[32]

There will be many references to Launder and Gilliat's screenwriting abilities in this book, but it will help to fix the motif to look briefly at a segment of the adaptation (in this case Gilliat's) for Carol Reed of a prestigious literary text, H. G. Wells's *Kipps*, where the temptation to overliterary adaptation might be thought irresistible. Early on in the novel there are two sections largely narrated through Wells's authorial persona: the 'Venus Epipontia' section describing in ornately witty terms Kipps's initiation into sexual interests, ending with a short dramatized scene where he and one of the girls from work flirt;[33] and then the account, wholly related by the authorial persona, of Kipps's vague dissatisfactions which lead him to Mr Coote's lecture on Self Help ('I suppose some such phase of discontent is a normal thing in every adolescence. The ripening mind seeks something upon which its will may crystallise, upon which its discursive emotions, growing more abundant with each year of life, may concentrate ... It led Kipps finally into Technical Education as we understand it in the south of England').[34] This scene is briefly reported, not dramatized. The screenplay, avoiding the temptations of an authorial overvoice, creates two adjacent wholly dramatic scenes out of what is mostly authorially related. In the first, Kipps and a friend take two girls on a Sunday promenade and listen to a brass band until the approach of a fee collector makes the men try to move the reluctant girls off, a dilemma that is happily solved by it starting to rain. As they shelter from the rain they see the advertisement for Mr Coote's lecture, which they think will be a magic lantern show, and decide to go in. The first scene with its slightly daring pleasures of flirting and smoking sets up the second where the others separate themselves from Artie by their giggling and mocking of Coote's rhetoric (with Carlyle and quotations from Gray and Shakespeare as well as the interruption of a stentorian nose blower added to the source):

> COOTE You have the ladder! I have a ladder! We all have a ladder!
> YOUTH (*to Girl*) You got yours? (*Girl giggles*).

When his female companion tries to draw Kipps's attention to the joking, he smiles politely but his interest immediately swings back to the speaker, so he completely misses his male friend's mimicking of 'you may mount ever higher and higher'. As the scene ends Michael Redgrave's Kipps leans forward, cut off from his less responsive companions, in rapt closeup, the thin handle of his umbrella pressed to his mouth. As elsewhere, it is difficult to separate the screenwriter's contribution from the director's, but at the least the screenplay provided the specific structures on which the director worked, and any claim that those structures are not cinematically conceived is impossible to sustain.

Nevertheless the structures provided and Reed's realization tend to the conservative rather than the radical. Launder and Gilliat's contemporaries Hitchcock, Lean and Powell are obviously more visually adventurous directors, as Gilliat suggests to Mac-Donald, confessing to a poor visual memory – the drawings of setups in his director's shooting script of *The Rake's Progress* certainly exhibit no draughtsmanly ability – and defining his own style, rather than visual, as narrative (which, of course, is not the same as verbal).[35] One doubts whether any film of Launder and Gilliat's ever began as an expansion of a visual image, and, though there are many instances in their films of highly skilled pictorialism and mise en scène (and in this respect Gilliat's late *Endless*

*Night* is something of a revelation), it's also true that relatively few of their visual images – as distinct from actors' performances – dominate the experience of the viewer as do those of the directors cited above. Viewing again Joseph Losey's triumph of art design in *Modesty Blaise* (1966), one could not imagine anything remotely similar (whatever the other virtues) if the project had remained with Gilliat. Gilliat recorded that Val Valentine conceived the idea of *Waterloo Road* from seeing crowds sleeping in the underground, but the script and the film treat the underground as one of many evocative spaces, not the central defining image of the narrative.[36] However, this said, one must guard against failing to see what is there because prejudiced by the part-deserved reputation of British cinema of the time for verbality over visuality. Later concentration on specific films will attempt an antidote to overstressing such tendencies, but one example suggests aspects easily missed. In *The Constant Husband*, after he's been kidnapped by the family of the Italian wife he deserted, Rex Harrison is led into the backstage of a circus, a bewildering environment to his amnesic self. Confronted by the passionate Lola (Nicole Maurey), who greets him as her husband, Rex Harrison in closeup faints. As he falls out of the bottom of the frame, a clown, previously wholly blocked out by the protagonist, is revealed. The move on from this is very swift. The scene doesn't linger, doesn't emphasize the juxtaposition of the images, as, say, the painting of the jester is repeatedly emphasized in a quite different melodramatic context in Hitchcock's *Blackmail*, but the pointing of the trope is not wholly dissimilar, and the discreet art here can be overlooked if one's framework of viewing is more conventional than what is viewed, which certainly invokes – though in a form mediated by the very upper-middle-class style of the whole film – tropes associated with the expressionist cinema, much more overt, and more strikingly and consistently developed in *Blackmail*, but nevertheless part of the sophisticated art of *The Constant Husband*. (Another example of an art of discreet near invisibility is the relentless chainsmoking of the otherwise very Englishly imperturbable enemy spy, Miller, played by Raymond Huntley, in *I See a Dark Stranger*.)

(iii) *Choice and use of actors*. This is a factor better treated in the discussion of particular films, but one basic generalization belongs here. Like most British film-makers Launder and Gilliat cultivated actors' skills of irony, understatement and allusiveness, particularly in comic modes. A list of actors they worked with contains more significant figures than it omits, particularly in the 1940s and 1950s: Rex Harrison, Stewart Granger, Eric Portman, Robert Donat, Herbert Lom, Cecil Parker, Basil Radford, Naunton Wayne, Leo Genn, Trevor Howard, Richard Attenborough, Douglas Fairbanks Jr, Jack Hawkins, Guy Middleton, Robert Morley, Maurice Evans, George Cole, Terry-Thomas, Bill Travers, Hywel Bennett, Patricia Roc, Rosamund John, Sally Gray, Deborah Kerr, Phyllis Calvert, Renée Houston, Flora Robson, Megs Jenkins, Anne Crawford, Jean Kent, Diana Dors, Kay Kendall, Jean Simmons, Glynis Johns, Peter Sellers, Hayley Mills, and many others. This list testifies to the variety of their work, but the actor most perennially associated with their films was Alastair Sim, whose range of meanings within the parameters of middleclass paternalism (both good and bad), as a comic actor who could shade to a sinister, almost vampiric inflection of his benign eccentricity, proved particularly fitting for their purposes.

(iv) The question of Launder and Gilliat's *deployment of mise en scène*, like their uses of particular actors, is better tackled in the contexts of individual films, where what can be generalized as a conservative bias inflected by sometimes unexpected elements, takes on forms shaped by the demands of different projects (whether the presence of the modernist female nude statue in *Folly to be Wise*, symbolizing the narrative's problematics of femininity and postwar modernity, or the expressionist and film noir-influenced lighting and photography of *I See a Dark Stranger*).

While we do not associate Launder and Gilliat with the avant garde as we do Hitchcock with his UFA connections, their cinematic sophistication – particularly Gilliat's – should not be underestimated. Brown's and MacDonald's interviews both corroborate Gilliat's interest in Lang, his visits to the Film Society and his admiration for German cinema of the 1920s and early 1930s.[37] The narrative structures of some of Launder and Gilliat's films,

particularly circa 1945–50, cultivate, within conventional parameters, marked elements of ambiguity. Because Launder and Gilliat
didn't much theorize about their work, those places where they
show particular sophistication tend to be overlooked, simply because
they almost never discussed themselves, and were never themselves discussed, in terms generally reserved for art cinema. This
is not to formulate their cinema as other than a mainstream, highly
conventionalized one, but to say that some of the sophisticated
influences that operated on Hitchcock and Powell and Pressburger had a lesser but not negligible influence on them.

Others, of course, did not. A concrete instance of the limitations
imposed by the British cinema of their period is evident in the
question of music. We know that Gilliat had a great interest in
opera, and in MacDonald's interview he uses a general question
about changes in the cinema to talk about the failure of narrative
film generally to develop 'a truly integrated use of music', showing
himself to be a formidable theorist of the subject, but just saying
of himself, 'I always wanted to try it, but it never got off the
ground'.[38] The generally conventional use of music in British
cinema of the time bore down heavily on Lauder and Gilliat's
films. With the exception of the special case of the musical *The
Story of Gilbert and Sullivan*, and the use of Bernard Herrmann
and the moog synthesizer for *Endless Night*, it is hard to see any
attempt to break the dominant pattern (often, though, expertly
produced, as in Alwyn's scores for *I See a Dark Stranger* and for
*Green for Danger* with its clever uses of the 'Paul Jones'), and
ironically it is a Launder project, *The Bridal Path*, that of all their
films has perhaps the freshest, most memorable use of music, the
Percy Graingerish extradiegetic folk singing that accompanies
Ewan/Bill Travers on his journeys.

But such conservatism should not be taken as symptomatic of
everything, particularly narrative construction. To formulate analysis
of Launder and Gilliat's films solely in terms of a simplified
version of the possible workings of British classical cinema may
blind one to many complexities, the number of variations possible
in even the most conventional classic practice. Questions of
particular stylistic choices are better discussed through individual

films, but it would seem to be true that at any generalizable building-block level, Launder and Gilliat's style is not distinct from that of their contemporaries. An interesting case here is *The Green Man*, a Launder and Gilliat production, scripted by them from their own screenplay, itself based on their stage play *The Body Was Well Nourished*, produced circa 1940. Here the directorial credit belongs to Robert Day (later the director of *The Rebel* (1960) and *Two Way Stretch* (1960)). However, because of Day's inexperience, much of the film was directed without credit by Basil Dearden, and some of it by Launder and Gilliat.[39] The point here – not exactly a crystal clear one because both Day and Dearden, aware that it was Launder and Gilliat's material, would probably have striven to give the film a Launder and Gilliat feel – is that it seems impossible to distinguish between directorial contributions, yet in writing, casting, and ethos the film probably strikes us clearly as Launder and Gilliat's.

The two contemporaneous sets of film-makers with whom Launder and Gilliat (with their comic bias) can most obviously be compared are the Boulting Brothers and Ealing, and I find views about group style and individuality similar to those that I have come to with Launder and Gilliat paralleled both in the recent volume of essays devoted to the brothers, *The Family Way*, and in Charles Barr's earlier *Ealing Studios*.[40] In the former the introduction attempts a definition of the Boultings' procedures, in the absence of marked formal differences, in terms of 'particular modes of performance and narrative control',[41] while David Lusted's chapter on *Fame is the Spur* (1947) and *I'm All Right, Jack* suggests that what is sometimes perceived as a simple style is, when closely inspected, a complex interweaving of realist, melodramatic and even occasionally 'surreal-expressionist modernism'.[42] In the latter, in passages by different film-makers (Hamer's *It Always Rains on Sunday* (1947), Dearden's *The Blue Lamp* (1949)) at the same studio, Charles Barr demonstrates similar skilful uses ('tact and balance' in the 'organization of simple elements within a static frame'[43]) of a classical British style, again with the implication that differences rest on subtle variations on the common style. All these insights are applicable to Launder and Gilliat, the point being that differentiation takes place within the parameters of the group style, but unsystematically, making generalization difficult.

### The Story of ~~Launder~~ Gilbert and ~~Gilliat~~ Sullivan

Though an examination of any of the films somewhat margin-alized by the plan of this book would say valuable things about Launder and Gilliat, *The Story of Gilbert and Sullivan* (1953) says the most, and in a particularly self-conscious, even self-referential way. It has a number of immediate claims on our attention – as one of the few notable British musicals; as a variant on the heritage film (brought out in Coronation year and to mark the twenty-first birthday of Alexander Korda's London Films); and as the most visually beautiful of all their films (only their second in colour, with Elizabeth Haffenden and Hein Heckroth credited for the costumes, and with Vincent Korda given a generalized credit, presumably for the overall design which has been compared with that of *Black Narcissus* (1946) and *The Red Shoes*). Last, but not least in interest, it is the often self-effacing Launder and Gilliat's most self-referential text.[44]

Largely critically disregarded – Brown sees it as a film in which the film-makers unusually lost contact with their public[45] – *The Story of Gilbert and Sullivan* has been opened up to re-estimation through the Gilbert and Sullivan biopic by the contemporary British film-maker Mike Leigh, *Topsy Turvy* (2000), a film which bears many signs of being a conscious rewriting of the earlier film. This is not a casual assertion, for Leigh quotes and reworks key scenes from the 1953 film, most specifically the Japanese sword sequence, which leads to the idea of *The Mikado*, Gilbert's wandering of mean London streets during his attack of first-night nerves, and the writer's and musician's quarrel over words and music. In an important review of the Leigh film Geoffrey O'Brien refers substantially to the earlier work, refusing to downgrade it to elevate the fascinating later film, but seeing it as a paradigm of the virtues of an earlier phase of British cinema.

The very traits once characterized as Stiff Upper Lip Cinema – the absence of high emotion or flamboyant Gesture, the dry and carefully researched presentation of Historical background, the tone balanced between blithe good humour and unflinching decorum in the face of life crises – have receded sufficiently into the past to seem rather bracing.[46]

Some of Launder and Gilliat's inflection of these qualities can be seen in the sequence where Gilbert conceives the idea of *The Mikado*, only nine shots long, both classically restrained and highly suggestive. In shot 1 Gilbert's (Robert Morley) legs pace about as his overvoice irascibly reads Sullivan's (Maurice Evans) letter demanding a story of 'human interest and probability'. In shot 2 he moves to his desk. Wind from an open window disturbs some papers. He gets up crossly. In shot 3, his back to the camera, he bangs the window shut. Shot 4, a close up, rapidly pans down with a Japanese sword as it falls from wall to floor. In shot 5 Gilbert looks, goes and picks it up, thinks of trying to replace it on the wall, but instead places it on the corner of his desk and sits down. In shot 6, beginning to reply to Sullivan's letter, he is distracted by the sword. Shot 7 is a closeup of the sword, the camera moving in on it. In shot 8 Gilbert picks it up, but the camera, which has moved to cover his action, continues along to a closeup of the table lamp, at first unlit, then, as the light fades, slightly, then fully, glowing. The camera moves back to Gilbert, now in shirt sleeves, writing. In shot 9 Mrs Gilbert enters with coffee. At various points in this sequence a familiar fragment from *The Mikado*'s overture asserts the dawning idea of a Japanese subject.

Inspiration passages – the birth of the poem, novel, song, symphony – are notoriously difficult to pull off on film, the necessary shorthand often seeming crude, even risible. Here the utilization of the innate qualities of Morley as an actor – he is not in any way a player who specializes in inward sensibilities – is backed up by a number of shots, or segments within shots, that don't feature his face at all, putting weight on the various objects, the window, the sword and the lamp. The sequence, avoiding any banal facial afflatus of creativity (Gilbert in the dialogue that immediately follows the entry of his wife employs a jocular mode between over and understatement when he asks his wife 'How does it feel to be married to a transsplendent genius?'), invokes without large-scale rhetoric two traditional metaphors of creativity, the mind-impregnating wind and the lamp of the intellect, full of romantic resonance yet here employed in a humdrum atmosphere of accidents and distractions.

Though the virtuosity of Launder and Gilliat's British musical is rather different from the space-expanding energies of the Hollywood musical (*Brigadoon* was released in the same year), the pair's mastery of narrative-number relationships rivals Hollywood's most sophisticated. Two very effective instances come to mind. When Gilbert quarrels with Sullivan and Carte (Peter Finch), Helen Lenoir says, 'Why don't you take a leaf out of your own book, *The Gondoliers*, Act 2, Scene 2', at which the narrative cuts to a quartet on stage singing 'In a contemplative fashion / And a tranquil frame of mind / Free from every sort of passion / Some solution let us find'. Later, after a momentary truce inspired by her suggestion, there is another cutaway to the stage quartet now fiercely quarreling. In the second case, at the gala revival of *The Yeomen of the Guard*, the news of Sullivan's imminent death is conveyed by a tearful Louis to a shocked Gilbert and Carte, while the tragic jester sings his version of 'I have a song to sing – oh': 'When a jester is outwitted / Feelings fester, heart is lead, / Food for fishes, only fishes, / Jester wishes he was dead', and then falls down dead.

O'Brien writes of Launder and Gilliat's film 'embodying the world of expectations with which Gilbert and Sullivan shaped their work, a work in which it is in some sense still a part, or at least wants to believe it is a part'.[47] This careful formulation does justice to the complexity of tone that *The Story of Gilbert and Sullivan* develops in its celebration of new Elizabethanism's optimism about national revival (as distinct from the celebrations of glorious failure produced in two related films of the time, the Boulting Brothers' Festival of Britain biopic of William Friese Green, *The Magic Box* (1951), and *Scott of the Antarctic* (Frend, 1948). *The Story of Gilbert and Sullivan* is the only one of Launder and Gilliat's postwar films which attempts (fragmentarily) anything like the inclusiveness that characterized the war films. Though the upper-middle-class and theatrical settings of the film hardly encourage this, what does is the sense that Gilbert and Sullivan's art appealed across a very broad class spectrum, something which is memorably rendered in parts of the early montage-dominated sequence which spans the duo's early successes from *The Sorcerer* to *The Pirates of Penzance*, in which their songs travel through all sections of society, from the most privileged to working-class pubs and a night-time fairground world that takes on almost expressionist underworld dimensions (recalling perhaps Gilliat's enthusiasm for Lang), the latter mixed with more decorous middle-class images like the two sporty young men tandeming while whistling one of the tunes.

Thinking of the use of montage in *Millions Like Us* to move the narrative to a wider perspective than that of the individual drama-centred entertainment film, while still retaining the latter's appeal, we can see how the later film reinvokes montage, prompted by the enthusiasms of Coronation Year. (Readers of the author's age will remember the winning of the Ashes, the ascent of Everest, Gordon Richards's Derby, Matthews's Cup Final, those films *A Queen is Crowned* and *Elizabeth Our Queen*, the latter with their now factitious-seeming rhetoric of grandeur.) *The Story of Gilbert and Sullivan* makes much of the previous female monarch of an optimistic late Victorian Britain, played by Muriel Aked with a mixture of distance and homely ordinariness no doubt trying to mesh mystique with democracy. But though the montage is managed felicitously, its operation is much more conservative, and the community gestured at much more precarious – constituted solely at the level of art – than in *Millions Like Us*. That this seems better than nothing accounts for the utopian feeling the sequence generates (at least for this viewer), but the dominant feeling of the film is inevitably nostalgic rather than forward looking, and this is demonstrated right at the beginning in the wonderfully composed sequence where Grace (Dinah Sheridan) rides in a carriage with her sisters to the Crystal Palace to hear Arthur's oratorio, *The Prodigal Son*, through scenes of insulated Victorian upper-class leisure, the idyllicness of which depends on the exclusion of the classes the later montage includes. The imperial theme is sounded as expected in 1953. In two parallel set pieces, one ending the film, first Sullivan and then Gilbert are knighted, the latter to the strains of 'In spite of all temptation he remains an Englishman'. The chorus, balanced between affirmation and irony even in its own time, is correspondingly even more ambivalent in a later, growingly post-imperial context. Whereas before the ironies were perhaps largely good manners, here they threaten to become searching. Like some other parts of the film this ending signals an interesting sceptical edge to its own celebrations.

In *The Story of Gilbert and Sullivan*, Launder and Gilliat, two British film-makers better known together than apart, making a film about the partnership of two other British artists also much better known together than apart, would have had to fight hard not to produce a text with self-referential implications. However, these are not just carried inertly by the makers/subjects parallel, but are intricately worked through the narrative. In a telling scene Gilbert acts out for his wife part of *The Gondoliers*, operating puppets in a toy theatre so that she can visualize it. Here he introduces two puppets, Marco and Giuseppe ('Giuseppe is the stout one'), and then, moving to the scene in the Grand Inquisitor's palace, pronounces the words 'Until it is ascertained which of you two gondoliers is to be King, I have arranged that you will rule jointly'. The question is asked 'As one individual?' and he confirms 'As one individual'. Launder and Gilliat's joint reign as 'one individual' seemed almost completely unrocked by the conflicts which eventually broke up Gilbert and Sullivan's and which provide the main dramatic tension in the film, tensions which basically arise from Sullivan's feelings that he should be committing himself to high rather than to popular art. A preview of the split which ends the partnership occurs when Sullivan invites Gilbert to write the libretto for his grand opera, an offer which Gilbert refuses in a way that causes a fundamental quarrel, Gilbert complaining that the partnership has always compromised his words (opera is 'the triumph of sound over sense') while Sullivan replies that it has always discriminated against his music (reducing it 'to a mere rum-ti-tum, so that every syllable of yours can be heard in the back of the gallery'). Though the quarrel is patched up, it breaks open again over financial matters (the film is realistic about these, something which adds to the film-industry parallels suggested below), and finally ends their creative association.

Though Gilliat's own attachment to opera, and his more obviously intellectual literary and cinematic interests lend credence to the idea of some self-identification with Sullivan, with Gilbert's wit and liking for farce making him closer to Launder, the fundamental subtextual meaning of the quarrel is surely that it plays out possibilities which basically never affected a more equable partnership, which didn't contain the same seeds of dissension. First of all Launder and Gilliat were not two practitioners from radically different spheres like Gilbert and Sullivan (or even Powell and Pressburger), but practitioners with equal writing, directing and producing skills (in this more like the Boulting Brothers). Second, with both coming out of similar commercial film-industry backgrounds, they were, for all that Gilliat was more high-culture oriented, neither really divided in outlook, with one satisfied by popular art and one driven towards high art, nor as a joint individual caught between these antitheses.

In giving weight to the role of D'Oyley Carte, the film lays emphasis on Carte's entrepreneurial abilities and provision of an institutional setting for the pair's work, at least until their quarrel. It is tempting to read this in the light of the sustaining umbrella relationship that Rank provided for the film-makers during their most productive years, even if the relationship cooled over 'Independent Frame'. Even the montage's treatment of Gilbert and Sullivan's trip with *HMS Pinafore* to America is readable in terms of a more easily successful parallel to Rank's eventually curdled dream of British penetration of the American film market. Here in a utopian prequel Gilbert and Sullivan invade America with hugely desired British products, their only competition the Americans' pirated versions of their own works.

Part of the film's celebration of Gilbert and Sullivan is that despite their on-and-off relationship they created a high popular art that became a kind of national institution. In his excellent article Geoffrey O'Brien acknowledges the power of Gilbert and Sullivan's art for his generation. 'The magic will of course not necessarily be apparent to all viewers. It's hard for me to imagine coming to Gilbert and Sullivan cold, in the middle of life, having been born into a world where they were part of its decor.'[48] (This recalls Dicky Randall in *Night Train to Munich*, who says at one point, 'You know, I once played Poo-Bah to the Foreign Secretary's Koko'.) O'Brien goes on to describe how they seemed to embody 'a kind of universal lexicon' of linguistic, musical, dramatic, melodramatic and farcical forms.[49] This inheritance, it strikes me, is close enough to the characteristics of Launder and Gilliat's art to strengthen that sense of identification between makers and subjects which I have traced.

The primary site in the film of the battle between, and resolution of, high and popular art is the virtuosic forty-eight-shot sequence which dramatizes Sullivan's desperate attempts to compose both *The Mikado* and the oratorio *The Golden Legend* simultaneously. Contrasting two performing spaces, the popular theatre and the great concert hall, the sequence also foregrounds a single site, Sullivan's rooms, taken over in turn by rehearsals for each project, with a subsidiary repetitive structure of the representative of the other project, the music critic Joseph Bennett, then Gilbert, then the music critic again, climbing the stairs to Gilbert's room to expel the occupying forces. These oppositions expand to oppose popular and classical, colourful motion and black-and-white formality (Sullivan's face, white shirtfront, bow tie and gloves picked out of the dome of blackness as he advances to the podium), the secular and the semi-ecclesiastical (*The Golden Legend* is Longfellow, not the Bible, but the mise en scène treats it like the latter), the lively Savoy girls and the massed angelic female choristers, orchestra and organ, pleasure and duty, culminating in the transition from the gaiety of 'He's going to marry Yum Yum' to the almost sacerdotal solemnity of the première before the queen. Of course, in one sense it is no contest, even though the sequence ends with the royal performance and shots moving upwards through the ranks of the chorus to the tips of the pipes of a great flower-bedecked organ, and Sullivan, arms dropping as he finishes conducting, is knighted in the dissolve-led following shot. We are left in no doubt that it is Sullivan's popular music that counts, something particularly clear in an ecstatic series of moments, after his manservant, Louis, has signalled to Sullivan, conducting on stage a rehearsal of the number 'Here's a pretty mess' (which makes apposite commentary on his predicament), that he must leave. Sullivan, still conducting as he is helped on with his cape and given his cane by Louis, weaves happily in and out of the performers and then exits in a high-spirited imitation of a vaudeville performer's signing off.

At the same time, though, the lyrics of the song, 'Here's a pretty mess, here's a how-de-do', though their obvious meaning comments on Sullivan's comic predicament of trying to fulfil two demands (i.e. here's a mixup, here's a jumbled-up state of things), can also be understood more positively – a *pretty* mess, a greeting, an introduction (of one kind of music to another) – which results in a popular art informed by Sullivan's serious aspirations, aspirations which he has mistakenly seen as ends in themselves rather than something to give substance to the operettas. Launder and Gilliat, of course, didn't move between an attempted British *Das Testament des Dr Mabuse* and a *Happiest Days of Your Life*, or alternate between ambitions for a native *M* and a *Two Thousand Women*, but their films exhibit a knowledge of the cinema that goes beyond the contemporary British one, a knowledge put at the service of the popular. At the same time, both the shadow of Sullivan's unachieved ambitions and the invocation of Englishness – the latter of which demands a reading both positive (Launder and Gilliat's self-identifying as very English artists) and ironic (that sense of secondariness inevitably pertaining to the British film industry) – play into these meanings, so that the passage analysed above and indeed the whole film may be read as an oblique self-defence and self-assessment.

## Notes

1 Iris De Cartier, 'Individual Films' publicity piece. See Launder and Gilliat microfiche, BFI Library.

2 See *Variety*, 8 June 1955; *Evening Standard*, 31 May 1957.

3 Geoff Brown, *Launder and Gilliat* (BFI, London, 1977). Brown had access to both Launder and Gilliat and thus to much biographical and production information, especially uncredited work. Much of the factual information in this chapter relies on Brown's book, and to avoid excessive footnoting a general debt is acknowledged here.

4 Brown, *Launder and Gilliat*, pp. 142, 145, 153; Kevin MacDonald, 'Interview with Sidney Gilliat', *Projections* 2, ed. John Boorman and Walter Donohoe (Faber and Faber, London, 1993), p. 146.

5 MacDonald, 'Interview with Sidney Gilliat', pp. 125–33.

6 Brown, *Launder and Gilliat*, p. 110.

7 Ibid., pp. 108–9.

8 Ibid., p. 138.

9 Ibid., p. 131.

10 MacDonald, 'Interview with Sidney Gilliat', p. 140.

11 Ibid., p. 134.

12 'Frank Launder. Portrait of a Brilliant British Film Personality', Iris De Cartier, 'Individual Films' publicity. See Launder and Gilliat microfiche, BFI Library.

13 Raymond Durgnat, *A Mirror for England: British Movies from Austerity to Affluence* (Faber and Faber, London, 1970), pp. 242–3.

14 Brown, *Launder and Gilliat*, p. 19

15 Ibid., p. 146.

16 MacDonald, 'Interview with Sidney Gilliat', pp. 129–30.

17 Brown, *Launder and Gilliat*, pp. 122–3, 129, 132–3.

18 Ibid., p. 124.

19 MacDonald, 'Interview with Sidney Gilliat', p. 136.

20 '"Two Thousand Women" (by one of them)', Gaumont British Press Information Sheet, 8 September 1944, and 'Film-making the Hard Way', *Picture Post*, 17 December 1948.

21 See Alan Burton, Tim O'Sullivan and Paul Wells (eds), *The Family Way: The Boulting Brothers and Postwar British Film Culture* (Flicks Books, Trowbridge, Wiltshire, 2000), *passim*. There are of course some interviews, e.g. 'Theo Richmond Talks to Sidney Gilliat and Frank Launder' (*Guardian*, 28 September 1970) and 'What Happens When Gilliat Faces [Sidney J.] Furie' ('Take 4 by Quentin Crewe'), *Daily Mail*, 30 May 1963.

22 Antonia Lant, 'The Female Spy: Gender, Nationality, and War in *I See a Dark Stranger*', in Robert Sklar and Charles Musser (eds), *Resisting Images: Essays in Film and History* (Temple University Press, Philadelphia, 1990), p. 180.

23 Durgnat, *A Mirror for England*, p. 243. Another phrase of his, 'Their partial autonomy from the concensus', deserves to be kept in mind.

24 On these projects see Brown, *Launder and Gilliat*, pp. 112–13.

25 David Bordwell, 'The Bounds of Difference', in David Bordwell, Janet

Staiger and Kristin Thompson, *The Classical Hollywood Cinema: Film Style and Mode of Production to 1960* (Routledge and Kegan Paul, London, 1985), pp. 70–84, *passim*.

26 Bordwell, 'The Bounds of Difference', *passim*.

27 Ibid., p. 80.

28 Ibid.

29 Leonard B. Meyer, 'Towards a Theory of Style', in Berel Lang (ed.), *The Concept of Style* (University of Pennsylvania Press, Philadelphia, 1979), pp. 9–24, cited in Bordwell, 'The Bounds of Difference', p. 78.

30 Brown, *Launder and Gilliat*, p. 104.

31 Ibid., p. 20.

32 Ibid., p. 137.

33 H. G. Wells, *Kipps* in *A Quartette of Comedies* (Ernest Benn, London, 1928), pp. 55–62.

34 Wells, *Kipps*, pp. 64–5.

35 MacDonald, 'Interview with Sidney Gilliat', pp. 140–1.

36 Brown, *Launder and Gilliat*, p. 110.

37 MacDonald, 'Interview with Sidney Gilliat', pp. 138–41.

38 Ibid., p. 148.

39 See Brown, *Launder and Gilliat*, p. 138.

40 Charles Barr, *Ealing Studios* (Tayleur and Cameron in association with David and Charles, London, 1977).

41 Burton, O'Sullivan and Wells (eds), *The Family Way*, Introduction, p. 9.

42 David Lusted, 'British Cinema Aesthetics and Hybridity: *Fame is the Spur* and *I'm All Right, Jack*', in Burton, O'Sullivan and Wells (eds), *The Family Way*, pp. 189–99.

43 Barr, *Ealing Studios*, pp. 86–9, especially p. 89.

44 There are lots of instances of generic self-awareness, some of which Gilliat himself notes regarding *State Secret* and *Green for Danger* (both Brown, *Launder and Gilliat*, p. 119), but how many intertextual references to their own films? For a start, list *The Young Mr Pitt* advertisement in *Millions Like Us*, the latinized reappearance of General Niva (from *State Secret*) in *The Green Man*, Miss Jezzard's (Muriel Aked's Deputy Head Mistress in *Happiest Days*) Home for Girls in *Lady Godiva Rides Again*, Jennifer Calthrop's metamorphosis into the May Savitt Qualthrope String Quartet, the reference to *The Blue Lagoon* in *The Pure Hell of St Trinian's* (1961), the metronome quoted from Bridie's dream that appears in Bramwell's dream in *Fortune is a Woman* (1957), and the repeated motif of Blake: the name of George Cole's character in *The Green Man*, the title and the song in *Endless Night*, and the placing of the microdot in a colon in 'Infant Joy' in *Ring of Spies*, plus the serendipity of the real-life spy's name.

45 Brown, *Launder and Gilliat*, p. 17.

46 Geoffrey O'Brien, 'Stompin' at the Savoy: *Topsy-Turvy*: A Film Directed by Mike Leigh', *New York Review of Books*, 47/3 (2000), 16–19.

47 O'Brien, 'Stompin' at the Savoy', 18.

48 Ibid., 16.

49 Ibid., 16.

1 *The Story of Gilbert and Sullivan*. As stormy a creative relationship as Launder and Gilliat's was serene. From left, at flashpoint, Gilbert (Robert Morley), then Sullivan (Maurice Evans), with Helen Lenoir (Eileen Herlie) and D'Oyley Carte (Peter Finch).

2 *Millions Like Us* 1. Celia (Patricia Roc) and Fred (Gordon Jackson), the film's young lovers, brought together by the war which also cuts short their happiness.

3 *Millions Like Us* 2. The double heroines, mobile women Celia (Patricia Roc) – Innocence, and Jennifer (Anne Crawford) – Experience, in the aircraft component factory.

4 Frank Launder and Sidney Gilliat – producer-writer-directors, modest auteurs.

**5** *2000 Women*. From left Rosemary (Patricia Roc), Freda (Phyllis Calvert) and Maud (Renée Houston) plan the escape of the airmen backstage.

**6** *Waterloo Road*. Jim (John Mills) strikes out against the coming postwar age by knocking Stewart Granger's spiv, Ted, downstairs as they struggle for possession of Jim's wife.

**7** *The Rake's Progress.* The Rake, Vivian (Rex Harrison), and Rikki (Lilli Palmer) drink a toast to their marriage of convenience.

**8** *I See a Dark Stranger.* Bridie (Deborah Kerr), Irish nationalist and German spy, is comforted by enemy officer David (Trevor Howard) after her room has been entered by a Nazi on her trail.

42

9 *The Blue Lagoon*. 'Aloha there!' Jean Simmons (Emmeline) and Donald Houston (Michael) pose exotically for the film's publicity.

**10** *The Happiest Days of Your Life*. Comic immortals Alastair Sim (Pond) and Margaret Rutherford (Miss Whitchurch), the Heads of Nutborne and St Swithins, ponder the horrors of coeducation.

# Keeping the home fires burning: the home front trilogy — *Millions Like Us, Two Thousand Women, Waterloo Road*

## 2

## Towards the home front trilogy

It would be an exaggeration to say that Launder and Gilliat were made by the war, since they both came into it with established individual careers and developed talents that might have gone in several directions. What, for instance, would have happened to Gilliat if he had gone to America to work with Conway or Hitchcock? But as far as Launder and Gilliat together are concerned, the statement is less extreme, for while the writers of *The Lady Vanishes* were hardly beginners, the war consolidated their partnership, giving them a foregrounded role in the British film industry's new life as articulator of the national struggle and psyche. Eventually in *Millions Like Us* it gave them the opportunity to write for themselves rather than others, to become writer-directors, thus setting the pattern for their postwar careers.

If *Millions Like Us* was the defining work of their partnership, their progress towards it was not quite arrowlike. After the outbreak of war they continued to work apart and together on projects whose only connection with the war was antithetical – the not to be underestimated role of the cinema of normality in a time of crisis – jointly scripting the Will Fyffe comedy-thriller vehicle *They Came By Night* (released June 1940), while Gilliat wrote the scenario for Reed's Margaret Lockwood melodrama *The Girl in the News* (February 1941) and then for *Kipps* (March 1941). Only gradually did the war dominate their projects. Launder wrote the story for the amusing *Inspector Hornleigh Goes To It* (Forde, May

1940), which involved army life and fifth columnists, and was also – with Carol Reed, the producer Edward Black and Rex Harrison – scheduled to make the RAF epic *Spitfire* in 1941, till a Darryl F. Zanuck project caused its cancellation.

The pair's movement towards concentration on war projects took two forms. First, there were the features written for Reed, the outbreak-of-war thriller *Night Train to Munich* (June 1940) and then *The Young Mr Pitt* (September 1942), which, like Korda's more romantic *That Hamilton Woman* (1941), suggested the French Revolution and Napoleonic wars as parallels to the modern struggle (with the French fleet poised to invade like the Luftwaffe, and Pitt's rebuilding of the fleet paralleling the rearming of modern Britain). Secondly, there was work (credited and un-credited) for Ministry of Information propaganda shorts, with more of Gilliat observable (perhaps because of Launder's involve-ment in *Spitfire*), for instance his scenarios for *From the Four Corners* (Havelock Allan, June 1941), a fifteen-minute non-combat film celebrating Commonwealth allies, and for *Mr Proudfoot Shows a Light* (March 1941), a short comic lesson about blackout regulations. Such films are the only tangible evidence of much uncredited work by both. However, one other short, all of eight minutes long, has a significance beyond itself. *Partners in Crime* (June 1942), a comic-didactic warning against the black market, was the first film directed as well as written by Launder and Gilliat. Now their work for the MOI and their reputation as writers for feature films brought them the offer from the MOI of writing and directing a feature-length documentary covering the home front war effort. Though this never eventuated, it metamorphosed into a work combining aspects of both their feature and MOI films, *Millions Like Us*. The success of this film established them as major writer-directors and led to the two films made in 1944, *Two Thousand Women* and *Waterloo Road*, which also left the combat film to others. (Of their MOI films only the script that Launder wrote for *Soldier, Sailor* (Shaw, 13 August 1945) is part situated on the war front.)

In the foreground of the background

The mainstream war film is a combat film, centring on a male group preparing for, and taking part in, combat. In such films women's roles are almost necessarily plangent and circumscribed, as in Coward and Lean's *In Which We Serve* (1942) where the wives, Mrs Kinross (Celia Johnson), Mrs Lewis (Kay Walsh) and Mrs Hardy (Joyce Carey), are only seen via the men's memories. They are essential inspirations to their husbands, but their own battle is wholly internal and stoical, waiting and not weeping. *The Heart of Britain*, a Crown Unit short of 1941, celebrates women's more material contribution, but in terms controlled by peacetime expectations:

> Behind this grim work lies an infinite number of patient everyday tasks for the women, dull jobs like typing lists of addresses, unending ones like sorting clothes for the homeless, routines which women fill with love and devotion, and the simplest, most difficult task of all, just staying put with the war around the corner.

The reality altered dramatically with the demands of total war, which led to female conscription in the *National Service Act (No. 2)* of 10 December 1941. This meant that by early 1942 all single women between 21 and 30 were at the government's disposal for entry into the auxiliary forces, industry or agriculture. The home front, the productive base on which the armed forces depended, was itself exposed to extreme war conditions through aerial bombardment. Naturally, therefore, it was a vital target for government efforts to maintain morale, and the immense deployment of the female population into previously male areas significantly altered the terms in which women were addressed, from passive to active partners, with all the complications such shifts from conventional notions of femininity entailed. Launder and Gilliat, in gravitating to the home front, and particularly to 'the fate – if you like to call it that – of the conscripted woman, the mobile woman',[1] were no doubt attracted by its domestic-epic qualities, by a sense of significant changes and perhaps by an aesthetic opportunism, the desire to cover areas less expected than those in other war films.

In concentrating on the female contribution to the home front (*Two Thousand Women* is a displaced home front narrative), Launder and Gilliat shared problems of representation with other wartime film-makers. Their works were part of the war effort, dedicated to the sustaining of morale, and subject to pressures of acceptability and censorship. Some writing, like Sue Harper's on the representation of women in World War II, tends to overlook, not just the priorities which governed everything loosely categorizable as propaganda, but the dominant structures of feeling of the time, as when it criticizes *Millions Like Us* for not representing the dislike many women had for industrial work.[2] Launder and Gilliat's brief was clearly to represent factory work positively, but such positive representation had to pass a reality test by convincing viewers that it contained a sufficient quota of the actual to be acceptable. Surely a watcher would have to be very unintelligent to think that the jobs done in *Millions* weren't tedious and fatiguing, even though that – understandably – is not what the film emphasizes. Though Jennifer's alienation from her work ('War effort's caught it in the neck again,' says Gwen as Jennifer is admonished) has much to do with class and temperament, and, anyway, is eventually overcome, it allows certain things about the work's unpleasantness to be covertly stated. However, it is important to bear in mind that, in a film viewing female war work positively, representations of dissatisfaction would have alienated the wartime audience who expected women to work as uncomplainingly as men. It's hard to see how the film could have sustained the positives emerging from the female group if at the same time the audience saw them as whingers. Harper's other criticism, that relations in the factory are patriarchally and comfortingly controlled by Charlie,[3] is true, but again surely reflects the reality of the time, which in a film founded in realism can hardly be dismissed. Alternative representations would have been fantasy. However, it should be noted that Charlie never questions the place of the women in the industrial process or their capabilities, and in this sense his paternalistic role is positive.

Two other particular problems were shared with all film-makers working on projects that embraced rather than escaped the war.

These were the twin necessities of constructing images of the United Kingdom which represented the unity of the different nations and regions, and which also represented the nation's class hierarchies in such a way as (a) to override divisions without improbably denying their realities, and (b), increasingly to suggest that a benefit of the war – justifying its hardships – would be social changes affecting class differences in a very stratified society, and also advancing women in the postwar world, though clearly not in such a way as to alienate median opinion. As in the other famous female-oriented wartime films, *The Gentle Sex* (Howard, 1943) and *The Lamp Still Burns* (Elvey, 1943), and of course the paradigmatic male group films, the groups in *Millions Like Us* and *Two Thousand Women* contain representatives of the other nations and classes besides the predominant English middle class. *Millions Like Us* includes Fred from Glasgow and Gwen from Wales, the concert at the Hippodrome features a Welsh male-voice choir singing 'Land of our fathers', and the ballroom sequence has a massed dance to a frenetically speeded up 'Loch Lomond'. The Northern Irish, with their more tendentious connotations, tend not to be part of this, though there are exceptions, as in *The Bells Go Down* (1943). Perhaps accidentally, *Two Thousand Women* registers the possible strains of producing such affirmations, in the characters' inconsistent uses of the terms 'English' and 'British' throughout the film, and in the climax where the Glaswegian and very unEnglish Maud leads, with hyperactive enthusiasm, the singing of 'There'll always be an England'. In *Millions Like Us* Charlie Forbes/Eric Portman (Yorkshire) and Annie Earnshaw/Terry Randall (Lancashire) represent the Northern regions. In the self-contained South London world of *Waterloo Road* questions of the wider nation hardly impinge, which is one reason why it feels more conservative than Launder and Gilliat's earlier works. In *Waterloo Road* the emphasis falls on the representation of the working class, though, because of the relatively sealed-off world of the film, there is little class interaction. It should be noted that while one of Launder and Gilliat's ambitions was to break the infrequently challenged mould of comic-condescending representation of the working class, they faced major difficulties in this, because as Gilliat himself noted, there were few non-comic actors from other than a middle-class background[4] – so that representations tended to be comic (Annie Earnshaw in *Millions*) or slightly unconvincing, and often to substitute a representation of the petit bourgeoisie, the lowest middle class, for the working-class. Patricia Roc's performance in *Millions Like Us* is wonderfully affecting, but, without a trace of working-class accent, she is an instance of this, and, as a contemporary reviewer noted, 'a little bit Ritzy' for the part.[5]

One of Launder and Gilliat's great abilities in dealing with the home front and the wartime woman is their unportentousness. The famous appearance of the occluded figure and voice of Leslie Howard in *The Gentle Sex* (1943), mediating the worries of a society sensing major changes, is a great cinematic moment, and not as conservatively reprehensible as is sometimes imagined from a later date where the paternalistic condecension in its speaking to widespread feelings, shared by both men and women, is exaggerated. But Launder and Gilliat, perhaps out a mixture of greater unflappability and a spirit both more radical and more superficial, seem to accept the changes much more easily (at least in the first two films which concentrate on them – *Waterloo Road* being, perhaps, another story). There is something liberating about representations so positive with hardly a trace of an idealized role model in sight. *Two Thousand Women* was always the least praised of the three films because it didn't wholly fit dominant modes of realism, but with the loosening of that hegemony, its brilliant interplay between realism and generic motivations is much more available for contemporary viewers. Equally, while the sense of realism that is such a great achievement of *Millions Like Us* still impinges very strongly on contemporary viewers, they are now perhaps better placed to appreciate other aspects of that film's complexity.

## *Millions Like Us* (Launder and Gilliat, 1942)

*L'entrée des usines Launder et Gilliat*

*Millions Like Us*, from its first reviews on, has been the most critically respected and discussed of all Launder and Gilliat's films, though it is probably not their most characteristic work. Symptomatically, the most distinguished piece of writing on the film, as well as some lesser ones, treat it as a kind of unauthored communal text, at least without feeling the need of sustained reference to its makers.[6] Such approaches reflect a sense of the direct pressure of structures beyond the authors, the authorship of the age in less mediated form than in their other films. To take two antithetical aspects: the profound influence of documentary in the film (explained by the project's origins and Launder and Gilliat's work for the MOI) is not something at the forefront of their films either before or after; and the surge of emotionality produced by the end of the film – arguably the most extraordinary release of feeling in the British wartime cinema – is not exactly characteristic of the film-makers' other work, where the understated comic inflection is so prevalent (though part of the complexity of the scene of Celia's reinsertion into the group is that it happens through a comic song burlesquing a jilted woman's grief rather than a widow's).

The most central of the discussions alluded to above, Andrew Higson's in *Waving the Flag*, is built around four perceptions. (1) The film's project is to construct an image for wartime of the nation. (2) The image of the nation is closely connected to the image of the family, most radically in the film's sense of a new and expanded family superimposed on the older one. (3) The mixture of radical and conservative elements running through the film reflects both the drive towards a changed society opened up through the war, and more conservative traditional needs. (4) The film's coalescing of documentary and feature film creates a work with the attractions of feature films (empathy, identification, heterosexual romance) but also with the ability of documentary modes (especially montage sequences) to register the larger public sphere which the feature film usually treats only as an adjunct of its individually oriented narrative.

These elements are not unique to *Millions Like Us* among war front and home front films, but they have especial force in it, and the discussion below takes for granted their importance. This discussion is in three parts. The first focuses on the opening sequence of documentary images, reading through them some of the particular as well as general meanings that documentary enacts in the film. The second examines some of the bridges the narrative makes between the private and public worlds, moving from its most protracted sequences of montage to a small scene played by a single actor in an unaltering location. The third, looking at the most commercial-feature-oriented parts of the film, the relationships between Celia and Fred and Jennifer and Charlie, which provide the main 'classical cinema' identificatory structures, argues that the second relationship in fact plays a key role, modulating perception of the whole narrative.

The nine-shot title-credit sequence shows workers arriving for a factory shift, reverse-echoing Lumiere's ur-documentary *La Sortie des usines Lumière* (1895). The camera setups viewing the workers are all static, the only movement the crowd's within the frames. Probably shot on 'field work' for the original MOI project, the visuals' graininess, natural uneven lighting, lack both of orchestrated camera work and obvious direction of the seemingly unselfconscious crowd, suggest a profilmic reality as little altered by camera presence as possible. In six of nine shots the camera looks straight on at the workers moving rapidly towards and past it.

While the visuals connote documentary, title and credits suggest the feature film, with the names of the stars preceding the film's title and other credits (Patricia Roc and Eric Portman in shots 1 and 3, the others in shot 2, the film's title in shot 4, and the other credits 6–9), all preceded by the entertainment connotations of the Gainsborough logo. Documentaries, of course without star billings, construct their credits differently (e.g. Jennings's *Listen to Britain* (1941): (1) logo of gun and violin, (2) Crown Film Unit and producer credit, (3) director, etc., credits, (4) Foreword).

Where the credits deviate is in shot 4, where the words 'And Millions Like You' are followed by the film's title 'in "Millions Like Us"' in shot 5. Here, rather than just playing entertainment film credits, albeit slightly modified towards unglamorousness, against documentary visuals, the credits themselves are modulated by documentary values expressed in the words 'And Millions Like You'. These play with the epic film's clichéd boast of 'a cast of thousands', but transcend it with reference to the 'millions' on the home front, to suggest that the audience (or, more literally, sur-rogates in whom they will immediately recognize themselves) are to be the supporting cast to stars implicitly more similar to than glamorously different from themselves. (In particular, Patricia Roc, Anne Crawford and even Eric Portman, though not decon-structed so much as to be without glamour, are presented, as Antonia Lant notes of Celia, to 'gleam less with the sheen of the fetish'[7]). The film, which very consciously chooses the identifi-catory attractions of the commercial feature in order to broaden its appeal, says, however, through these titles, that star identifications will be significantly more inflected by realism than usual, the real having a particular appeal and value in the extreme reality of the war.

The shot setups are generally so simple and the resulting images so natural, seemingly 'found' rather than constructed, that it requires some effort to articulate the meanings they propound – the ordinary, durable drabness of the workers; the starkness of their surrounds lit only by winter sunlight, the large number of women among the factory employees, all with their connotations of a quotidianly unidealized war situation. Others are established by absence rather than presence – the lack, for instance, of any military personnel (the millions of the title specifically referring to the home front participants). Yet others emerge by a negation of the more monumentally heroic, pathos-ridden Soviet and Nazi documentary traditions, known to the film-makers and in glimp-ses at least to much of the audience, not to mention a down-to-earth distancing from the ennobling working-class images of the 1930s British documentary tradition, to which, of course, in other ways the sequence is indebted. Launder and Gilliat's emphatically non-documentary background doesn't prevent them from grasp-ing effective documentary principles very quickly (after all, as Brown emphasizes, they shared with Hitchcock in particular a fascination with showing English lower-middle-class reality),[8] but it does distance them from what they might have considered the rather high falutin political-aesthetic extremes of the Grierson tradition.

Like other more elevatedly heroic documentarists, though, Launder and Gilliat do surround their images with some heroic-aesthetic connotations, here deriving from Beethoven's Fifth Symphony on the sound track. The difference, though, is that there is an unclosed tension between image and sound, with the camera resisting picking out images obviously justifying the music's aura, so that an ordinariness touched by grandeur, reinterpreted by it rather than transfigured by it, results. As their site Launder and Gilliat chose an industrial workplace devoid of high historical-cultural associations, or traces of the pastoralism so often invoked in British war-time films, and added no sense of specialness or pageant to it (in this, and many other ways, differentiating it from the Nuremburg site of *Triumph des Willens* (1936)). The crowd are not involved in watching or being part of a spectacle. They just walk, then hurry, to work. As they advance the camera refuses to distinguish any of them from the others, either for beauty or pathos, *à la* Riefenstahl, with the crowd moving so quickly, the camera view so broad, and the shots so brief (some last ten seconds, but the average is under five) that only fleetingly, remembering that the titles interfere with scanning the detail of the shots, are individuals likely to impinge on the viewer. For instance, in shot 2 a woman in a dark hat at screen right dabs her eye as if it is irritated, a younger blonde woman moves forward dragging on a cigarette (like others with fags in their mouths enjoying the small unhealthy pleasures of austerity) and a man passes the camera at screen right with his hand up, palm outward, to his mouth – as if trying to dislodge something from his teeth. In the last shot, as the crowd, particularly the younger women, start to run (presumably nearly late for work), a man walks unhurriedly, rather eccentrically, from screen left to right, hand on breast in a mannered, opaque gesture. Such moments signify as the serendipities of the real, rather than by any weight of symbolic meaning (though the last might suggest tolerance of the odd, the unregimented, even in a state of war society), but this sense of the unorchestrated unadorned is constructed – such meanings, we must remember, are not essences, but are constructed by the film – into vital ideological meaning through the sequence, to signify the monumentality of the unmonumental, the will of a nation imaged in ordinariness, yet, as the Beethoven declares, with its own formidable understated power and unemphasized pathos. Only twice, in shots 5 and 7, are high angles used, with their propensity to form the movement of crowds into abstract lines of force, readable as the advance of destiny, the tide of history, etc., and the sequence equally eschews Soviet-style metaphor. All but one of the other shots have the workers moving towards the camera not as a single force but, though forward and with purpose, in differing directions, left, right and centre, as if to suggest there can be will without absolute regimentation.

Alongside the almost self-contained sequence of the production of the bomber later in the narrative, these opening nine shots constitute the film's purest documentary sequence, but elsewhere there is pervasive use of documentarily shot material to reinforce the film's realistic look, sometimes even at the risk of slightly uneven transitions to non-documentary shots. The documentary parts, however, generally imitate to a significant degree the lighting and framing of the non-documentary parts of the film, many of which take place in documentary settings like the factory, the canteen, the dancehall and the pub, where it can be difficult to decide where documentary shots end and feature film ones begin. If the viewer or analyst is in danger of taking the extensive influence of documentary for granted, looking again at the complex shot that follows Celia's being told of Fred's death, which overtly employs the rhetoric of the melodrama in moving from a closeup of the photograph of the wedding party to Celia lit and posed highly articifically in statuesque grief, will solidify the point by its extreme difference. The point is, of course, essential. Not only was the construction/reflection of the real a central value in British wartime cinema, and one with a high emotional charge to it, but it was also seen as distinguishing the British war film in credibility from the American. On the other hand, at various points, though licensed by a certain accord with naturalism, the overtly melodramatic can – in the case at hand aurally – invade the scene, as in the repeated instances where the sound of Wellingtons flying overhead prefigures Fred's death. Melodrama and realism do not necessarily cancel each other out, but meet in 'the melodrama of everyday life', one of the terms in which Higson discusses the film.[9]

## Public and private

*Millions'* interestingly unstable opening third mixes documentary montage and narrative sequences to an unusual degree. The credit sequence gives way to the slightly fatuous documentary passage on prewar seaside pleasures, which, presented in quotation marks, underlines the film's awareness of its narrative strategies – that condescendingly jolly upper-middle-class commentary will not recur. It resolves into the Crowsons' departure for their summer holiday, followed by another set of (uncommentated) seaside documentary shots, then the arrival at the boarding house, moving to the scene of Phyllis and Celia's evening at the pier, where Phyllis is surrounded by men and Celia only courted by the boring boy from Market Harborough. The glimpses of the Pierrot show on and off stage that follow, though in the same general space of the pier, are in no sense presented from Celia's or Phyllis's viewpoint: and particularly illustrate the narrative's desire to at least partly dissolve the boundaries of the individually oriented feature film. The female performer's choric quoting of Gray's 'Ode on a Distant Prospect of Eton College' ('Alas, regardless of their doom, / The little victims play! / No sense have they of time to come, / Nor care beyond today'), followed by the beginning of war signified in the disappearance of the lights on the pier and then by the individual coming out of the shop while the camera goes in to find the sign saying 'no blackout material', could, clearly, have been given in a personalized mode through the Crowsons, as in the moment where the landlady gets the news of Hitler turned off so that she can listen to the dance music ('Ah, Ambrose!'). *Millions'* use of Charters and Caldicott

(Basil Radford and Naunton Wayne) from *The Lady Vanishes* and *Night Train to Munich* can be seen in the same light: familiar, comfortable figures, but here not tied into any plot mechanism or relationship with the main characters at all, and used, blatantly, to extend the scope of the narrative, to present other aspects that the plot, in its most limited sense, would be closed off from.

The most highly structured single example of the intersection of documentary montage and narrative is the 'Purple Alert' and subsequent bombing raid, which briefly causes the evacuation of the factory. This sequence of ninety-eight shots, over approximately seven minutes fifty seconds (an average shot time of about four and a half seconds), insists, despite its being the occasion of significant happenings in the private sphere – Jennifer's baiting of Charlie into carrying her out of the factory by force, and Gwen's conversation with Celia in the shelter about Fred – on placing these actions within a wider set of perspectives than those of the main character–focalizers. Instead there is a panoramic view of the raid, with multiple sites of interest, some returned to, some only seen once: the controller figure in his room, playing records, using the phone; the roof spotters; women setting up a barrage balloon and finding the range for anti-aircraft guns; the firefighters after the bombs have fallen; the women in the factory, some known to the watcher, some not; Celia and Gwen, Charlie and Jennifer; the emptying of the factory as production stops; waiting in the bomb shelter; the return to the factory after the raid.

Though the later narrative becomes more conventionally struc- tured, especially as Celia and Fred's romance becomes central, residues of documentary montage in excess of simple establishing shots continue to play a part, and the wartime inescapability of the public realm is stressed even in a sequence which seems to be predominantly private. After their quarrel, Fred waits for Celia outside the factory and persuades her to come to a quiet country pub to talk. Even here the film takes the opportunity – where, as far as establishing is concerned, shots 4 and 5 (even just 5) would suffice – of inserting a very brief montage prelude: (1) shot closing in on shift indicator board; 'Night' being slid in; (2) closeup; Bell going off; (3) girls leaving their machines; (4) dissolve to crowds coming out; (5) Fred watching for Celia. Thus this moment of domestic tension has a pronounced context of work, routines, crowds. When Celia allows herself to be persuaded, she and Fred ride off on Fred's motorbike to an apparently deserted country pub. It turns out to be chokingly full of soldiers, and when Fred only half goes in he is berated: 'Make up your mind, chum, are you coming in or not?' When he and Celia do, the rest of their conversation is staged so that, whether shots are medium or medium closeup, others are always in the frame with them. When Fred goes to order drinks, a soldier tries to pick Celia up, and when Fred asks, 'You wouldn't like to marry me, would you?', before Celia can answer they are interrupted by a soldier moving between them, and then asking Fred to help pass his pint. When Celia agrees, the song on the wireless or pub record player (clearly diegetic, though we don't see the source) culminates with the line 'What more can I say', a last detail encapsulating the private/public tensions of the scene. The device expresses, of course, a sense of pleasure and accord, but also registers the public ownership of the most intimate emotions (cf. the big 'Combined Operations' dance scene at which Celia and Fred remeet and the final canteen sing-song scene where Celia's personal grief is contained).

In the first sequences above personal narrative is intersected by public montage in a formally inventive and unconventional way. In the sequence with Celia and Fred, montage is vestigially retained at the beginning, but the hemming in of the private world by the public is expressed chiefly in terms of the placement of intimacies within an overbearingly public context. In a third scene, given the context created elsewhere, related meanings may even be produced in a context as restricted and unpublic as the little solo (except for the cat) performance of Mr Crowson's (Moore Marriott) lonely homecoming after all his daughters have become in one way or another 'mobile women'. Coming in from the wet and parking his rifle, he fails to notice a telegram on the floor. A saccharine version of 'Home sweet home' plays. He greets the cat, and clears a space for his parcel of fish and chips and bottle of beer amidst the chaos on the table. Visiting the formidably neglected kitchen, he picks up an unwashed plate from the sink, runs it and a knife and fork under the tap, shakes them and dries them unhygienically, drinks, complainingly, some beer, takes his boots off – a close-up revealing a massively undarned sock – chases the cat off the table, picks up a chip with his fingers and eats it. Going back into the hall he finds the telegram and reads it. 'I am getting married on Monday. Don't be cross. He's ever so nice. Can you come up? His name is Fred Blake. He's a sergeant gunner in the RAF. Love, Celia.'

The scene is simultaneously satiric and replete with pathos. It makes the point pungently that the father is domestically helpless without the females in the house, exposing the aged patriarch in all his weakness, so that he becomes, we may feel, a way of imaging the sloughing-off of outmoded aspects of patriarchal control (with Charlie representing what are felt to be more essential ones). At the same time, the deserted, disarrayed house, bereft of family and women, is replete with a pathos relating to other characters' (Fred's and Celia's, and even Jennifer's and Charlie's) visions of homes after the war. The comic-parodic 'Home sweet home' – to be used in *Two Thousand Women* a year later with very affirmative connotations – is highly ambivalent, reminding us that, whatever feelings about change are invoked in *Millions Like Us*, the homes that are imagined after the war are for the mass of viewers not some version of secular kibbutz or national crèche, but better versions of the present. Higson's extended comparison in *Waving the Flag* demonstrates how much less conservative a film *Millions Like Us* is than the Coward/Lean *This Happy Breed* (1944), where the home is the unchanging physical centre of the narrative.[10] The home imaged here in *Millions Like Us* in its all but absence, in the context of the alternative societies coming into existence for the duration of the war, asks what the new postwar homes will be like just as the relationship of Jennifer and Charlie asks similar questions about the postwar relationships between men and women, alongside the class questions it also raises.

## Celia and Fred, Jennifer and Charlie

> I had scarcely thought it possible ... that such a clearly confected affinity should be justified with such tart, ironic insight. (C. A. Lejeune on Jennifer and Charlie, *Observer*, 3 October 1943)

One of the defining aspects of the classical narrative film is a romantic plot closely bound up with the other plot material of the film.[11] (The war front film can constitute an exception, but romance and family can be smuggled in, usually by flashback.) The home front narrative obviously finds it easier to bring in such material as part of the action, and all three of Launder and Gilliat's films do so (even if in *Two Thousand Women* by devices owing more to generic convention than to realism). Had Launder and Gilliat followed the original MOI brief, *Millions Like Us* would probably have made equivalents of the less erotically ideal Gwen and Annie momentary heroines rather than supporting roles. Instead, however profoundly affected by documentary *Millions Like Us* is, it is very much marked as a mainstream entertainment film, with not just one but two love plots, pulling the audience into a complex of emotional identifications spread over the four characters Celia, Fred, Jennifer and Charlie, and perhaps even an unruly fifth in Phyllis.

*Millions Like Us* thus addresses the audience's sexual, romantic and familial desires, but, like other British war films, in a significantly constrained way, so that they are subject to the depredations, deferments, uncertainties and tragedies of war. It's an exaggeration to suggest, as has been done, that Celia is *punished* for her personal desires,[12] but the three films have different versions of the priorities encapsulated in Charlie's admonition to Celia, 'it may make the world go round, but it won't win the war'. In *Millions* Celia has to be content with brief happiness, and stoically bear Fred's death, while the outcome of Jennifer and Charlie's relationship, produced by the war, is suspended. It should be noted too, as another aspect of Launder and Gilliat's realism (in the particular senses of a sometimes lively unidealism and, no doubt, a reflection of common behaviour), that the war's encouragment to short-term relationships and promiscuity is given more of a presence in their films than in other war films, with Phyllis's multiple boyfriends in *Millions Like Us*, Ted's activities in *Waterloo Road*, and Bridie's desires in *Two Thousand Women*.

Even in the film's early more unorthodox phases, as it resists settling into linear narrative, Celia is marked out as its central strand. The dutiful, shy, dreamy younger sister, whom Phyllis mocks for cuddling up with fantasies of Charles Boyer, domesticated, child-centred, devoted to her father, finds herself designated a 'mobile woman', assumes her place in the factory, and then meets the un-Boyerlike young airman, Fred (Gordon Jackson). As the narrative becomes less fragmented, their relationship becomes increasingly dominant, although, as argued above, it is never separated from the public world. In her essay on women in the World War II cinema Sue Harper is scathing about Celia and what she implies about the film's attitudes to women, noting how 'difffident' and 'agreeable' she is, and how 'Her body language – consistently lowered gaze, closed posture – speaks of demure primness'. 'Only a female constructed in such a way can inspire the war effort.'[13] This is a rather partial view of Celia: after all she does, despite that lowered gaze, leave home, bring her father round to supporting her call-up, adapt to the new society of the factory, and decide to marry Fred without getting her father's permission. But, accepting its main outlines, the point is oversimple for two reasons. First, Fred is quite as gauchely innocent as she is (in fact it is Celia who initiates their relationship). The fact that she is parallelled by a male character, whom we would hesitate to label as similarly representative, suggests that her absolute representativeness needs questioning. Both she and Fred are regarded by other characters almost as children. Both Jennifer and Gwen call Celia 'kid', and Higson insightfully, in developing his family images for the characters, sees Celia as the younger sister and Fred as the younger brother in a persuasive putative audience identification.[14] Secondly, seeing Celia as the film's ruling female stereotype extracts her from the context of the other women, most of all Jennifer. Despite Celia's predominance, the viewer's experience with the film is surely likely to be that the group, though narrower than that in *Two Thousand Women*, essentially confined to Gwen and Jennifer (and, outside the group, Phyllis), displays a variety of qualities often not identical with Celia's. (As Phyllis says impatiently to Mr Crowson early in the film, 'Celia's not me!')

It should be difficult to miss the parallelism set up between Celia and Fred and Jennifer and Charlie. In the first there are youth and inexperience, characters from roughly the same class sector, and a tragic trajectory that leaves Celia a war widow. In the second, greater maturity, interesting frictions of temperament and class (Jennifer, London upper middle class; Charlie, Yorkshire upper working/lower middle class), and the couple's destiny is emphatically unresolved, semi-allegorically linked to the question of whether the war has changed the nation enough to make it viable in the new peacetime context. The war brings Celia and Fred together, uprooting her from ordinary town life and Fred from Glasgow to the Midlands, but we feel that Celia would probably have met his local equivalent in peacetime. This is hardly so with Jennifer and Charlie, who inhabit not just different geographical areas but class sectors so distinct that only the dislocations of war could have brought them together. (In fact Jennifer's 'natural' partner is seen in the offficer-class Harry with whom she has been out on a date just prior to her pretending to go to sleep on Charlie's shoulder.)

The intensely structured parallelism begins about one third of the way into the narrative, from where it is intimately traced in thirteen scenes, and half traced in more if we see the rebellious daughter, Phyllis, metamorphosed into Jennifer as the private family is replaced by the larger surrogate workplace family, with Phyllis after that only making short appearances in the later narrative.

1   Celia, Gwen and the other girls arrive at the hostel by coach. Jennifer arrives by taxi and is immediately established by this, her manners and ultra-fashionable clothes as an upper-middle-class outsider. An immediate connection with Celia is made when the taxi driver (though much younger than Mr Crowson) echoes Celia's father's suspicions that women's war work is a front for sexual misbehaviour.

2 Celia's roomsharing with Gwen is immediately contrasted with Jennifer's with Annie Earnshaw, the working-class Lancashire girl, and their mutual incomprehension of each other.

3 In the factory Celia's good training-school report, noted by Charlie, is contrasted with Jennifer's bad one and her sardonic, uncooperative attitude.

4 The 'Combined Operations' dance sequence. Celia and Fred's growing romance is played against the antagonism between Jennifer and Charlie (with its indicators of sexual interest beneath the hostility) as they snub each other by choosing different dancing partners. The parallelism between Celia and Jennifer is formally expressed by Jennifer passing Celia and Fred as she enters the dancehall and they leave it, and then by her leaving it as they come back in. Charlie makes a joke about Jennifer's lack of interest in children, which implicitly contrasts her with Celia. It even extends to the same tipsy middle-aged man dancing first with Celia, then trying to dance with Jennifer.

5 In a reversal of the situation in 3, Celia is reprimanded by Charlie for daydreaming, while he has no criticism to make of Jennifer's work.

6 In the 'Purple Alert' sequence, in contrast to Celia's and the others' obeying of regulations, Jennifer provocatively stays at her machine, parodying the duty that Charlie has tried to instill in her. When she replies mockingly to his asking her whether she wants him to use force ('Oh, Mr Forbes!'), he carries her out. In the shelter her anger cools and her expression suggests she realizes that there is a component of desire in Charlie's anger. The camera pans from her to Celia and Gwen discussing Fred.

7 As Celia and Gwen return by train from the Hippodrome concert, Jennifer gets into a compartment occupied by Charlie. Cut from her pretending to fall asleep on Charlie's shoulder to Gwen and Celia talking about Fred.

8 The canteen sequence where Celia's honeymoon is discussed. Jennifer sits next to Celia on one of the two occasions where the two (who are not represented as intimate) talk. Jennifer lends her her underwear and her nightdress.

9 Celia's wedding party. When the happy couple leave, Jennifer and Charlie comment on them rather fondly and parentally as they will do again in the film's penultimate scene, and Charlie asks Jennifer to the pictures.

10 In the factory after Celia's honeymoon, Celia is embarrasssed when Jennifer asks her if Fred liked the underclothes, while Jennifer is amused by Celia's shy inexperience. ('You are a funny kid').

11 Charlie reacts sharply to Jennifer's familiarity in the workplace. Celia is called to the office to be informed of Fred's death over Germany.

12 The shot of Celia alone, listening to the sound of children, dissolves to Jennifer and Charlie on the hill above the town, discussing Celia and Fred and their own relationship. Charlie tells Jennifer that he won't marry her because of their class differences, until he knows whether the wartime changes will continue after the war, but in such a way as to leave the issue open.

13 Jennifer is present in the group around Celia in the canteen during the community singing, in which Celia submerges private grief in group affirmation.

It is not only a question of an extended structural parallel. While Patricia Roc's and Gordon Jackson's performances were much commented on at the time of the film's release for their innocence and fetchingness, both Jennifer and Charlie are embodied in compelling representations by more mature actors. Anne Crawford, tall, languid, oval-faced, had a register that could embrace the vapidity of the man-crazy Margaret in *Two Thousand Women* ('Did I ever tell you how I fought for my virtue in a bungalow in Harpenden?'). Usually though, her almost excessive sartorial elegance – witness her tight broadchecked suit, highly mannered hat, and supercilious cigarette holder as she arrives at the workers' hostel in *Millions Like Us* – is accompanied by formidable characteristics, as with her self-indulgent but self-knowing Vera in Gainsborough's *They Were Sisters* (Crabtree, 1945). Literally and metaphorically sophisticated, the later film's scene where she is given a facial massage by a servant, derives obliquely from the moment in *Millions Like Us* where Annie is as amazed by her night-time beauty aids as Jennifer is by Annie's sleeping in her underwear. In her Hollywood role of Morgan Le Fay in *The Knights of the Round Table* (Thorpe, 1954), just before her premature death, this combination of languorous spoiledness and wilful intelligence is angled towards an impressive picture-book evil. More centrally, though, her rich bitch aura creates more ambivalent effects, typing her at once as pretentious, but also, in the complex context of *Millions Like Us*, where her upperclassness undergoes some populist chastisement ('War effort's got it in the neck again'), giving her an independence which fascinates Charlie. When in *Sisters* a suitor tells her, 'You're very amusing, you're lovely and you're as hard as nails', she replies, 'How right you are. Now is it my turn? Physically you'll pass in a crowd, a little over sophisticated perhaps, and there's a danger of your head swelling to the size of a balloon.' This directly imitates the tone of her reply to Charlie in *Millions*' penultimate scene: 'As for you, you've no looks, you're oldfashioned, morbidly suspicious, dull, and your pipe makes horrible bubbly noises.' The repeat version testifies to an excitement felt about the transgressive aspects of her behaviour in *Millions* where, under the cover of her outsiderness, a great deal else is smuggled in.

The other half of the couple, Charlie Forbes, is Eric Portman, a central British 1940s screen presence, hood-eyed, purse-mouthed, brooding, full of veiled intensities, e.g. the Leutnants's Nazi fanaticism in *49th Parallel* (Powell and Pressburger, 1941), the antic fervour of Culpepper in *A Canterbury Tale* (Powell and Pressburger, 1944), and the dark doublenesses of the slightly later crime melodramas, *Wanted for Murder* (1946), *Dear Murderer*, *Corridor of Mirrors* (1947) and *Daybreak* (1948). Portman's native Yorkshireness gave him easy authority in the part of the factory foreman, and the constant sense of intelligence he gives off intersects happily with the particulars of Charlie's position and self-confidence as the ascending product of the most highly educated sector of the working class. The clash of the highly defined characteristics of these two notable actors gives the overtly symbolic,

almost allegorical representation of war-induced class dislocations promising possible postwar reorientations, a memorable
particularity (as witness Lejeune's just comment in the epigraph
on page 59). The film's penultimate scene (number 12 in the list
above) is in various ways antithetical to the extraordinarily 'voluptuous' (to use Higson's well-chosen word)[15] final scene of Celia's
reinsertion into the group, being a scene of debate, very self-
consciously working over large social questions. It is also wonderfully acted, its minute unspoken or half-spoken complexities as
memorable, at least to later viewings, as the emotional finale, and,
at least in retrospect, pulling the viewer back from complete
submergence in it.

Registering the importance of the second love relationship is
crucial. It makes it impossible to argue that participation with the
narrative involves a simple regressive attachment to a heroine
constructed as a malleable ultra-patriarchal fantasy. Celia is arguably more complicated than that (as is the narrative's attitude to
her, which, however loving, stresses her naivety, as in the two
fantasies she daydreams), but Jennifer, and her relationship with
Charlie, are certainly so. As the structures that parallel Celia and
Jennifer suggest, they are intimately related opposites, and the
meanings articulated around Jennifer, and Charlie, are as important as those produced around Celia and Fred.

### *Two Thousand Women* (Launder, 1944)

#### Uncaptive hearts

It is assumed that *Two Thousand Women* inverts the conventions
of the prisoner of war film, by taking 'classic formulas common to
the male prison camp dramas and transform[ing] them by
substituting the exploits of the women'.[16] Its female POWs may
not have the urge to escape which is predominant in male POW
films, but they keep up morale, outwit their captors by hiding RAF
flyers in the camp, expose a stool pigeon, and finally, under cover
of a camp concert, effect the flyers' escape. However, the trans-
formative relationship between *Two Thousand Women* and other

texts is retrospective, since the films that *Two Thousand Women* is taken to transform – *The Captive Heart* (Dearden, 1946), the first British WWII POW film, the later recapitulatory *The Wooden Horse* (Dalrymple, 1950) and *The Colditz Story* (Foxwell, 1954) or Wilder's *Stalag 17* (1953) – actually followed Launder's. Renoir's *La Grande Illusion* (1937) might possibly be an influence, with its transvestized men on the concert stage singing the Marseillaise at reports of a French victory, while in *Two Thousand Women* the female performers and audience sing 'There'll always be an England' as the RAF men escape, but Launder's stressing of real life over intertextuality is convincing. He said the idea came 'through two show girls who visited Shepherd's Bush. They were escapees from the women's internment camp at Vittel, where approximately two thousand women, caught at the time of the fall of France, were held captive. From the anecdotes they related, and their method of escape, I built the story'.[17] (One of them, Nicky Nicholson, credited extrafilmically as the film's 'technical advisor', introduced it at some early first-run performances at the Gaumont, Haymarket.)[18] Rather, then, than subverting earlier films, *Two Thousand Women* appears, remarkably, to have produced the variation before the theme.

Unchronological though the relationship is, some comparison with Dearden's *The Captive Heart* is enlightening. *The Captive Heart*'s overvoiced dedication to 'Prisoners of War' might almost be equally applied to *Two Thousand Women*: 'Their unbroken spirit is the symbol of a moral victory for which no bells have pealed ... It was a war in which no decorations could be given, but to have come out of it with a whole spirit is its highest honour.' But only 'might almost', because, though applicable in essence, the dedication's tone, at one with the relatively stable tone of *The Captive Heart*, is out of key with *Two Thousand Women*'s calculatedly unstable mix of melodrama, realism and comedy, black humour and proto-feminist thematics. Compare, for instance, the handling of the popular 'national' song 'There'll always be an England'. Dearden's marching prisoners whistle it stoically, wordlessly, as if the lyrics are too private to each individual to be publicly uttered. *Two Thousand Women* shows no such retractedness. The song is presented not in one, but in two modes: first Rosemary's sentiment-filled rendition, then the group's defiantly raucous bawling of it, schizophrenically unlike versions reflecting a deviation from the admired understated realism of *Millions Like Us* which alienated some early reviewers. Maud's shout to the new inmates of 'Welcome to Holloway' (the London women's prison) sets the tone for the earlier film's irreverence. 'Welcome to the gentlest English suburbs replicated' would more suit the atmospheres of Dearden's film. *Two Thousand Women* also refuses *The Captive Heart*'s borrowing of the flashback structure of earlier war films like *In Which We Serve* (1942), which allowed movement between the main narrative and memories of wives and homes. Of the dozen or so British women foregrounded in *Two Thousand Women*, a statistically improbable number seem independent of marriage – single, divorced or, with various of the older women, their status unclear so that they seem to all intents single. During the performance of 'Home sweet home' the camera lingers on a woman holding her daughter as she listens (presumably thinking of home and husband), but this is exceptional as *Two Thousand Women* insists on the centrality of the female group in their 'women (almost) alone' situation. It's true that the narrative manages to get three British airmen into the camp, but the male actors are overshadowed by the film's extraordinary females: Patricia Roc from *Millions Like Us*, Phyllis Calvert, already a Gainsborough star, Jean Kent beginning her run as the charismatic 'bad girl' of British cinema, Renée Houston, the clever, abrasive Scottish actress, memorable as a gold digger in the Launder-written *A Girl Must Live* (Reed, 1939), Anne Crawford familiar from *Millions Like Us*, the renowned Flora Robson, Muriel Aked (Miss Jezzard in *Happiest Days* and the queen in *The Story of Gilbert and Sullivan*), and various others.

## The narrative

*Two Thousand Women* brings together in a displaced version of the home front a group of British women arrested in France, 1940, as the Germans invade. The group, a microcosm of British society, gestures to the home nations and regions, if less inclusively than *Millions Like Us*, with Maud (Renée Houston), a tough Glaswegian, a dominant character, while Mrs Buttshaw (Thora Hird) represents the North of England. There is, too, a rare wartime representation, or half representation, of Irishness, in Jean Kent's Bridie Johnson, with implications discussed below. Class is densely if partially represented, and declared by Maud to be one of the two main problems of the community (sexual frustration being the other) — 'Not all of us are out of the same drawer'. Mrs Hope Latimer, once a lady in waiting to a countess, claims upper-class rank by contagion. Upper-middle-class gentility is the mark of Miss Manningford (Flora Robson), her companion Miss Meredith (Muriel Aked) and Mrs Hatfield (Kathleen Boutall). Beside them stand the more numerous middle class, and then the petit bourgeois characters who in films of this period tend to stand in for the manual working class (Mrs Woodbury, the butcher's wife, whom the women watch fighting with her class superior, Mrs Ogilvy, and Mrs Buttshaw who has owned a tea shop). Professions are hazier, but at the centre there are four younger working women, three of them, rather unrepresentatively, from the entertainment world (reflecting Launder's narrative source). The fourth, Freda, is a journalist. The film, in its robust, unsentimentalizing way, avoids aspects of the noble selfless group (if we believe Bridie, Freda isn't even a respectable journalist but 'a sobsister for a yellow rag') – so they're certainly not a group of nurses replaying *The Lamp Still Burns*. A spectrum of age is also represented, so that though the leading figures are youngish, the two Misses, Haddy and Mrs Hope Latimer are all middle-aged and the narrative takes care not to marginalize them.

*Two Thousand Women*'s narrative is difficult to summarize adequately, since, as a group film, its diffusion of interest across many characters, and the importance of small-scale interactions in the interstices of the main plotlines, complicate description. The abstract below can't suggest the important process, mostly achieved with minor characters, by which the divisions within the community are overcome. However, it usefully corrects some semi-authoritative misdescriptions (perhaps more interestingly seen as feminist fantasies about a text which both provokes and resists such reveries). Thus one critic has declared that Rosemary refuses James's proposal outright (so that the narrative's successful heterosexual love is denied, rather than marginalized), while another critic invents a scene that Launder tempts us to imagine, but certainly never gives us: 'in a scene of delirious awkwardness, a novice nun (Patricia Roc) is required to take her place behind the ostrich plumes. The "purity" of the agent clearly neutralizes the "pollution" of the act'.[19]

1  France, 1940: the German invasion. A nun (Patricia Roc, who later reverts to her name of Rosemary Brown) is arrested by French soldiers as a fifth columnist. Her claims that she is English are not believed and she is imprisoned, perhaps to be shot.

2  When the Germans arrive she becomes their prisoner and is sent to Marneville internment camp for British women along with Freda (Phyllis Calvert), a journalist, Bridie (Jean Kent), a stripper, and two middle-aged spinsters, Miss Manningford (Flora Robson) and Miss Meredith (Muriel Aked).

3  Arriving, the new internees are introduced to the other inmates, particularly Maud (Renée Houston) who acts as a sardonic presenter, and Teresa (Betty Jardine), later revealed as a Nazi plant. When the women are alotted rooms Bridie's seduction of the German sergeant types her sexuality as suspect. The new arrivals are treated to a bath by the longer-term internees.

4  A radio is mysteriously discovered – it will later be revealed to have been left by the elderly patriotic owner of the converted chateau, Monsieur Boper. However, as soon as it is used the guards confiscate it, proving the existence of a stool pigeon, 'Poison Ivy', in the group.

5  Suspicion briefly falls first on Rosemary, who reveals that she is a novice nun, then on Bridie.

6  During an air raid Miss Manningford and Miss Meredith are apprehended breaking the blackout to help the RAF, an act that will lead to their being sent to a 'punishment camp'.

7 Two of the RAF men, Jimmy (James McKechnie) and Alex (Reginald Purdell), having baled out, make their way by accident into the internment camp. Jimmy ends up in Rosemary's and Freda's room, while Freda is absent, thus enabling a love relationship, which will continue as the women hide the men and arrange their escape, while Alex ends up with the two Misses. A third flyer, Dave (Bob Arden) is as yet unaccounted for.

8 At a secret meeting, an inner group of the women plan the escape to coincide with the camp concert, and Monsieur Boper pledges help in hiding them.

9 In order to move them it is necessary to borrow Teresa's keys. Searching her room, Rosemary finds evidence that Teresa is a Nazi Party member.

10 Suspecting the presence of the flyers, the authorities order an assembly so that rooms can be searched, and the men attend this in grotesque transvestite disguise. While a message is passed around informing the other women about this, a counter message is sent that Teresa is a spy. At the moment when it seems that the second message will not prevent the disaster of the first reaching Teresa, Rosemary stages a situation-saving faint. While the meeting goes on the compromised German sergeant finds that Bridie is still in her room. She claims to be injured and he allows her to stay. After he leaves, Dave's presence is revealed. Importantly he has overheard part of a compromising conversation, and suspects Bridie of collaboration, putting an end to his romantic interest in her.

11 The meeting over, the two other flyers are shifted, and Bridie reveals that she has another in her room.

12 Alec remembers where he has seen Rosemary before. She is 'Mary Maugham', a stage entertainer, who was involved in a scandal with a married man and then joined a convent.

13 James angrily confronts Rosemary with her past, but then relents and continues to court her. She is attracted but initially resists.

14 The arrival of the German sergeant in Bridie's room causes a major crisis. He sees Dave, and Dave strangles him just as the

other men arrive. Dave fiercely resists Bridie's interest in him.

15 When the men are relocated they have to take the sergeant's body with them, and in a blackly comic scene they play cards with the corpse. Dave, who killed Hentzner, nearly cracks up.

16 With the concert – the front for the escape – imminent, the women, needing an act that will preoccupy the guards, decide to ask Bridie to do a striptease.

17 However, when Freda asks Bridie, she refuses, saying that she doesn't care if Dave doesn't escape. Freda bribes her by promising to arrange a meeting with him.

18 As the two Misses are sent to punishment camp, the women sing 'For they are jolly good fellows'.

19 As the camp concert begins, the men are moved to their final hiding place.

20 Freda brings Bridie and Dave together, but he angrily abuses her, not realizing how important Bridie is to the escape.

21 Distraught, Bridie puts a note betraying the escape under Teresa's door, just as Freda gets Dave to write Bridie a note pretending affection for her in order to secure her cooperation.

22 When Bridie receives this she tries to prevent Teresa from giving the warning. They fight, but Teresa wins and staggers out to warn Frau Holweg, the senior female authority.

23 When Holweg tries to enter the auditorium Maud knocks her out.

24 With Bridie unable to perform, Rosemary ambiguously announces that she will stand in for her.

25 Before doing so, she visits the men to arrange the last phase of the escape and commits herself to James when the war ends.

26 Rosemary, rather than stripping, sings 'There'll always be an England', and, in an extended sequence, intercutting action in the auditorium with the escape outside, Teresa bursts into the hall moments too late to give the alarm, and is set upon by the women. The film ends with the women defiantly singing 'There'll always be an England' while the escape is successfully completed.

## Calculated Instabilities

Looking back, Launder thought he 'should have treated the subject more seriously ... that it would have been a bigger film if I had concentrated less on the comedy and more on the drama'.[20]

Here he was surely wrong, perhaps overreacting to reviews which saw the film as superficial beside the realism of *Millions Like Us*. Edgar Anstey, who accused it of being 'aimed at the till rather than at the top flights of cinema',[21] noted that 'Launder cannot avoid giving rise in our minds to more solemn considerations than he is on this occasion prepared to tackle'.[22] The *Observer* (17 September 1944) saw the female group as public schoolgirls, 'played in the highest of spirits by Gainsborough's Young Ladies' and having 'a simply wizard time', a view echoed by the *Evening Standard* (16 September 1950) which, picking up connections with *The Happiest Days of Your Life*, described the film as '"The Head Girl of St Chad's" or some book by Angela Brazil all over again'. Outside the reviewers, a male student answering J. P. Mayer's questionnaire disliked the film both for its excessive realism in deglamorizing the women, and also on the seemingly incompatible grounds of its heightened stereotyping.[23] The spectrum of opinion adds up to a film that takes on more than it can handle, indulges too much superficial comedy, has too much and too little realism, is both too odd and too stereotyped, and lacks the 'sincerity and art' of *Millions Like Us* (*Daily Telegraph*, 18 September 1944). Read positively against the grain, however, the catalogue gives an insight into the film's calculatedly mixed, unstable mode, justifying Launder's first thoughts over his last.

The film's opening is as good a place as any to demonstrate something of its characteristic juxtapositions of mode and mood. Nothing could be less like the documentary beginning of *Millions Like Us* than the heightened generic melodrama of the beautiful nun wandering the forest at night, arrested by soldiers of whose identity it is impossible to be certain. (We probably catch their French, but are they French-speaking Germans? French fascists?) Cut to a room full of silent military personnel casually listening to a radio. Dance music ends with the announcement 'You have been listening to dance music played by Coriano and his Pampas Serenaders'. Coriano says goodnight in a cockney accent. John Snagge begins to read the news; the men cluster round to listen and then start talking in French. (The rest of the scene will establish exactly where we are – France 1940 – with the Germans closing in and Patricia Roc thought to be a Nazi sympathizer by the French soldiers gleaning news from the BBC.) As soon as Patricia Roc is brought in, a relaxed scene, dominated by the joke about Coriano's fake Latinity, and by quieter parallels to the unbalancing of the viewer in the previous scene through deliberate ambiguities in establishing place and nationality, shifts back into more melodramatic atmospheres. Seemingly threatened with execution, Roc faints. The third scene has her languishing in jail like a tableau from *Dialogues des Carmelites*. Alerted by heavy military footsteps both Roc and the viewer expect the worst. Surprisingly, Roc is confronted not by French but by German soldiers. The suspense only resolves in the next scene where she is farewelled politely by a German soldier as she gets into the van taking her to Marneville. The journey is predominantly marked by the comedy of Freda and Bridie's obsessive bitching at each other, though the comic tone is interrupted by the two Misses' stoic farewell to their domestics, with that pathos in turn slightly subverted by the unsentimental observation of degrees of tyranny in Miss Manningford's control over Miss Meredith.

These and other movements, large and small, between melodrama and comedy, empathy and detachment, realism and stereotype, accompanied by consistent wrongfootings of the spectator, foreshadow the mode of the following narrative. In selecting from his informant Nicky Nicholson's account, Launder omitted harsher material where the Germans are seen in a sadistic light (stealing Red Cross food parcels, ogling the women bathing, etc.),[24] a decision which by modifying tendencies to a black/white:us/them structure (really only hammered in the closing moments) allows emphasis on relationships within the group and the film's multiple types of femininity. The prevalence of comedy even within the film's tensest situations (most heightened where the airmen play cards with Sergeant Hentzner's corpse) encourages detachment even when the action is fastest-moving.

Anstey's critique that the film raises issues without resolving them may or may not have been aimed at such effects, but almost certainly chastised the slippages by which serious consequences for the women's acts are raised and then deflected. The two Misses aid the RAF by breaking the blackout, Maud KOs Frau Holweg, Teresa is assaulted, and it is more than possible that the women will be held partly responsible for the sergeant's death. Even where such possibilities are realized with Miss Manningford and Miss Meredith being taken off to punishment camp, the implications tend to be deflected by other material, the speed of the narrative and the rousing 'There'll always be an England' climax. In a sense Anstey is right about the evasions, but, on the other hand, the comic tone and instabilities work to create a locus in which the wartime female can be explored, celebrated and problematized without taking painful possibilities into areas which would undermine the carefully modulated strategies. What's gained justifies what's lost.

## Female affirmations

The arrival of the RAF men objectifies a sense that the females are being observed and judged. This does not take an extreme manifestation like Howard's overvoice in *The Gentle Sex*, but certainly the women see themselves as under male scrutiny – as when Margaret claims that Boper has been sent into the women's quarters 'to see we don't make a muck of things', or when Rosemary tells Freda that 'the boys don't think we can do it'. Here the presence of male characters in the diegesis, and the views attributed to them, replicate opinions held or half held, no doubt, by some, both male and female, in the audience. One of the novelties of *Two Thousand Women* for its original audience must have been seeing the women acting so resourcefully. For instance, Haddy isn't just painting canvases, she has also mapped the camp, while Freda exhibits exact knowledge of the camp perimeter's searchlights. There is also Jimmy's surprise that when Rosemary found him in her room she did not 'scream or something', to which her reply is simply 'Why?' Such moments are all the more impressive because the film resists idealization. The over-'feminine' Margaret does scream when Alec appears, and Maud's constant comments on sexual frustration and class antipathies quash any ideas of an Amazonian utopia. Nevertheless, in the crisis the women solve, at least temporarily, their problems of internal unity, with Mrs Hope Latimer, as well as Margaret and Annette (both younger characters slightly suspect both in terms of class and sexuality), playing important roles in the escape. A further demonstration of female abilities comes as conventional female weaknesses are self-consciously used to advantage by the women. Thus Rosemary, who genuinely fainted under interrogation, later *fakes* a faint to prevent Teresa finding out about the RAF men; Annette utilizes her sexuality, not like Bridie for personal advantage, but for the group's, by luring the chauffeur into a trap; and the female vice of gossip becomes a facade behind which vital messages can be sent in the assembly scene.

The (largely subverted) male scrutiny built into the narrative is parallelled by a second very literal inspection of the female when the newcomers are offered baths. Whether a male is present or the viewer is external, the female bathing scene is a traditional site of voyeurism, particularly in the French painting tradition of Fragonard, Courbet and Ingres, whose 'The Turkish Bath' may be alluded to when Maud describes the inmates as 'like a very large harem with the sultan away for his annual holiday'. What ensues is particularly interesting in its defusing of erotic expectations as Patricia Roc and Phyllis Calvert undress and bathe, and Jean Kent waits her turn half undressed. It is extremely unlikely that Launder planned an assault on male erotic scopophilia or programmatically attempted to show the female body in a largely unvoyeuristic framework. What can be said, though, is that the film's narrative context, with its insistence on the women's capabilities rather than just their sexuality, its wartime ethos of the deflection of personal aims (including sexual desire), and its viewing context of a predominantly female audience, encourage the creation of as unconventional – i.e. as ordinary – a female bathing scene as possible, with the only male who enters it, the elderly M. Boper, too preoccupied to notice the disrobing women. Indeed the only interested diegetic look is Margaret's, a reflex action sizing up the competition. The scene is structured so that multiple activities deflect interest from any voyeuristic centre (Maud being caustic, Teresa fulminating against tea drinking and eulogizing team spirit, the two Misses shocked by the lack of privacy). When Rosemary and Freda go in to bathe the camera stays behind with other characters, and when they are distantly seen in the bath, Phyllis Calvert is actually drinking a cup of tea. Attractive though the women are, it is a far from Bathsheba-like scenario. It would be wrong to exaggerate the scene into too pure a spectacle. Bridie poses provocatively. Freda does a Windmill Theatre imitation of Bridie's stripping ('My first: "Innocence"'), though this, in underlining the subject of 'stripping' for an audience, enacts a parody of it, and the scene ends when the screams of the two females fighting below draw the women to the window. Here Patricia Roc is for a moment barely covered by her towel, Annette stands with her arms folded across her bare breasts, and Lucy looks perversely excited by the fight. Such unruliness subverts any too didactic possibilities. Nevertheless the scene is extraordinary in conveying a rather salutary sense of unerotic ordinariness, as the women (whose diegetic viewpoints are to dominate the film) simply take a bath, with exhibitionism, narcissism and voyeurism – though impossible to banish from the scene and in fact self-reflexively made part of it – demoted to the margins.

## The first Bridie

When the 'new girls' are allotted rooms two kinds of female power are dramatized. First, Flora Robson's Miss Manningford defeats Sergeant Hentzner with matriarchal authority and an unerring eye for male moral weakness. Her 'my man' putdown draws admiring looks from the other women, though I think we are meant to appreciate the irony that it has been honed in the civilian world as a class weapon. Almost immediately the sergeant is defeated again, as Bridie, to get a single room, vamps him, the seduction compared by Freda to a rat entering a trap after 'the oldest cheese in the world'. In the first instance a female power based on a perception of male weakness operates without deployment of the erotic. In the second the erotic is flagrantly used and commented on in such a way as to mark not only the group's disapproval of it but the film's self-consciousness about the subject of female sexuality. This has its most excessive representation in Jean Kent's Bridie Johnson, a petulantly sensuous striptease artist whose narcissism is signalled by the pinups of herself performing on the walls of her room, and whose deployment of her charms on the enemy immediately renders her problematic.

*Two Thousand Women* adds to its national, class and temperamental female types a wide range of sexual types within a situation of duress that activates at high pressure the meanings surrounding 'reinvented' femininity in a war ambiguating gender boundaries and demanding images that affirm a lessening of traditional binary male/female oppositions without suggesting their dissolution, something undesired by most men and women. Ranged around Rosemary (traditional good, with complications) and Bridie (traditional bad, also with complications) is a spectrum of sexuality – the wholly desexed Nazi women, the indiarubber, rump-slapping Teresa and the stick insect Frau Holweg; the repressed propriety of Miss Manningford and Miss Meredith, who would be shocked by any reading of them as crypto-lesbians, a motif very dimly alluded to when Freda remarks of Teresa 'to think I once had a crush on a girl like that at school!'; Maud's hyper-experienced post-sexual cynicism ('I've seen enough of men to last me a lifetime'); Freda's rather brusque tomboyish asexuality; the wanly sexualized Margaret; and Annette stereotyped by Maud as French (i.e. interested in clothes and missing the men). All these are exhibited in a context that makes much play with sexual realism (making allowances for the greater politeness of 1940s representations), but also with more than realistic categories, especially in the extraordinary construction of Rosemary who (whether via authorial sophistication or the text's unconscious) is presented with a remarkable density of symbolic representation – madonna at the beginning of the narrative, a novice nun seeking to help children, then at least seeming whore when exposed as the scandalous Mary Maugham (a stigma she is rescued from by her explanation of innocence, though interestingly Alec reports that while he believed her, his wife did not). Finally she becomes the representative of the wartime dream of romantic love, deferred, as war circumstances demand, till her future reunion with Jimmy.

Rosemary's romantic forbearance, indulging yet disciplining the dream, is like other of the group's sexual interests, firmly disciplined by war responsibilities. Whatever sexual flutters the RAF men arouse are controlled as everyone applies themselves to the patriotic task. Everyone, that is, except Bridie, played by Jean Kent, surely the most potently erotic of all British actresses of the period, a Susan Hayward in a cinema unable quite to find a sustained place for her. Very early on Bridie's flaunted, feral-coated sexuality is typed as disruptive, then becomes actively dangerous, causing the crisis of the German sergeant's death, a scene which involves an extraordinary image of the German and Allied soldiers wrestling for a phallic pistol waving over the nearly naked pinups of Bridie on the wall. Bridie is also increasingly defined as pathetically manipulable, almost comically dependent on male approval, and then as menacingly unstable as her rejection by Dave causes her to betray the escape. Here a subterranean aspect intersects, for Bridie's Christian name and her stage name of 'Bubbles Kelly' identify her as Irish. These linked suspicions of her Irishness and of her sexuality are simultaneously proferred and withdrawn, never mentioned again, and untraceable in Jean Kent's English accent. Half present, but undefined in Bridie Johnson, the interlaced instabilities of female sexuality and Irishness would be reworked in another Bridie in *I See a Dark Stranger*.

For all the group's condemnation of Bridie, it is hard not to feel that contemporaneous audiences (more dominantly female than male) would have found attractive as well as disturbing Bridie's explosion of self-oriented desire, safe to indulge because encircled by obvious disapproval. The negative group response is articulated primarily by Freda, who, however, seems to go beyond the call of duty in her constant harping at Bridie ('little love hungry', 'little passion fruit'), suggesting beyond the acting out of the general will a too intense animus, an embodiment of the neurotic aspects of the repressions demanded by the war. It is another mark of the complexity of the film that, within the primary material of the punishing of Bridie's excessive sexuality, traces of such counter elements exist.

## Marneville–Manville

As the new internees arrive Mrs Hatfield greets them with 'Welcome to Marneville, the only British colony uninhabited by man'. The statement is not quite true, for the camp is controlled and guarded by men, of whom the German Sergeant Hentzner is the most conspicuous. At the concert these authorities, including the visiting Gestapo, assemble in force. Also in the camp is Monsieur Boper, at first hostilely regarded by the women, who, however, turns out to be a patriot. Most importantly there are the three RAF men, Jimmy Moore, Alec Harvey and Dave Kennedy. These male presences remind us that Haddie's humorously invoked Amazonian colony has its limits. It is created and surrounded by the war, in which the main fighting forces are men, and in which the warring societies are, within their vital differences, patriarchal. The film is both a war film and a film about women, the second arising out of and heavily implicated in the first, but not quite identical at all points with it. This can be demonstrated at the beginning when Rosemary is arrested by both sides in turn, and a certain tension exists since, at this point, the Allied good and her own best interests are opposed, with more immediate danger posed to her from the French than from the Germans. For just a moment there is an image of a woman under male authority, irrespective of whether Axis or Allied. This is a more extreme implication than exists elsewhere, where the war of the sexes within the war of nations and ideologies is given in good-humoured, but none the less sharp, terms, through the many instances of female competence outlined above, through examples of unexpected male incompetence – like the dropped male glove that gives away the flyers' presence, and by the way Alec's rather tired clichés of female secondariness are so clearly beside the point. One way in which a male–female competitiveness is both signalled and defused is its being imaged in terms of children's rivalries, games between girls and boys, with 'boys' – for the British airmen – consistently used by the women.

Once inside the camp, the RAF men enjoy a primacy both as objects of desire and as the fighting men whose escape is the most important consideration. But they are also very much second-arized, wholly dependent on the women's skill and fortitude, with Jimmy and Alec at one point grotesquely feminized in transvestite disguise. Not surprisingly the text offers compensations for this, as when the men briefly take command after the sergeant is killed. However, even here, mythologies of absolute male self-control and female vulnerability are destabilized. Bridie becomes hysteri-cal, but the other women cope, and a little later it is Dave who comes close to breakdown. A more relaxed reversal of female control happens when, with Jimmy apparently asleep, Rosemary and Freda gaze at and discuss the erotics of a seemingly uncon-scious male body, until, after they have put the light out, he answers their last speculation about his height – 'five foot eleven and a half. Good night ladies', reversing the advantage they seemed to hold.

The actors cast as the flyers are notably uncharismatic, and Carl Jaffe as the German sergeant sexually manipulated by Bridie, though a more compelling actor, plays a weakly ascetic, sensually compromised authoritarian, no match for the women. Of the others, Reginald Purdell has a homely, comic persona, the actor playing Dave is almost embarrassingly wooden, while James McKechnie as Jimmy has a lightweight West End comedy air, encouraged by romantic dialogue that borders on cliché (of the 'a room like this and a girl like you' kind). Given the sharpness of the dialogue elsewhere, particularly when Maud or Freda are around, and whenever sex, gender and romance are the subject, this can hardly be accidental. Alec, a homely, henpecked husband and rather a kneejerking chauvinist about women, is central in two comic episodes. In the first the two Misses' decision to let him stay the night in their room ends in intense embarrassment for all. Miss Manningford has insisted on turning the light off to prevent his (unlikely) voyeurism while everyone undresses, but Freda's sudden 'what the butler saw' entry exposes them all in half undress. The comedy here derives partly from the spinsters' repressions, but equally from a comedy of male repressions, Alec's timidity as a compromised married man. The second episode is one of the most memorable in the film. Scouting the outside of the building, Alec suddenly appears at Margaret's window, reflected in her mirror which is decorated with her photos of male film stars, thus producing a startling image of his unglamorous face surrounded by icons of idealized masculinity. This highly wrought composition, in which an unideal male reality is juxtaposed with idealized images, reversing a comparison more associated with the female, underlines the wit of the film's dealings with sex and gender.

## Shows and blows

At the film's end the concert's primary function is to cover the escape, but it has its own significances, made through the three numbers fragmentarily staged (Renée Houston belting out 'Too many women and not enough love to go round', Lucy performing 'Home sweet home', and Rosemary singing 'There'll always be an England', the last joined by all the British women). Echoing *Millions Like Us*, *Two Thousand Women* also ends with musical numbers sung from a stage, the last turning into choric group affirmation. In other respects the endings are unlike; the scene in *Millions Like Us* confined to a single space – the singers on stage, the massed canteen, Celia and her workmates – with everything building up to a concentration on Celia's grief and its placement within the affirmation of community; whereas, though it moves to an analogous group affirmation, the concert in *Two Thousand Women* is a fragmentary part of an extremely multi-focused set of sequences – the escape, Rosemary and Jimmy's romance, Bridie's and Dave's bustup, Bridie's act of betrayal and attempt to atone, Teresa's attempt to give the alarm, etc., joined to the concert through quick intercutting between various spaces and the auditorium, concentrated only at the end into two sites, the body of the auditorium and somewhere outside where the escape proceeds.

The film's last shot – lights of a vehicle moving off in the dark, carrying the RAF men back to the fight – parallels the final shot of *Millions Like Us* with the bombers flying off into the night.

The numbers comment directly and indirectly on many of the narrative's interests. In the first Renée Houston, in part imitation Dietrich drag, sardonically sings a song of heterosexual lack, 'Too many women and not enough men to go round'. This is only part imitation Marlene because she wears, with her top hat and cane, tights, a jacket with a very female cut, and a cravat sporting a huge stone. Maud is a curious character, a faded sexbomb, claiming immunity from sexual longings ('I've had enough of men to last me a lifetime'), yet the constant detached observer of the women's sexual frustrations. She is also the character most associated with violence, the most extreme instance of the binding of male wartime traits onto female ones, and her costume, the content of her number, and her performance provide extra unstable commentary on all these.

The concert justifies other characters also appearing in stagey costume. In contrast to Maud, Lucy appears (curtseying) in high heels and a girlish white dress, hands coyly clasped, as she sings 'There's no place like home', in sweet soprano antithesis to Maud's brassiness. Here the camera registers the reactions of the listening British women, moved by the evocation of home and family (otherwise rare in the film), with even hardbitten Freda fighting down a gulp. The song with its past, present and future visions of both the national and the domestic home, raises implicitly the question (which floats around a number of WWII films, including *Millions Like Us*) to what degree the positives of the temporary new 'home' of the camp – community, greater egalitarianism, greater female autonomy and responsibility – will influence the postwar restoration? In the final number, Rosemary, dressed in a chastely alluring white gown, sings 'There'll always be an England', again in a sweetly plangent soprano and a clasped-hands style that echoes Lucy's. The situation is fascinating because it has seemed that Rosemary intends to perform a striptease in place of the indisposed Bridie. When she doesn't, the number takes on the additional meaning of the replacement of one kind of sexuality (carnality) by another (romantic love), though the instability courted by the film is such that one might feel that the final effect is less regulated and that different versions of sexuality (brassy Maud, girlish Lucy, romantic Rosemary and Bridie's memorable loose-cannon sexiness) are jammed up against each other rather than arranged hierarchically.

This number takes place against a series of violent acts, not just the guards stomping through the auditorium, but primarily woman on woman. Earlier Maud, imitating a boxing commentator, presented Mrs Ogilvie and Mrs Woodbury fighting, and announced, 'This is life in the raw. This is life as the cannibals live it'. Maud is constantly associated with violence, expressing a desire to injure Bridie, nearly assaulting M. Boper and threatening to attack anyone spreading rumours about Rosemary. Even the gentle Haddy comically fantasizes an escape plan that involves cutting the guards' throats. Towards the end of the film all this escalates. Bridie and Teresa are involved in a desperate fight, and when Frau Holweg tries to force her way into the auditorium, Maud's elbow jolts her unconscious. Moments later, as Teresa staggers out after giving the alarm, someone trips her and the women attack her.

There is a fascinating ambivalence about this violence. Attached to Maud, it can be enjoyed, but also disowned because of Maud's unrepresentative Glaswegian hardness. It is enjoyed for denying the sentimental essentialist view that women are by nature non-violent. But equally it is disavowed because it threatens one of the most basic gender divisions, the fact that women, for all the blurring of absolute masculinity and femininity created by the war, are still felt not to be — and wished not to be – as violent as men. The wartime logic of this is that women conscripts are used as auxiliaries – operating the rangefinders for the anti-aircraft guns in the 'Purple Alert' sequence in *Millions Like Us* – but not as troops, expected to kill in an unmediated way. Antonia Lant's *Blackout* is very good on the psychic complications the restructuring of gender lines in the Second World War caused, not just the obvious – female exhilarations at expanded opportunities, masculine fears both of male loss of role and defeminization of women – but less obvious female fears of defeminization as the price of appropriating masculine roles.[25] Such complexities are intricately registered as the film manoeuvres first to close the gender gap between the males and females, and then to commend the scaling down of the excesses of femininity that the war demands (most obviously in the condemnation of Bridie), while simultaneously imaging strong traditional elements of femininity (Rosemary being central here, and perhaps irresponsible interests in Bridie). As for violence, clearly breaking the taboo is exhilarating and amusing if done a little (especially by Maud), but, pushed too far, it becomes frightening, collapsing a deeply felt difference. The scene where Teresa is attacked poises itself between – without resolving – these contradictions (cheers as the women punish the traitor, fears that they might tear her to pieces). In Wilder's *Stalag 17* there is a chilling scene when the young stool pigeon is driven to his death. The scene is terrifying, but most viewers will find it tolerable because men are expected to be more violent than women. Here the attack on Teresa is circumscribed by the presence of the guards, who will surely break it up. Additionally it is committed by women not known to the audience, and the camera cuts away from it so quickly that its seriousness remains uncertain. Do the women intend to kill her, or is it a dormitory scragging out of *St Trinian's*? We can't know, and other matters quickly engage the attention. It is one of the less consciously articulated moments in *Two Thousand Women*, but nevertheless illustrates how intensely the film invokes the problematics as well as the exhilarations of wartime femininity.

### *Waterloo Road* (Gilliat, 1944)

'We were fighting for you, you and all the other babies'
(Jennings, *A Diary For Timothy*)

The third of the home front films was Gilliat's *Waterloo Road*. Here Private Jim Colter (John Mills), informed by his sister that his wife Tillie (Joy Shelton) has been receiving the attentions of Ted Purvis (Stewart Granger), a smooth black-market operator, goes AWOL to rescue a marriage which has foundered on his unwillingness to have the child his wife desires in the uncertainty of wartime. The action follows simultaneously his attempt, while avoiding capture by the military police, to find his wife, and Ted's project of seducing her. As Jim tries to find them, the narrative moves through the environs of Waterloo, both celebrating the endurance of the community suffering the Blitz, and revealing intriguing lowlife aspects of the city's underside. It finally brings the two men together as, during an air raid, they fight over Tillie. Despite Ted's boxing background, Jim rather improbably defeats him, thanks to inside information given to him by Dr Montgomery, one of those ambivalent Alastair Sim authority figures that Launder and Gilliat are so fond of. While Ted's punishment continues with the grimly humorous revelation that his fake medical certificate actually tells the truth, and that he really does have a heart condition that will compromise his womanizing lifestyle, Jim and Tilly, reunited, forgive each other. The film has an opening and closing frame in which Dr Montgomery looks back from the present, 1944–5, with the threat of invasion over and the end of the war in sight, to the moment of the narrative's duration, the Blitz of 1940–1. In the closing frame we learn that between past and present the Coulters have produced a son who is apostrophized as inheriting the difficult future, like a working-class equivalent of the middle-class infant Timothy in Humphrey Jennings's *A Diary For Timothy* (1945).

### 'A symptom of a general condition'

Determinedly unAmerican though *Waterloo Road* is, with Dr Montgomery even acting as a sardonic commentator on the competing cinema when a couple he greets tell him they are going to watch a Mickey Rooney film, it has a climax more Hollywood than Gainsborough when the hero, small John Mills, the paragon of retracted decency, finally knocks the physically more impressive Stewart Granger down the stairs while the object of their battle, Joy Shelton, watches. Even given Ted Purvis's sybaritic lack of fitness, and the defensive weakness that Dr Montgomery, a Blackfriars boxing aficionado, has passed on to Jim, the defeat of the ex-professional boxer is unlikely and underlines the wishfulfilment of the narrative's attempt to solve its problems. Granger's Ted Purvis becomes the symbolic locus of these problems and, additionally, the means by which others are displaced, and thus to some degree takes on the role of scapegoat. Like Bridie in *Two Thousand Women* he embodies an antisocial individualism allied to an overt sexuality. With his spasmodically transatlantic accent, his shoulder shrugs imitated from American gangster films (Jean Kent, an embittered ex-girlfriend, asked where he is, says he might be at the cinema picking up hints from Victor Mature), and the electric razor he is using as he is introduced into the narrative, he also embodies a fear of a sweeping Americanization of the future in the later war years (an example of which can be found in George Orwell's famous essay 'The Decline of the English Murder').[26] In this opening appearance he dismisses regally a letter from the Inland Revenue, then poses imperiously waiting for his shirt to be put on. Though he rules over an alternative world, the representation of which is one of the unusual features of *Waterloo Road* – 'The Lucky Star' pinball arcade, 'The Alcazar' dancehall, Toni's women's hairdressing salon in which he has an interest – he is subtly not presented as a pariah. His first appearance is in the communal centre of the underground (where the postman makes a detour to deliver letters to him), the barman at The Canterbury Arms seems genuinely friendly towards him (though no doubt Ted is good business), and there is little ambiguity about the attraction he exerts over women. Jean Kent's cameo leaves no doubt that hers is the angry reaction of a still smitten cast-off, while Ted's casual ownership of a girl who tells him that Tillie is 'not the type you usually go for' is expressed by his reply, 'I like 'em hard to get once in a while' and a proprietorial slap on her bottom. Tillie's interest in him will be investigated below.

This doubleness is important. Ted is placed outside the society and values of the film, subversive of the norms and values of trust, community, duty, cooperation and self-sacrifice, but he is also presented as inside it, as if he represents tendencies that cannot be wholly disavowed by a community now looking to the end of the war, as its communal structures, brought about by the privations of the Blitz, begin to seem fragile and perhaps, in the future, expendable. The film is structured round the battle for Tillie (social stability, home, the child: very much a shrinking of the wider meanings given to the female in the two preceding films) between John Mills and his persona of stoical, retracted virtue, and Stewart Granger and Ted's handsome, shifty opportunism. The antithesis is made more meaningful by their similar working-class origins. Ted, while romancing Tilly, spins her a line about his deepdown domestic desires, but there is no reason to doubt what he tells her about his tough beginnings, fighting preliminaries at the Blackfriars ring, and his entrepreneurial escape from that past. Jim has worked in a locomotive shed, studying, with ambitions to be an engineer, to lift himself up by hard work, as opposed to Ted's leaping class barriers into a kind of classless wealth by dubious methods. In the long view Jim is identified with the solidity of a profession that builds and structures, Ted and the two taxis he has invested in for the postwar years, with the black side of the emerging consumer industries.

Under the weight of Dr Montgomery's view that he is 'a symptom of a general condition' and advice to Jim that 'you don't want the Ted Purvises of this world to reap the benefits when it's all over, or now for that matter', other problematics of social organization and gender foregrounded in Launder and Gilliat's, and various other war films of the time, tend to be forgotten, which is what gives *Waterloo Road* a more conservative bias than the two earlier films. However, it is difficult not to feel that, though Ted is given many negative traits, particularly in the scene where he hits Tillie when she finally refuses to sleep with him, he is also 'a symptom of a general condition' in another way, a complex focus of desire as well as disavowal, especially for the females within the narrative and for the predominantly female wartime audience of the film. Interestingly, a schoolgirl answering Mayer's questionnaire said that she disliked *Waterloo Road* precisely because of a doubleness she perceived in Granger who 'should either play a villainous part as in *Madonna of the Seven Moons*, or a happy sentimentalist as in *Love Story*, but not an "in between"'. The 'inbetweenness' that disturbed her, others may have found more attractive.[27] Connected with sites of pleasure, the pub, the cinema, the pinball arcade, the dancehall, clothes, good times and female glamour through the hairdressing salon, Ted has escaped both general wartime and working-class austerity, making himself a kind of pleasure principle to which Tillie ambivalently responds from the beginning of the film where she agrees to meet him. When she arrives, she says that she has only kept the date in order to tell him that she isn't going to keep it, but then lets herself be talked into a drink, a dance and a meal, and finally into going up to his place for his supposed birthday party. When it becomes clear to her that the whole thing is a setup and that he expects her to sleep with him, she fails to resist, telling him that she knows what he is doing. Though her acceding is ambivalent, redolent of guilt and accompanied by the waiver 'It doesn't mean anything', she swooningly collapses back in anticipation, and it is only the incongruous announcement to the background radio music Ted has strategically arranged that triggers the fit of hysterical laughter that draws her back to her desire for family and stability in the long haul of the postwar future. It seems that the text recognizes the attractions as well as the menace of Ted when, at the film's end, having digested Montgomery's news about his enforced change of lifestyle, Ted, momentarily forgetting himself, starts flirting with the pretty nurse tending his wounds, who is obviously eager to join his list of available girls (the film thus insisting on a female fascination with Ted even after he's been judged and punished). His eye caught by the doctor, Ted with wry humour drops the nurse's hand and resignedly waves her away, acceding to necessity, but his humour and self-awareness make him something more than just the butt of the joke.

## The doctor exhorts

Jim's defeat of Ted is presided over by Alastair Sim's Dr Montgomery, who within the main narrative variously encounters the members of the triangle, allowing him to intervene with what is going on. Thus he observes Ted and Tilly making their date in the Underground, attends Jim's injuries after he has been beaten up at The Lucky Star, deflecting the police in the process, passes Ted and Tilly as they head for Ted's place, and then sets Jim up for his encounter with Ted. In the prologue and epilogue Montgomery declares himself a kind of surrogate father of the Colters' baby son. He has, as he says, 'played quite a part in this little story myself'. In the last moments of the film he actually addresses the child (who, smiling, is granted the film's very last shot) – 'Well, Jimmie, m'boy, you've got the future, it's all yours'. As already suggested, the moment constitutes an intriguing anticipation of Humphrey Jennings's *A Diary For Timothy* (1945), built around the idea of an address to a newborn baby inheriting the postwar world and its problems, though it is noticeable that Jennings's film alludes to basic structural problems of society in a way that *Waterloo Road* doesn't. Montgomery's rhetoric is very much one of rebuilding, but only at the most basic level – the increasing by reproduction of a population depleted by war. Inflecting the phrase 'Millions Like Us', he announces, 'Ay, we'll need good citizens when this is all over – millions of them!'

As surrogate father to the infant Colter, he is literally paternalistic, but this paternalism extends further in ways the earlier films avoided. Here there is very much a sense, quixotic and shabby-eccentric in his middleclassness though Montgomery is, that he speaks on behalf of the inhabitants of the film, and through a somewhat condescending rhetoric, calling the Colters 'little people' and referring to Tillie as 'the little wife'. It is an interesting example of split imperatives, the film achieving a degree of innovation in its more than usually authentic attempt to represent working-class life with less of a petit bourgeois feel to things than in *Millions Like Us*, yet at the same time distancing itself from that life both through Montgomery's superior view of it, and through the disappearance of the sense of needed changes present in *Millions Like Us*.

Montgomery's condescension seems to spread to women generally. His patient Mrs Fogarty is 'an old hag', and in the prologue he also mutters disapproval of a rather elderly looking mother for the way she is looking after her child – 'Bless my soul, woman, don't bounce it!' – prefiguring his criticism of Tilly's child-handling in the epilogue where he booms, 'How many times have I told you, don't cuddle him. The more they cuddle, the more they cry, the more they cry, the more cuddle. It's a vicious circle. Probably explains Hitler ... He'll be a good citizen if you bring him up like I tell you'.

We should be more than a little suspicious of writing that ignores the tremendous desire for domesticity that the long struggle of the war involved, which sees women, particularly married and marriageable women, as almost forced against their will back into the domestic sphere. Whatever the later frustrations of this might have turned out to be, there was clearly by the end of the war a mass desire for domesticity, a feeling which *Waterloo Road* picks up and shapes. Tilly's feeling, expressed to Jim as they go past the house they have chosen for themselves, is that 'it'll be lovely to have a place for our own'. Though a memory of com-munalism hangs about the Underground shelter, in other ways the excitements over new formations and groupings, both in the home and at work, now seem distant. The extended, largely female family Tilly lives in – mother-in-law, sister-in-law (with whom she fights), brother-in-law (asleep after night shifts), sister-in-law's young daughter, and the rather feminized neighbour, Tom – is not exactly a site of female cooperation and sympathy, more one dominated by conflict. Work, whether male or female, is presented very mundanely, no longer seeming to be vitally con-nected to the war effort, but simply something to be got through (messing up Fred and Ruby's sex life as well). We see Ruby at her job when Jim questions her about Tilly, selling train tickets at Waterloo, a job that easily might be shown as essential, but here the only people annoyed by her neglecting to serve them are civilians, a rather bossy woman and a slightly prissy elderly man who misses a train to Basingstoke. In a meaningful intertextual reference back to *Millions Like Us*, Tom, the gentle pigeon-fancying lodger, having glimpsed Jim and Tilly's troubles, has the following conversation with the AWOL Canadian.

TOM Females are a problem all round. Bloomin' crossword puzzle. La Donna Eh Mobeel.
CANADIAN What's that?
TOM Italian.
CANADIAN What does it mean?
TOM It means woman is mobile.
CANADIAN Who said that? Mr Bevin?

The significance of this is that the phrase 'mobile woman', so exciting and meaningful in the earlier film, has returned completely to its more traditional meanings, of woman wholly contained in the sexual-domestic sphere. Even army life from the point of view of late 1944/early 1945 is presented implicitly as waiting for the war to end (so that the mood of the film belongs more to the time it was made than the time it mainly represents). Though at one point Jim suggests a reason for not having a baby is that he might be killed, he seems in no great danger of being posted to the war front, and 'Canada', whom he meets when avoiding MPs, has gone AWOL solely to get the excitement that lack of combat has denied him. Even the dangers of the Blitz seem mainly orchestrated at the end to provide an accompaniment to the fight between Jim and Ted for Tilly, as if to say that the main purpose now of the war is to get Tillie's baby conceived and born. It seems to me less useful to hypothesize about differences in Launder and Gilliat's views here from those of the earlier films, to speculate on these differences as reflecting a personal growing conservatism (which might or might not be true), than to see *Waterloo Road* rather as responding to sets of feelings in the air, the sense of the ending of the war getting close, a desire for domesticity, a declining radicalism, though it's clearly true that the more radical the artists, the less likely they would be to dramatize such feelings without contesting them.

Though the doctor modernizes his look between the frame sequences and the narrative, abandoning his oldfashioned wing collar and dressing in lighter-coloured, more modern clothes, he utters a very traditional masculine critique of Tilly's too-feminine dealing with the child which he asserts may do him later harm. Here we have not just the reassertion of the domestic, but on top of that a masculine overlooking of even the most traditionally female sphere. Perhaps there's a feeling that this is a necessary assertion against the feminizations the relaxations of peace might bring, a call to masculine hardness, a ban on female cossetting because of the austerity that lies ahead, felt even at the onset of victory. However read, it is difficult not to see *Waterloo Road* as drawing back from the various optimisms and dynamisms of *Millions Like Us* and *Two Thousand Women*.

These feelings might seem prophetic enough in the retrospection of a last late war film directed by Launder in 1965, *Joey Boy*. This coarsely reductive comedy, with similarities to the earlier, more groundbreaking Boulting Brothers film, *Private's Progress* (1956), deals with the various scams committed by Joey (Harry H. Corbett) a knowing East End criminal rather than Ian Carmichael's naive graduate in the Boultings' film, when he and his gang (itself a parody of the multi-nationed wartime group) are forced to join the army to avoid prosecution, only to find that the army offers them a protected environment for their schemes (gambling, prostitution, etc.). Here the 'myth' of wartime unity is replayed through the prism of modern British society, and revealed to be, at least from that perspective, only a front for exploitation and pocketlining. Beside Joey even Ted provokes nostalgia.

## Notes

1 Brown, *Launder and Gilliat*, p. 108.
2 Sue Harper, 'The Representation of Women in British Feature Films, 1939–1945', in Philip Taylor (ed.), *Britain and the Cinema in the Second World War* (Macmillan, Basingstoke and London, 1988), p. 175.
3 Ibid.
4 MacDonald, 'Interview with Sidney Gilliat', p. 136.
5 *Sunday Times*, 10 October 1943.
6 This is basically true of Andrew Higson in *Waving the Flag: Constructing a National Cinema in Britain* (Clarendon Press, Oxford, 1995), of Sue Harper in 'The Representation of Women in British Feature Films, 1939–1945', in Philip M. Taylor, *Britain and the Cinema in the Second World War* (Macmillan, Basingstoke and London, 1988), and of Christine Gledhill and Gillian Swanson in Geoff Hurd (ed.), *National Fictions: World War Two in British*

*Film and Television* (BFI, London, 1984).

7 Antonia Lant, *Blackout: Reinventing Women for Wartime British Cinema* (Princeton University Press, Princeton, New Jersey, 1991), p. 72.

8 Brown, *Launder and Gilliat*, p. 11.

9 Higson, *Waving the Flag*. In fact 'The Documentary Ideal and the Melodrama of Ordinary Life' is one of Higson's chapter titles.

10 Higson, *Waving the Flag*, particularly pp. 243–71.

11 David Bordwell, 'Story Causality and Motivation', in David Bordwell, Janet Staiger and Kristin Thompson, *The Classical Hollywood Cinema: Film Style and Mode of Production to 1960* (Routledge and Kegan Paul, London, 1985), p. 16.

12 Higson says this in *Waving the Flag*, p. 233–4. It is true that Celia registers the ticket office sign saying 'Is Your Journey Really Necessary?', but 'punished' seems an excessive reading of this and other ironies.

13 Harper,'The Representation of Women', pp. 174–5.

14 Higson, *Waving the Flag*, p. 233.

15 Ibid., p. 243. 'But the pleasure of the sequence derives also from a voluptuous sense of national unity.'

16 Marcia Landy, *British Genres: Cinema and Society, 1930–1960* (Princeton University Press, Princeton, New Jersey, 1991), p. 208; Harper, 'The Representation of Women', p. 182.

17 Brown, *Launder and Gilliat*, p. 109.

18 '"2,000 Women" (by one of them)', Gaumont British Press Information, 8 September 1944.

19 Landy, *British Genres*, p. 208; Harper, 'The Representation of Women', p. 182.

20 Brown, *Launder and Gilliat*, pp. 109–10.

21 Anstey, *Spectator* review of *The Rake's Progress*, 14 December 1945.

22 Anstey, *Spectator*, 22 September 1944.

23 J. P. Mayer, *British Cinemas and Their Audiences: Sociological Studies* (Dobson, London, 1948), p. 192.

24 See 'Film Notes: Women in the Nazis' Prison Camps' by C. Campbell Dixon, *Daily Telegraph*, 2 June 1944.

25 Lant, *Blackout, passim.*, but especially pp. 85–113.

26 George Orwell, 'The Decline of the English Murder', in *The Collected Works of George Orwell*, vol. 18, ed. Peter Davison, assisted by Ian Angus and Sheila Davis (Secker and Warburg, London, 1998), pp. 108–10.

27 Mayer, *British Cinemas and Their Audiences*, p. 161.

# Very individual pictures: *The Rake's Progress, I See a Dark Stranger*

## 3

## War and peace

With the confidence of film-makers working at the height of their powers Launder and Gilliat moved into production, forming their own company, Individual Pictures (April, 1944) and leaving Gainsborough for the loose association of Independent Producers Ltd, joining with Cineguild's Ronald Neame, Anthony Havelock Allan and David Lean, Gabriel Pascal Productions, and Powell and Pressburger's Archers, as part of the larger Rank Organization, where they stayed until 1950, by which time the creative freedoms enjoyed early on by the associates were in decline, and they moved to Korda's London Films.

Even beside the most distinguished products of the Rank arrangement — *The Red Shoes, Black Narcissus, Great Expectations, Oliver Twist* (1948) – the new company's first two films justified the implicit boast of their name. *The Rake's Progress* (1945) and *I See a Dark Stranger* (1946) are indeed works of considerable individuality. *The Rake's Progress*, part satiric critique, part ironic elegy, is *sui generis* one of the most fascinating films of the classical British cinema's richest period. *I See a Dark Stranger* seems to fit more easily within Launder and Gilliat's inclinations towards comedy-thriller-romance, but here the mode works at peculiarly high pressure on material bursting with ideological tensions and contradictions —a wartime spy thriller in which Deborah Kerr's appealing, rather than appalling, Irish heroine joins a Nazi spy ring in order to pursue her personal war against the British.

A shared underlying factor adding to both films' resonances is that both had their origins in late wartime, but were finally devised for peacetime viewing (*The Rake's Progress* had its première on 7 December 1945, while *I See a Dark Stranger* was released on 5 August 1946). This peacetime release is crucial, allowing *The Rake's Progress* a meditative relaxation in which the war is already recent history, to be seen within longer views. In the later *I See a Dark Stranger* it allows a certain licence (greater than would have been possible during wartime) to resolve difficult political thematics playfully. In real life the treason of the Irish–British William Joyce, with its echoes of Sir Roger Casement under whose portrait Bridie stands in the Dublin art gallery, ended in his execution rather than in Bridie's escape from punishment by the British state. At the same time these edge of peacetime films move away from the certainties of war to the more various, if less deadly, problematics of peace, which the narrator of Jennings's *A Diary For Timothy* (1945) so clearly expressed. ('Now that the enemy in Europe's breaking, life is going to become even more dangerous than before because now we have the power to choose and the right to criticize, even to grumble.')

Whereas the home front trilogy generally concentrates on the group, these films centre on individuals, in conflict with group structures, even their own. One male, one female; one an insider, quintessentially English, the other an outsider, Irish; both sexually troublesome in different ways; one opaquely cut off from interiority, the other highly subjectivized; and both only precariously reordered into the dominant community by narrative closure, Vivian by death in service, Bridie by her marrying her British officer.

The protagonist of *The Rake's Progress* is a creature of marked political incorrectness (the film even omits the shooting script's moment where he at least gives half a crown to an unemployed Welsh miner[1]), out of step with historical processes, describing himself as 'a type' who 'has become obsolete'. Dying to make way for the new democratic order (the Labour election win was in July 1945, nearly six months before the film's première), he is, however, not so easily disposed of in his implications, playing as he does on complex nostalgias, not all of them dismissable as wholly regressive, and enacting in his ambivalent way concerns that will become part of the postwar world: individualism, hedonism, the problematics of commitment, the difficult structures of sexual relationships, and those questions sounded in Jennifer's meditations at the beginning and end of the film about social determinism and individual will. These are the questions of a world at relative peace, and Vivian, while representing in class terms a dying world, in obliquer ways also represents disturbing aspects of the new one.

As for Bridie in *I See a Dark Stranger*, Antonia Lant has formulated the way in which the peculiarly unstable problematics of Ireland and femininity are fused together in Deborah Kerr's heroine.[2] As Lant reads the ending of the film, the question of Bridie's female independence is settled patriarchally by her marriage to David, but the question of Ireland remains to trouble the postwar era.[3] Both films' endings, in giving versions of closure and incorporation (Vivian's 'redemption', Bridie's marriage into Britishness), and then subverting them to a degree, demonstrate the ambivalences built up around the two protagonists which the rest of this chapter will trace.

## The Rake's Progress

### Ways of seeing

In the 1993 interview, Gilliat, responding to MacDonald's emphasis on the film's ambiguities, spoke of *The Rake's Progress* as a film which 'often seems a different picture from what it was the time before'.[4] This agreement between interviewer ('That's the strength of a great film – that it changes with the times and keeps a certain ambiguity') and interviewee seems more than an idiosyncratic reaction. A look back at the film's first reviews suggests an enigmatic text, provoking fundamental disagreements and an often moralizing tone in its discussion (beyond the film's supposed sexual immorality which worried both the American censors and Rank himself, supposedly on account of his wife's disapproval of it).[5] This tone, perhaps alien to later viewers, undoubtedly sprang from the clash of communitarian wartime values with the film's interest in its depoliticized, individualist anti-hero, an interest certainly not devoid of moral and political implications, but also not wholly dominated by them. Of these reviews that of Edgar Anstey (*Spectator*, 14 December 1945) the documentary director, left-wing critic and pillar of the postwar British film culture establishment, is the most interesting, admitting the film's finesse, but, like C.A. Lejeune (*Observer*, 9 December 1945), and Elspeth Grant (*Sketch*, 1 December 1945), rejecting the film's ending as a sentimental glorification of an unworthy hero. Anstey (who greatly admired *Millions Like Us* and *Waterloo Road*), viewed *The Rake's Progress* as a satiric study derailed not just by aspects of its treatment, but by the casting – 'It clearly is *not* possible to remain admonitory if the villain is played by Mr Harrison at his most endearing'. The moral feelings the film aroused in Anstey were so considerable that they led him to extremely distorted descriptions of the hero: 'A man who would have been equally honoured in the ranks of the SS' (Vivian actually makes his decision to help Rikki after looking down from his hotel window on a Nazi parade) and who has 'killed his father, robbed and ruined his wife and seduced the wife of his best friend' (Vivian has a responsibility for his father's accidental death, but he doesn't murder him; he does rob Rikki, but he also saves her life and we have no knowledge that she is 'ruined' when she exits the narrative; and Jill can hardly be seen as a reluctant seducee). Anstey clearly cannot conceive of any legitimate treatment of Vivian beyond the stereotypes of 'a worthless and unrepresentative creature', 'a certain kind of gilded young aristocrat of the 1930s, the politically unconscious gangster who lived on his small wits and his father's reputation'. But E. Arnot Robertson's view of the film as both 'honest' and 'wise' (*Mail*, 1 December 1945) shows that there were alternative responses.

For such a fascinating film there is surprisingly little later comment (though Gilliat notes both Olivier's and Bertrand Tavernier's admiration of its complexities).[6] However, Landy's brief treatment in *British Genres*[7] suggests approaches that go beyond arguments about Vivian's unworthiness by placing the film as a male 'tragic' melodrama centred on a hero in tension with societal values. She makes three useful generalizations: that the Rake's actions are a critique of middle-class and patriarchal values, that the hero is unconscious of the motivations that drive him, and that the Rake's women are 'victims of the protagonist's resistance to patriarchy and conventional social codes'. Only the second of these can be accepted without some revision, but they all open up ways of seeing the hero in terms of meanings and effects rather than just moral critique. A last strand of opinion is powerfully formulated in the MacDonald interview where we are told that Olivier said he was always moved to tears by Vivian's father's death with its strange poignancy of Geoffrey Tearle's last words to his son, and Gilliat stated that the scene had the same effect on him.[8] Here there is evidence that the film's negative but powerful oedipal thematics are capable of moving spectators obscurely, even if much of the narrative proceeds in the satiric-detached vein suggested by its Hogarthian title (though the atmospheric and rather lonely Topolski drawings behind the title sequence suggest that the up-dating will not be wholly dominated by satire).

At the same time various socio-political markers are laid down, ensuring that the film's ability to move never effaces the social text. Four events, three explicit, one implicit, have an underlying importance in what is, among other things, a portrait of a period. Chronologically, the first is Armistice Night 1918, where Vivian meets the two common soldiers, whose mention of Lloyd George's promise of 'a plot of land and a cow' for returning soldiers looks ahead to the disillusion of social hopes in the 1920s, underlined by the appearances of the pensionless organ-grinding veteran in the Oxford sequence. More opaque, but enacted throughout the narrative, is Vivian's ritualistic kissing of the regimental badge given to him by them, before any dangerous undertaking, an action which forms an unarticulated bond between him and a class he elsewhere seems hardly aware of. The second is the October 1931 general election, the results of which are being broadcast when Vivian visits his father after being sent down, Colonel Kenway having just been returned as a Conservative MP in the huge victory for the National government headed by Ramsay MacDonald but overwhelmingly Conservative in makeup. This result – wholly approved by Vivian's family (in a moment cut from the shooting script Uncle Hubert sings, to Al Jolson's 'Sonny boy', 'I'll follow you, Stanley [Baldwin] boy') – sets the 1930s and Vivian's adult life in motion. This is, various hints suggest, a decade characterized by upper-class complacency, working its way blindly to the shock of the third of the explicit landmarks, the 1939–45 war, with its by-products of accelerated social change. Finally, beyond the end of the narrative, but part of every original viewer's experience, was the July 1945 election, its landslide Labour victory rhyming with the National landslide of 1931, but with promise of more substantial social reforms. It is this moment – in conjunction with the war, out of which, in many senses, it came – that consigns Vivian to history.

One might have difficulties with Anstey's description of Rex Harrison as a particularly 'endearing' actor, but Anstey is right that Harrison's casting as the Rake is crucial, as in *The Constant Husband*, and indeed in *Night Train to Munich*. Harrison's forte was upper-middle-class comedy. Noel Coward's double-edged praise famously judged him as the best light comedian in the world, bar himself, who if he had not been that might have ended up as a second-hand car salesman. *The Rake's Progress* (like *The Constant Husband*) plays on this witty perception. In the earlier film car salesman is one of the jobs a down-at-heel Vivian drifts into, and the joke is repeated in *The Constant Husband*.

Coward's first remark underlined Harrison's skills, the second signalled uneasinesses in the Harrison persona, the slight facti-tiousness in its confidence and elegance, its tacking along the borderline of gentleman and cad, as it is lived out on screen, stage and in the tabloids' fascination with the long-playing domestic epic of 'Sexy Rexy' and his women. It is clear that Harrison's reputa-tion for 'fatal charm' (the title of Alexander Walker's biography) was consciously used to give resonance to a role which explores the Harrison persona to the extent that, as Walker notes, 'the film has acquired over the years the character of a surrogate autobio-graphy'.[9] Some of these possibilities are visible in *Night Train to Munich*, where Dickie Randall, though a more stable and likeable adventurer than Vivian, still has edgy aspects to his sang froid, seems happiest role-playing, and cultivates with knowing distance his role as the great lover, his introduction in the narrative being his cover of singing banal love ditties as a seaside entertainer. Later, disguised as a Nazi officer and supposed to be exerting irresistible powers on Margaret Lockwood to further German war aims, he moves efficiently round the bedroom vetting it for . bugging devices while uttering automatic endearments: 'My darling, you look as charming as ever – those same sweet lips like warm carnations [opens door to look for microphone], those sweet mysterious eyes darker and softer than the bluest dusk of august violets, as the poet has it, and I hope he was Aryan [sits on bed and picks up phone]'. Here the play-acting situation softens the implication that Harrison's characters exploit, without being moved by, the effects his presence causes, especially for women, and which constitute the ambivalent attraction, more often associated with female stars, of a mystery that may just be style, a facade hiding emptiness. Accompanying this, a certain laconic insolence is always half asserting a lack of respect (itself a further provocation?) for the women entranced by him. 'Well, I tried to clean it up after the provost had asserted his authority. That's what women are for,' Vivien Leigh says to him in Storm in a Teacup, an irony that he tops with 'Oh that's what women are for, are they?'

Such aspects are interesting, but not exactly 'endearing', in tune with the less recognized but crucial aspect of his underlying querulousness, his faint-burning, rebarbative, almost neurotic, choler so memorably exploited in Preston Sturges's Unfaithfully Yours (1946), where Harrison enacts an extraordinarily black comic study in male narcissism assailed by insecurity. The extremity of that role sheds light on how a kind of put-upon-ness, occasionally reaching into darker insecurities, is actually a thoroughgoing part of the actor's presence, made concrete in a vocal habit recurrent throughout the films from his 1930s roles to My Fair Lady, where his voice constantly breaks register to betray a simmering annoyance. (His Sprechgesang singing style in the latter is an easily consulted repository of such effects, nowhere more pronounced than in his rendition of 'Let a woman in your life'). Such characteristics, and the tensions within the patriarchal style they act out, are heavily played on in his Hollywood role just after The Rake's Progress, as King Monkut (Rama IV) in Anna and the King of Siam

(Cromwell, 1946). Like Sir Alfred, only more so, the king is a powerful individual, in his case an all-powerful potentate with not just a beautiful wife, or numerous women, but a harem. If interesting effects are played on Harrison's persona of arrogance in Sturges's film, where the unknowability of his wife's (Linda Darnell's) feelings disturbs it, in the earlier work he is constantly pushed off balance by a moralizing female, Anna (Irene Dunne), and frequently explodes with anger and frustration. The veneer of Harrison's highly polished charm fascinates partly because of the cracks that are visible, and such suggestions are crucial in his performance in *The Rake's Progress* where tremors of subterranean, inchoate dissatisfaction within the hero's seamless style are part of the film's deepest meanings.

Against these various implications the picaresque plot unwinds.

1  Framing segment A. France, World War II. Vivian Kenway (Rex Harrison), commanding a tank, goes beyond literal orders and decides to 'recce' past a deserted bridge.

2  Framing segment B. Jennifer Calthrop (Margaret Johnston), whose role in the narrative will clarify, reads about Vivian being lost in action and muses about him in an interior monologue as she rides on a bus.

3  Vivian as a young boy strays into Piccadilly Circus on Armistice Night and, adopted by two ordinary soldiers, is christened by them 'Young 'Opeful'.

4  Oxford. Vivian as undergraduate climbs a tower to win a bet from one friend, Fogroy (Guy Middleton), and has an affair with the girlfriend, Jill (Jean Kent), of another, Sandy Duncan (Griffith Jones). He is sent down.

5  Visiting his father, Colonel Kenway MP (Godfrey Tearle) on the night of the 1931 general election to break the news, Vivian meets his father's secretary Jennifer Calthrop, and his family debate a career for him. Attracted by his father's reminiscences about his time on the South American coffee plantations of his friend Sir John Brockley, and attracted by the country club and cricket, Vivian decides on a South American career in coffee.

6 Porto Ibano, somewhere in South America. To his own surprise Vivian, under the tutelage of the firm's boffin, becomes interested in plans to increase the coffee crop. He learns a lesson in capitalist economics when he finds that a scarcity of coffee has made burning of surpluses necessary, in order to keep the price up. In response to this and to the sacking of his mentor 'Brommy', Vivian drunkenly heckles the visiting Sir John and loses his job.

7 Returning to London and his father, Vivian meets Jennifer again, and resists the family's plan for an immediate new career.

8 A montage of Vivian as playboy ends in a court appearance where he meets Sandy again.

9 Taken home by Sandy, Vivian re-encounters Jill, now married to Sandy, and has an affair with her. This is discovered by Sandy, who decides to divorce Jill. When Vivian announces he has no intention of marrying her, the two fight, but end up reconciled. Sandy and Jill drop out of the narrative.

10 Vienna, 1938. Now a racing driver with Fogroy, Vivian's participation in the Vienna Grand Prix is cancelled by the political situation. As he plans a runner from his hotel debts, a young Jewish woman, Rikki Krausner (Lili Palmer) proposes a marriage of convenience, in return for the payment of his debts. He agrees.

11 In London three things become clear. Both are now almost penniless; Rikki has fallen in love with Vivian; and Vivian is fond enough of her to stay with her rather than terminate the marriage.

12 Rikki, Vivian, Colonel Kenway and Jennifer go for a holiday to the family home in Cornwall. Tiring of Rikki, Vivian begins an affair with Jennifer which leads to Rikki's suicide attempt. Rescued from drowning, she denounces Vivian to his father and Jennifer.

13 Vivian, who has been drinking, crashes the car in which he has been driving his father and Rikki to London.

14 In hospital Vivian is present as his father dies.

15 Jennifer relates Vivian's decline into a series of unsalubrious

jobs, and then tracks him down to a dancehall where he is a professional dancing partner.

16 Jennifer takes Vivian back to Cornwall and nurses him through the breakdown caused by his father's death. Suddenly, recovered, he announces that he is leaving. He changes his mind and asks Jennifer to marry him. She agrees and catches the London train for a clothes-buying expedition. Returning, she finds only a letter from Vivian, saying that he is sorry but he cannot go through with it.

17 Return to framing segment A. Fogroy brings a senior officer to see where Vivian has died.

18 Jennifer's overvoice, which has been prominent in several sequences, ends the film meditating on the meaning of Vivian's life and death.

## Classical equivocal

Picaresque narratives are of their nature expansive, so it is unsurprising that Launder told Brown that he and Gilliat 'wrote a greatly overlength screenplay, and spent many hours cutting it down'.[10] Even Gilliat's personal shooting script has numerous differences from the film, showing last-minute adjustments. Some of these (mainly) deletions can be put down to economy – e.g. the nice idea of all three women, Jill, Rikki and Jennifer learning in turn of Vivian's death in characteristic surroundings (Jill in a nightclub waiting for a date with an American) is dropped for Jennifer alone. Shots omitted in the South American section — Vivian with Miss Fernandez, Vivian batting — come into the same category, but others seem motivated by a desire to delete elements pushing interpretation in a single direction. Thus the film's scene where Vivian shares a taxi with Jennifer after the scandal of his and Jill's adultery omits Vivian's crass pass at her, a decision one feels retrospectively was right. The moment makes Vivian uncharacteristically crude, and acts against the sense elsewhere that his women are the pursuers, perhaps more than the pursued. Elsewhere, after returning from South America, Vivian tries to explain to his father how he feels. 'Well, what sense is there in sweating to grow four beans where only three grew before ... while they're burning them by the ton. Crazy world, may as well act crazily.' (He repeats the last sentence almost verbatim when he visits Fogroy's car shop, a scene also cut from the film.) The omission of these rather memorable words, important enough to appear twice in the script, is significant. However cogent and attractive they are they militate against subtler effects, first, by breaking the film's discipline of denying self-explanation by Vivian, and second, by creating a too easy diagnosis, likely to stick in the mind to the detriment of other material. Jennifer, it's true, at the beginning and end of the film meditates on the meaning of Vivian, but what she says is essentially different even where it shares a broad sense of social determinism ('We're made mostly by what we inherit and the circumstances that surround us from the cradle on. That's how it was with Vivian'). For one thing, these are the words of another character, interpreting Vivian, not the words of Vivian himself; for another, they are also more opaque, altogether more difficult to interpret unambiguously than the words cut from the film.

Without suggesting that *The Rake's Progress* imitates the art-film ambiguity of a *Rashomon* or a *L'Année dernière à Marienbad*, I still want to argue that it bends classical narrative form significantly in structuring itself round a character presented as an enigma, both in and to himself and in the effects he generates in others, and that, while proferring explanations for Vivian being as he is which are both sociological and psychological, various fine balances are kept, making Vivian always a little more mysterious than the categories used to explain him. Here it is interesting to see how 'the book of the film', a shortened, inevitably simplified version of the narrative, written to cash in on the film's release, quickly moves to a single psychological explanation for Vivian's actions, heavily stressing the emotionally traumatized reactions of a motherless child.

> [S]ince the day, when, as a lonely and sensitive and motherless child, he had first found it necessary to build-up a protection against the sadness of neglect ... He knew now that he felt for Jennifer in a way that he had never felt for a woman before, but still the sense that any kind of monogamous life was not for him

proved very insistent. Sometimes the conflict was so strong that he had an inkling of its basis – the inner conviction, handed down by that unloved boy, that the simple warm things of the world were not for him.[II]

These overt explanations (suggesting that the writer did not expect his audience to be as hostile to Vivian as some of the early critics) depend on an authorial/narratorial intimacy with Vivian's conscious and unconscious motivations quite different from anything in a film careful to withhold such knowledge. This doesn't mean that the author was a wholly incompetent reader of the film. His brief was to make the opaque comprehensible to an audience wanting conventional motivations. Searching for explanations, he picked up clues that are undoubtedly there in the text, noticing that Vivian is indeed motherless – shown in the post-Oxford sequence as having only a father, the question of his mother being clarified, though without details, when, apropos of Vivian informing him of his marriage to Rikki, Colonel Kenway talks briefly about his late wife. There is no clue as to when she died, but there is a curious moment in the Armistice Night sequence when one of the soldiers asks Vivian if his father knows he is out. Of course the soldier can't know whether Vivian's mother is alive or dead, and his reference to the father rather than the mother is rationalizable in various ways, but in the whole context of the narrative the question is suggestive, pointing to other material, particularly clustered around Jennifer. However, as distinct from the novelization, the less univocal film text, though willing to invoke the lost mother, sometimes powerfully, is unwilling to wholly privilege the psychological at the expense of other meanings, such as the chain of socio-political indicators noted above. Here as elsewhere the film holds to its enigmatic mode against the temptations of closure and complete explanation.

And rightly so. The figure of the Rake is constituted in ambiguity from the start, attracting fascinated opprobrium for his amorality, his asocialism, his solipsism; and admiration, envy and identification for his profligacy, his freedom, his refusal of the social law. He may also be a tragic figure, driven by forces that he does not comprehend, powerful but nihilistic, dissatisfied and self-wounding. His actions may be in some sense an attack upon the patriarchal order, but since it is that order which enables his power, the attack may be self-destructive. Further, as a figure embodying certain of the contradictions in the culture, his meanings exist as much in the attractions and repulsions he arouses in the characters around him as in himself. Hence the logic in the *The Rake's Progress* of presenting Vivian almost without self-reflection (the only exception perhaps being his statement that he's 'a type who's become obsolete'). The transhistorical character of the Rake becomes in Launder and Gilliat's version a precise English interwar type (Gilliat quotes the novelist John Masters's statement of recognition of a particular charisma known among his Sandhurst contemporaries[12]) interacting obliquely but tellingly with a crucial phase of British history, and signifying beyond the rather constricted moral debate already noted.

## 'All the nice girls love a sailor'

Although in obvious senses *The Rake's Progress* with its male protagonist breaks a pattern of female-oriented films, it contains in the Rake's lovers three important female characters, Jill, Rikki and Jennifer. As has been noted of the various forms of melodrama, the concentration on a female centre in the 'woman's film' or a male centre in 'male melodrama' by no means limits the insights of the narratives to the prioritized sex.[13] In a kind of displaced gloss on this, Fogroy, Vivian's friend and fellow officer, as he steers his tank behind Vivian's through the French countryside, sings the well-known song

> All the nice girls love a sailor,
> All the nice girls love a tar,
> For there's something about a sailor,
> And you know what sailors are.
> Bright and breezy, free and easy,
> He's the ladies' pride and joy ...

This identification of Vivian with the subject of the song is traced through the film in Vivian and Fogroy's repeated catchphrase, 'Up the Navy!' In the context of Vivian's appeal to women (the only heretic is Aunt Angela, distanced from him by age, temperament and consanguinity) it suggests an interrogation of the song's lyrics. Why do 'nice' girls, especially, love a sailor? What is the 'something' about a sailor, and what is it that we are assumed to know that 'sailors are'? The song's implicit widom is that the sailor (like Vivian) excites female desire because he is what the 'nice' man, and, more especially, the 'nice girl' are not; free, un-fixed, promiscuous. Thus his special attraction for her lies in his disregard for the social norms to which she is bound, even more than the male. Jennifer and Rikki obviously qualify as 'nice girls'; Jill, selfish, ultra-calculating and promiscuous, does not, but she pretends to it, publicly becoming a 'nice girl' through her marri-age to the dull Sandy, behind the facade of which she has her affairs.

While it is true that *The Rake's Progress* may differ from some other male tragic melodramas in not blaming the possessiveness or control of women for the hero's marginalization,[14] it's not actually clear that the women wouldn't control him if they could. In fact all three of them try to secure him, but the effort is in vain, since marriage and possession (which, anyway, don't restrain Vivian, as we see with Rikki) are the antithesis of what he is un-consciously admired for. If they possessed him and he changed, *they* might lose interest in *him*. As it is, their affairs with him are dangerous for the women since, unconsciously attracted by his infidelity and scepticism, they lose their hearts to such qualities at their peril. So, if they are his victims, their state needs to be glossed as active rather than passive, for they actually seek him out fascinatedly, Jill cultivating him as the antithesis to Sandy, Rikki choosing him and not some suitable other for her attentions, and Jennifer literally searching high and low for him when he disappears. Jill, from the slightly insulting way that Vivian typically speaks to her, can have no illusions about him, Jennifer several times makes statements that she knows exactly what the fate of any one who fell in love with Vivian would be, and Rikki, the least experienced, in order to research her plan of proposing a marriage of convenience to Vivian, has found out all about his debts and lifestyle, so that, in the ordinary sense, even she knows what she is doing. Indeed one might go further and suggest that what she has found out, while on one level it may make him a suitable object for her business proposal, also propels her to fall in love with him. The women's primary victimization is that impelled by unconscious forces towards embodiments of their own desire in the Rake figure, they suffer the inevitable consequences of his scepticism and lack of commitment. To overidealize the women in the narrative, as Jennifer does Rikki when she speaks of her as 'Romantic, sensitive, pushed more and more into the background and loving Vivian with all her heart' (one might feel that in saying this she is using Rikki to dramatize/ idealize part of herself), to see the women as victims in any absolute sense, is to simplify both them and the film's implicit analysis of them.

In contrast to Jill's and Rikki's more attentuated presences, Jennifer Calthrop appears throughout the narrative, from the 1931 sequence on, in the background at first as Colonel Kenway's secretary, then in the foreground. What is initially a detached, observing role ( JENNIFER: It has nothing to do with me. It's not for me to pass judgement. VIVIAN: No one ever said that who hadn't already passed it.) is later merged with its opposite as she becomes first Vivian's lover and then, after their affair has been ended by Rikki's attempted suicide, a kind of maternal saviour, rescuing Vivian from the breakdown that follows his father's death. Later she is almost married to him, before becoming the last of the women he abandons. But her already multiple role extends further than this. She also has a privileged place in the home front part of the 1944 prologue–epilogue, meditating on his meanings at the beginning and the end of the film. The whole flashback narrative of Vivian's life thus unrolls between her interior monologues. If this voice (an experiment in female subjective commentary which will be repeated in Bridie in *I See a Dark Stranger*) is never quite pervasive enough to insist on the story told as *her* account, it is present enough to make her the primary, if not the absolutely authoritative voice of the film, with the most privileged view of Vivian, even though the film, following its strategy in other places, holds back from completely vindicating its authority.

Early on, Jennifer (often referred to slightly forbiddingly as 'Calthrop') functions largely as an ironic authority figure, associated with the father, acting out sardonically the disciplines and critiques Colonel Kenway cannot bring himself to enforce. (VIVIAN: You paid my bills! JENNIFER: It was time somebody did it. VIVIAN: Yes, but you docked my allowance to do it.) Her early exchanges with Vivian are marked by ironic banter (VIVIAN: I wonder what's cooking? JENNIFER: Not the fatted calf, I'm afraid). They gradually become more hostile as Jennifer's comments, especially in the taxi scene, take on an increasingly moral tone, with Vivian later suggesting that she should be reading *Eric or Little by Little* to the parish ladies. Eventually her detachment breaks down even further as she becomes Vivian's lover and then, after their affair has terminated, metamorphoses into an extraordinarily overt mother figure, rescuing him from his psychic collapse, and nursing him until he recovers. The oedipal reverberations of this are intensified by her position as (non-sexual) replacement for Colonel Kenway's dead wife, thus making her a kind of stepmother to Vivian; by the site that she rescues him from, a dancehall where he entertains, prior, presumably, to sleeping with, women old enough to be his mother; and by his retreat into infantile speechlessness during the period when she nurses him.

With her final role, in which, like Jill and Rikki, she becomes a rejected object of desire, Jennifer embraces a range of positions *vis-à-vis* Vivian more various than those of the other women in the narrative, whose different more limited roles she amalgamates – the unentranced critic (Aunt Agatha), the erotic partner–betrayed love object (Jill and Rikki), the father to whom she is closely bound (a number of times chastising Vivian for neglecting him), and the lost mother haunting the margins of the film. The Australian actress Margaret Johnston's cool, aloof beauty was underused by the 1940s English cinema, but it is particularly suited in its mixture of distance and plangency to such a mysteriously resonant role with its undertones of maternal solicitude. Along with the famous last words of Kenway Senior to his son, her musings about Vivian at the beginning and end of the narrative are the most moving moments in the film, precisely because they seem to

encompass so many positions. Here too the characteristic ambiguity of the film is preserved, since Jennifer's words, for all their
persuasiveness, are marked by wishfulfilment and dubiety, as
when she claims, after finding that Vivian has left her, that his
abandoning of her was a proof of his love for her, a statement that
stutters from apparent certainty into mere possibility. ('He led a
mental life which I could never enter ... But I know he loved me
and believed for a little while we could have made each other
happy. Then perhaps quite suddenly, he found himself again and
knew he hadn't changed, and so for once made a choice against
his own wish for my sake. I say perhaps. I'll never really know.') If
*The Rake's Progress* acts out paradigmatically the close relation of
the familial and personal with the social, it also resists the too easy
extension of this often made in the assumption that the interacting texts simply reflect each other. Rather, the narrative presents
them as symbiotic, but in conflict. Vivian is the object both of
satiric critique and of Jennifer's multifaceted mourning, and this
ambiguity, which takes us back to Gilliat's and MacDonald's
agreement that 'it often seems a different picture from what it was
the time before', is the life of the film.

## Fathers and sons

Discussion of film melodrama has until recently concentrated on
Hollywood models, but its main variants, the family melodrama,
the woman's picture and the male melodrama exist in British
cinema. The male melodrama's two broad types have been defined
as narratives of male initiation in which the hero successfully
attains his place in society (Gilliat's script for *Kipps* is a classic
example), and their 'tragic' inversion, in which the hero cannot
take that place and suffers accordingly.[15] *The Rake's Progress* clearly
fits the latter trajectory. In it the initiation drama's optimistic plot
is only ironically, or very vestigially, echoed in Vivian's 'good death'
and Jennifer's posthumous valediction ('Yes, that was Vivian, in
peace a misfit, a man who wanted to live dangerously in a world
that wanted to play safe. He was a fine soldier. Perhaps that was
his destiny'), and in his dull friend Sandy's un-rakelike progress in

the business world. The film centres on a powerfully charismatic yet marginalized male, empowered by his social position to live profligately, in opposition, if not to certain aristocratic codes, certainly to dominant middle-class ones, rejecting work, fatherhood, monogamy, responsibility (there is a biting moment where Jennifer says she pities Rikki her fate and Vivian says 'I've no intention of being her fate. I've more consideration for the girl'), but with diminishing social authority and material resources. Money is constantly a problem for Vivian, and at the nadir of his fortunes he takes on a series of jobs depending on parodically diminished versions of his charisma, selling second-hand cars and vacuum cleaners (shades of George Cole in *The Green Man*), and becoming a dancehall partner–gigolo. At the same time elements of the charisma survive marginalization; a quick audience eye will spot the irony that the newspaper in which Jennifer reads that he is 'missing presumed' is the Labour-supporting tabloid the *Daily Mirror*, demonstrating a fascination alongside political disapproval which encapsulates the clashing perspectives of the film.

Just as from one perspective the narrative is structured round Vivian's women, so from another it is built around Vivian's relationships with males, all of them, except for his contemporaries Sandy and Fogroy, father figures, the patriarchs (or their surrogates) of the society in which 'Young 'Opeful' is expected to take his place. Moving chronologically, these are: the lower-class soldiers who adopt him on Armistice Night; the proctor acting for the unseen dean of the college, who nabs Vivian for climbing the tower; Sir Hubert Parks, his father's brother-in-law; Sir John Brockley, the South American coffee magnate; his right-hand man in South America, Edwards, and 'Brommy', the firm's boffin; the policeman who interrupts Vivian's and Jean's pastoral idyll; the managers of Harrods and the hotel in Vienna, from both of whose establishments Vivian tries to do a runner; the senior officer whom Fogroy takes to see Vivian after his death; as well as three off-screen figures, Sandy's father (whose business Vivian contemptuously refuses jobs in); Uncle George, the black sheep family legend who made a fortune in diamonds in South Africa in less constricted days, and with whom Colonel Kenway indulgently compares his 'harum scarum' son; and Rikki's 'good father', who sacrifices all his capital in order to get her out of Austria where he will presumably die under the Nazis.

When listed like this, it strikes one forcibly that the narrative is so patterned that, when not with the women, Fogroy or Sandy, Vivian is inevitably in the company of his elders, typically occupying the position of the rebellious child – being caught in the act, looking for apt ways to confess, being called to account, running away, being rude, refusing to cooperate, managing to charm his way out of things – and that the narrative is selectively constructed to create that emphasis, repeating versions of that scene of the truant boy with the soldiers, the hero assuming and depending on the same indulgence. The fraughtness that attends many of these relationships (notably excepting that with Sir Hubert, a bluff old baby, a reductio ad absurdam of Vivian's refusal to attain his adult role, occupied when we see him with a yoyo, then having to be dragged away from a bagatelle board) reflects the doubleness of Vivian's position, produced and supported by his class, inheriting and exploiting the position of the fathers yet acting in rebellion against them, though a rebellion that has no conscious aim or end except getting 'a kick'. The only point where it could be said to clarify into consciously articulated opposition is in his drunken attack on the obnoxiously complacent, authoritarian Sir John Brockley, the coffee magnate, after he has sacked Bromfield, the one father figure able to influence Vivian (perhaps more susceptible because he is in a foreign environment) towards productive work, so much so that the Rake commits himself, at least temporarily, to a career as the executive arm of Brommy's research, 'growing four beans where only three grew before' in a version of the parable of the talents to go alongside Jennifer's joke about the prodigal son. Are we to believe that this might have been Vivian's salvation, or is the evidence elsewhere that his newfound métier would have bored him in the end?

At any rate, returning to England, Vivian rejects the careers the family suggest, and lives as a playboy, his only employment as a racing car driver, teamed up with Foggy, who, along with his other Oxford contemporary, Sandy, turns up at various points throughout the narrative, though never together, since they are obviously anti-thetical. Fogroy who, embodied by the same actor, Guy Middleton, will play more of the same as Hyde-Brown in *The Happiest Days of Your Life*, is Vivian without the complexities. Associated with betting, moneymaking schemes, fast cars and girls, he seems to have no family at all, suffers no oedipal guilts or tensions, and simply skitters from one scrape and excitement to another. Sandy, decent, constrained, dully successful, is also, in a way quite opposite to Foggy, without the oedipal tensions that mark Vivian. Sandy seems merely the mirror image of his unseen father, taking over the family business (soap, expanding into chemicals) and early on in the film, while boring Jill, quoting his father's conservative political opinions as if they were his own. Sandy is also distinguished from Vivian by his masochistic thraldom to Jill, which he expresses in terms of the hero's abject passion in Maugham's *Of Human Bondage*, whereas Vivian's lovemaking with Jill in the punt is surrounded by (ironic) allusions to *Antony and Cleopatra*. (In *The Constant Husband* Harrison's dog is called Mark Antony, marking him as Cleopatra!) Vivian's relation to the antithetical Fogroy and Sandy is, however, not wholly contained by simple antithesis. Some of the sense of his two companions as almost automata of upbringing and habit rubs off onto Vivian, especially where he and Sandy, after their brawl over Vivian's not marrying Jill, effect a reconciliation over a drink. Here they recognize a kind of kinship in their perception of the significance of their simultaneously uttering the words 'same again', as if in commentary on their lives, defining them both, rebel and conservative, as creatures of convention, and reminding the watcher of Jennifer's statement, at the beginning of the film, of social determinants.

Vivian's literal father figure, Colonel Kenway, despite his bluff simplicity, is, in spite of himself, the most complex of these characters. An oldfashioned Tory MP, his knowledge of politics seems restricted to the bland enthusiasm with which he salutes the election result: 'I honestly think that today has saved the country from disaster, and now it's up to us to set the nation on its feet again'. As he speaks, his butler, who's been asked by Vivian to get Colonel Kenway to see him, mimes the concept of other matters requiring the master's attention with rather disturbing facial gestures, creating a moment that could be read (perhaps for an unsettling moment is read by the MP) as the servant's disagreement with his views. Though a reference to Kenway Senior's opposition to Churchill, with its implication of his being an appeaser, was never carried over from the script to the film, there is little doubt that most viewers will see the colonel as the kind of politician whose blinkered conventionality helped lead, at least indirectly, to the decade's tragic end. Yet the viewer is not allowed to rest in this superior post-1945 position. For all his faults, Colonel Kenway (whom the well-read Gilliat saw as having his genesis in Thackeray's ever indulgent Colonel Newcome in *The Newcomes*[16]) is a generous, kindly, tolerant man, patient and uncomplaining at the many disappointments his son causes him, his essential decency shown when, despite his wish for Vivian to marry an Englishwoman, he is so protective of the foreign and Jewish Rikki. Indeed the one time that he can bring himself to criticize his son is after her attempted suicide. His virtues may go hand in hand with a lack of imagination, in the realm of the film's many implicits his upper-middle-class English male inability with emotions – perhaps exacerbated by the loss of his wife – may be in part to blame for Vivian's excess of detachment, but it would be a false sophistication that merely laughed at his simplicities (his statement for instance of his monogamous love for his wife), and when he dies the film seems to be suggesting that, whatever benefits the hoped-for changes of 1945 will bring, they may be missed.

The conversation between Gilliat and MacDonald cited earlier very much circles round Colonel Kenway's dying words to his son – 'You've hurt your hand' – and their obscurely touching qualities which moved Olivier and Gilliat himself to tears. Why are they so moving? They are, of course, a classic case of English understatement, linked to a paradoxical mixture of strong but defective emotions. Neither father nor son is able to articulate what they feel, and Colonel Kenway, in a motion which touchingly suggests his own selflessness as well as his desire to return to a moment when Vivian was a small boy and paternal filial relations less difficult, addresses him as if he was a child who'd slightly hurt himself. It is also one of those scenes that dramatizes quietly – this being part of the source of its unexpected force – the unfinishedness of all human relations. The larger point made earlier about the symbiotic link between the personal and the social in melodrama is also exemplified by the scene and its consequence, Vivian's psychic collapse, endlessly reliving the moment in the hospital room (as Jennifer tells us this we see Vivian looking at his hand). The extremity of Vivian's collapse, we might feel, goes beyond the personal in its implications, owing something to the sense that it has representative social meanings, that his father's death, beyond its private meanings, marks also the passing of his own time of privilege, the beginning of the end of the class hegemony that has sustained him. Here the extremity of the film's oedipal theme (in a sense, behind the accident, Vivian is the killer of his father, the disowner of his class heritage) sounds on both the personal and the social political levels of the film, so closely interwoven, but never allowed completely to merge.

### *I See a Dark Stranger*

The comic-thriller narrative

1. Pretitle sequence. The narrative begins with an enigmatic scene only explained later in the film. Night in a French town. In heightened expressionist thriller/film noir mode a man moves through the streets. Shot and wounded, he will be recognized later as the German spy, Oscar Pryce. In the scene's chief enigma Pryce looks at a signpost which reveals that the French town is in the Isle of Man.
2. Title sequence over idyllic Irish countryside. An avuncular Irish male overvoice announces that the story has started in the wrong place and commences the history of Bridie Quilty, a 'very strange little character'.
3. 1938. Bridie's father, Danny Quilty (W. O'Gorman), retells to a captivated pub audience his (fictional) tale of his actions in the 1916 revolution, and leads the singing of a revolutionary song first sung by 'a blackhaired angel of a girleen'. His

daughter (Deborah Kerr) listens entranced, mouthing the familiar words of the story as her father speaks them.

4   1944. Bridie's twenty-first birthday party. She announces her intention of leaving for Dublin that night and, in spite of protests, does so.

5   On the Dublin train she meets Miller (Raymond Huntley), shortly to be revealed as a German spy. She reveals her anti-British feelings to him.

6   Bridie visits the Dublin art gallery where Michael Callaghan (Brefni O'Rorke), a revolutionary hero, supposedly her father's ex-comrade, is assistant director. She asks him to help her join the IRA. He refuses, telling her that Ireland is not at war with England. As she leaves angrily, she pauses significantly before the portrait of Sir Roger Casement, hanged as a traitor for treason with the Germans in 1916.

7   In a bookshop another spy gives Miller the mission of rescuing Oscar Pryce from prison in Winbridge Vale in the West Country before he is sent to London for trial. Bridie coincidentally visits the shop to buy German-language books. Miller, needing an unknown accomplice, follows her out.

8   [The scene of his recruitment of Bridie is assumed, its actual terms suppressed from the audience.] Winbridge Vale. A statue of Cromwell is vandalized. Bridie, the unknown culprit, is established as working at a hotel where Miller is also staying. A convalescing artillery officer, David Baynes (Trevor Howard), arrives and immediately shows an interest in Bridie which she rebuffs.

9   Bridie goes out on a date with a British soldier. Miller, observing David, decides wrongly that he is an intelligence officer sent to watch for any attempt to spring Pryce.

10  Returning from her date, Bridie meets Miller in his room and gives him information about the moving of Pryce which she has extracted from the soldier. Miller shocks her by ordering her to prostitute herself with David to keep him out of the way.

11  On the evening arranged for the escape Bridie and David go for a walk in the country. They briefly quarrel about Cromwell,

on whom David is writing his Cambridge thesis, but then get more friendly. Concurrently, aided by lax security, Miller helps Pryce escape. They drive off pursued by security men. Price is killed and Miller escapes fatally wounded.

12  Evading David, Bridie goes to her room to find Miller dying. He instructs her to make contact with an unknown spy on a train and also to dispose of his body.

13  Pretending that she is taking the grandfather of the family who employ her out for an airing, she does this (though how is not revealed till her nightmare).

14  Evading a now suspicious David again, Bridie goes to bed but suffers a nightmare.

15  Next morning she leaves alone, but David follows her.

16  On the train she fails to make contact with the spy who is surprisingly revealed when a little old lady (Katie Johnson) is arrested.

17  When Bridie and David (who has caught up with her again) stay the night in Liverpool, a Nazi spy, seen following them in the previous sequence, frightens her by breaking into her room. Finding that because of a ban on travel to Eire she cannot get back home, she resolves to follow the information Miller gave her, and go to the Isle of Man where Pryce's notebook is hidden in the visitor's gallery of the Tynewold Parliament. Her plan is to smuggle it back home and give it to the German minister.

18  Next morning, evading David again, she leaves for the Isle of Man. The police and security close in on her, with the island's inefficient security men, Spanswick and Goodhusband, ordered to arrest her.

19  In the Parliament Bridie finds the notebook. Followed by the spy, she reads the notebook and looks at the unremarkable military site it mentions. She then realizes the truth that the military base contains a mock-up of a French town for training for the D-Day invasion. Envisioning not only the British soldiers but, crucially, the Irish volunteers who will be killed if her information goes to the Germans, Bridie decides to become 'a retired spy'.

21 As she attempts to burn the book she is visited by the un-observant security officers, but temporarily satisfies them with a false identity card claiming that she is Mrs David Baynes. When David, having tracked her down, arrives, he supports her story.

22 When he impresses on her the danger she is in, she suddenly disappears.

23 In the dancehall below she dances with Goodhusband, the security officer, and attempts to confess, but her partner is too preoccupied to listen. The spy takes advantage of a 'changing partners' number and dances with her, then somehow spirits her away.

24 David traces her to a boat at the docks. He is captured by the spies and taken with Bridie to Eire.

25 As the spies and their prisoners travel overland by horse and carriage they get caught up in a funeral procession which turns out to be a cover for a border smuggling operation. When the police get involved, Bridie and David escape in the confusion.

26 At a pub in what they conceive to be the Republic, David mediates between love and duty by phoning the police in order to hand Bridie over to the Irish rather than the British with whom she would be in mortal danger. After the call they discover they are in Northern Ireland. David urges Bridie to cross the border, but (not wishing him to compromise him-self) she insists on waiting with him for the police. Suddenly the radio announces the launching of the D-Day invasion, meaning that Bridie's information is no longer vital. As the police arrive, David helps her escape across the border, and then, with the police, captures the spies.

27 1945. Peace. David and Bridie as honeymooners stop at a hotel. As David goes to put the car away, Bridie notices something and registers anger. When he returns he sees her striding away with her suitcase. She tells him angrily that she will not stay in such a place. A shift of camera position reveals that the hotel is called The Cromwell Arms.

*I See a Dark Stranger* is illuminated by comparison with Launder and Gilliat's other Irish film *Captain Boycott* (Launder, 1947), released almost a year later. At a certain level of generality both films fit the prototype described by John Hill whereby the British Irish film diagnoses an endemic irrational Irish predilection for violence (the point confirmed here when Alastair Sim's Father McKeogh jokily says from the pulpit, 'And I know that even though you are Irish, it could be that one or two of you might think to resort to violence'), which leads to such films neglecting analysis of the social and political determinants of this violence.[17] Both films' optimistic narratives have their Irish protagonists convert-ing from violent action against the British to non-violence, Hugh Davin (Stewart Granger) by aligning himself with Parnell's Land League's non-violent protest, Bridie by deciding to become a 'retired spy' and marry an English officer.

*Captain Boycott* is a more interesting film than treatment of it either as simply passively fitting the schema above (which can't include its numerous surprises like Hugh's mother's unswerving commitment to revolutionary violence) or, as here, demonstrating the greater interest of *I See a Dark Stranger*, will allow. But for all its intelligent virtues, Launder is no Pontecorvo and the film is vulnerable to weaknesses of the kind Hill suggests, four in parti-cular. (1) Though it is careful to avoid any suggestion of heroic English agency, the casting of Robert Donat as Parnell, devoid of the slightest trace of Irish in his Anglo-Irishness, actually manages to suggest what is elsewhere scrupulously avoided. (2) Boycott's (Cecil Parker's) bluff foolishness tends to exculpate not just him but the whole English enterprise in Ireland — not to deny it and its cost, for the film contains memorably stark scenes of tenant eviction, but to make it seem an accidental foolishness, easily righted by the politics of goodwill. (3) The 'motiveless malignity' of Watty Connell, Boycott's Irish right-hand man who eggs on his foolish master into extreme actions with the result that an Irish-man becomes ultimately responsible for the Englishman's actions, embodies an oxymoronic Irishness that coalesces both irrational-ity and extreme Machiavellianism. (4) The human sympathies expressed for the Irish and against Boycott by the English soldiers, while touching, are too softcentred to satisfy a critical audience's sense of reality.

Though it is a costume film set back in the 1880s, *Captain Boycott* is the closest that Launder and Gilliat ever come to a film *à thèse*, so that these contradictions in its attempts to provide optimistic solutions compromise the film heavily, since so much is staked on its not being infected by the subterranean prejudices and sentimentalities that creep back into the text and make the overt political film about Anglo-Irish relations so difficult for British film-makers. Even the recent independence of India invoked by the film,[18] and attributed in part to Gandhi's non-violent protest movement (implicitly suggested as a moment a liberal modern Britain may be proud of), tends to be misleading in the context of Ireland where the question of Irish partition (the meaning of the Irish problem even in a nineteenth-century film for a modern audience) relates much more to the question of Indian *partition* than independence.

*I See a Dark Stranger* may look to a superficial view even more blatant in some of its designs than *Captain Boycott*, set as it is in the just-finished war in which Irish 'neutrality' was a major source of anger and suspicion, and especially with its 'imperialist' marriage plot of the male of the more 'advanced' culture taking a woman of the more 'primitive' one into his own. However, its sophisticated manipulation of so many intersecting and competing, even dislocating, elements – war film, spy thriller, female-centred drama, Anglo-Irish propaganda, self-consciously artful play with and meaningful confusion of national myths (there is a wonderful moment when Bridie tells Miller that her aunt living in England has told her that the English 'upper classes are cringin' and always moanin' about their troubles and the lower classes are arrogant and think they own the earth') – allows, as the narrative of *Captain Boycott* doesn't, the kind of intricate effects that Durgnat noted in a passage quoted in Chapter 1, so that the film escapes the inevitable disappointments that the earnest but compromised liberalism of *Captain Boycott* traps that film in.

Exactly how the comedy-thriller-romance manages to do this is an interesting question. Having as the protagonist, main focalizer and often fully subjectivized centre of the narrative, demanding considerable audience identification, a girl so possessed by hatred of the English that, failing to join the IRA, she becomes a Nazi spy, would seem to stretch sympathy for her (and the film-makers?) to breaking point, but hardly seems to have done so. The odd contemporaneous English review fretted over the film's indulgence with her, but much less so than one might expect. Antonia Lant's vision of the English critics squirming under the film is exaggerated. Only the *Daily Telegraph* review sounded a moral note; Jympson Harman's, with the title 'Naughty Deborah Aids the Nazis' (where the 'naughty' would seem to betray its unseriousness), is much more worried by the satiric treatment of British intelligence men fuelling American prejudices of national inefficiency. In fact it's a more striking aspect of the reviews that they rather overstress the film's comedy and underplay its very real suspense.[19]

In trying to define the way the film works, it must first be said that its situation is very different from the one in the British war film that, in this one respect of having an enemy at the centre, is closest to *Dark Stranger*, Powell and Pressburger's *49th Parallel* (1941). There the basic narrative association of the audience with the Nazi group crossing Canada, while it may play on some unruly unconscious fascinations, is formal, not sympathetic, as can be seen in the relief offered the audience by switches of position throughout the narrative as Eric Portman and his men encounter groups and individuals (and occasionally aspects of themselves) that are surrogates for the audience's own values. Deborah Kerr's vivacious and spirited Bridie (a composite of wilful child and resourceful heroine, winsome sweetness and transgressive boundary crosser – the polarities are essential to the film's strategies) is the centre of both narrative identification and sympathy. But the sympathy is a rather complex and divided one for the historical and preferred audience since they wish her to escape the consequence of her deeds at the same time that they hope she will be not too drastically prevented (hopefully by conversion) from committing any that are too irretrievably destructive. In order for the narrative to be genuinely suspenseful, the gravity of what she is doing must always be within at least the peripheral vision of the audience (as in the scene where Katie Johnson is arrested and Bridie's interior speech registers that it is 'horrible', presumably because she imagines herself hanged as the old lady will presumably be[20]), but must be outweighed by her romantic naivety, by the fact that she is not a Nazi but merely seeking through them a way of fighting the English, by her role as romantic heroine eliciting both male and female sympathy, and by her status as child, which, while it may be condescending both in feminist and nationalist terms, is essential in the positioning of the audience and the generation of sympathy.

The film's system is built, consciously or unconsciously, to be evasive – at the most obvious level by its expert oscillations between suspense and comedy. These are particularly evident in the virtuosic train scene where Bridie's attempts to contact an unknown fellow spy are conducted in atmospheres of considerable suspense, with eruptions into film noir visuals, particularly when the train plunges into tunnels, but in a carriage filled with stereotypical comic characters (crusty naval officer type, pruriently gossiping middle-class women, little old lady with thermos flask and picnic), and comic as well as dreadful resolutions (the strange lady's aberrant eye movements – madness? a code? – resolved by her book's title, *Exercises for the Eyes*). Such instabilities are repeated at other levels of the text and many of them are traced in Antonia Lant's reading in her major essay on the film, 'The Female Spy', of such details as the symbolic place of the Isle of Man and other border or metaphorically borderline situations in the narrative.[21]

To remain, though, with the most basic of the instabilities, that of comedy and suspense, the comic element, which serves various purposes – e.g. creating an indulgent framework for Bridie's crimes, for instance in the avuncular Irish storyteller's voice that commences her narrative; and offering a clashing perspective to the noir and expressionist elements in the film – also works in a double contradictory action either (a) to dissolve 'serious plot' difficulties into comic indulgence, or (b), on the contrary, to assert in a pleasurable form material that might otherwise be unpleasurable, slipping it, as it were, past the censor, with the apparent unseriousness of a joke. An instance of (a) is the way in which a whole set of logical worries about the narrative resolution – Would the authorities really take the view that the informational redundancy of Bridie's espionage once the D-Day invasion starts means that her spying is of no further interest? What about the search for Miller's and Pryce's accomplice? Wouldn't she be arrested once back on English soil? Would David really have escaped undetected and unpunished? – are eased aside in order for the couple's marriage, with its accompanying Anglo-Irish peace allegory, to take place. (One or two reviews at the time criticized the film's plotting for being full of holes, presumably meaning points like the ones just made.[22]) But this optimistic closure is in fact the site of (b) – comic effects working, through the joke of the quarrel about Cromwell that ends the film, to complicate rather than dissolve, and in harmless guise re-establish, without wrecking the narrative resolutions and harmonies on which the film's final pleasures depend, both personal and political problematics.

## The bride's dream

At a crucial point in *I See a Dark Stranger*, Bridie, now inescapably a German spy, returns late at night to her room. She has just – though the viewer can't know how – disposed of Miller's body. Horrified, she notices that Miller's hat – emphasized by a minatory zoom – is still on the table. Stuffing it up the chimney, she wipes the soot off her hands, her attention caught as she does by a picture on the wall of a bride in her wedding finery. Her unmistakeable fascination with it is broken by an ominous sound which an exterior shot reveals as the creaking in the wind of the sign of The George Hotel, with its painting of St George stabbing the dragon. As Bridie lies in bed in a trancelike state, images race through her mind, preceded by another shot of the swinging sign, a diagonal shadow whipping across it repeatedly. This is followed by a closeup of a metronome, its ticking hand mimicking the shadow's movement, which resolves into a part of the following image where the adolescent Bridie plays piano scales while her music master beats time with his finger, its movement rhyming with the shadow and the metronome hand. Bridie then sees the dying Miller in a shot we recognize from a preceding scene. Then there is a longshot of her wheeling the corpse along a cliff top and a flashpan to a vertiginous drop below. Cut to the now disturbingly canted picture of the bride, followed by a shot of another picture, difficult to decipher because of the brevity of the shot, but certainly of a woman, perhaps a female statue in some sort of sea and cloudscape. This is followed by shots of Bridie, looming from a low angle above Miller in the chair. Then she pushes Miller's body down the cliff. As he falls, the hat tumbles back out of the chimney with a cloud of soot and Bridie jerks up in bed, fully conscious.

*I See a Dark Stranger* is, with the exception of *Endless Night*, the most subjectively constructed of all Launder and Gilliat's films, extending Celia's daydreams in *Millions Like Us* and the oneiric elements centred around the heroine in *The Lady Vanishes*, the latter wonderfully developed by Hitchcock, but certainly originating in the scenario. Although the development of strict p.o.v. and interior voice are sporadic, they work very powerfully, particularly in a number of key scenes – for instance when Bridie meets Miller on the Dublin train, the second train scene when she tries to communicate with the unknown spy, her journey through Winbridge wheeling Miller's corpse, the moment where she imagines the D-Day forces being ambushed, and above all this one. The second and third of these sequences in particular are built around complex actions involving finely calculated suspense, in several places rivalling Hitchcock at his best – for instance when, wheeling the corpse through Winbridge, she is first approached by a man looking for a pickup, then rescued by a solicitous policeman, and then caught in a crowd of servicemen and women exiting from a cinema as the enemy's national anthem plays; or when the plainclothes policemen on the train, as they arrest Katie Johnson, speak to the unlikely seeming spy, but the framing and cutting of the action are so arranged that the audience shares Bridie's occluded viewpoint. Here, frozen by fear, she looks nowhere at all (the camera is pinned on her, so that we think, as Bridie does, that they are addressing her), until the camera reveals to the audience what Bridie is simultaneously realizing, that they are arresting not her but the old lady.

The bedroom scene differs in not taking place in a context of external action (except for having to get rid of the hat), but in being a moment of oneiric excess in which fragments of Bridie's unconscious emerge, in a location obviously connected with sexuality and fantasy, and also, through the hotel being called the George, with the film's political material. These fragments, within the context of a narrative in which a transgressive heroine attempts to assert herself while, ironically, always working under the shadow of numerous father figures, coalesce into a series of almost subliminal representations of father figures, questions of marriage and sexuality, guilt and fate, and male and female power and impotence, with father figures the linchpin of the sequence as they often are in the narrative for 'Danny Quilty's daughter' as she significantly introduces herself to Michael Callaghan. It will be remembered that in Bridie's first (girlhood) appearance she is presented as completely in thrall to her father, actually mouthing his words, or, as the current phrase is, being spoken by him. There is significantly no reference to Mrs Quilty.

There is a pronounced sexual component in Bridie's first reaction to another obvious father figure, Miller – initially sexual fear at being alone with a male stranger, then liking his hair, even though it is grey, and even admiring his nails. This sexual motif is reversed in a number of the film's patriarchs who are interested in her rather than vice versa, the jovially erotic Intelligence man, Goodhusband, on the Isle of Man, and the various older men in Ballygarry who have made passes at her. ('He [Miller] doesn't look that sort of man, but how can you tell? Mr McGee didn't look that sort of man, and Mr Claverty was a terrible shock to me.') There is also a slightly sexualized tone to the paternalistic humour of the elderly gallery guide who shows the schoolgirls ('me loves, me doves, me darlins') around the Dublin art gallery, a group to which Bridie significantly becomes appended. While there is none in the reprimandingly paternal figure of Michael Callaghan, who sternly refuses to help her to join the IRA, there is surely some fugitive combining of the paternal and the sexual in the portrait of Sir Roger Casement (one of several candidates for the unrevealed 'dark stranger' the title promises Bridie in its play on the words with which the fortuneteller traditionally promises a young female client marriage or a lover) that she stands in front of on her way out of the gallery, her shadow falling across it in a memorable image. Interestingly in the 'Gallery of the Famous' there is a portrait of a woman to her left that Bridie ignores completely, drawn to the central male figures, rather than the peripheral female ones, like the 'blackhaired angel of a girleen' in her father's narrative who sings the song that starts the revolution made by the men.

Bridie's nightmare, impelled by the fear and guilt of her situation, coalesces images of father figures, sexuality, girls and brides with oneiric economy. Miller's hat, a classic Freudian symbol, is stuffed up a vaginal chimney, only to descend, fatefully, orgasmically, in a cloud of soot which Bridie wipes away as if it is the stain of sin. The metronome, an image of discipline and order, resolves into part of the film's one subjective memory of her childhood, a scene significantly involving another in a chain of male authority figures – her music teacher. Like the other images streaming through her consciousness in her half waking, half sleeping state, this one is extremely ambivalent in meaning. Do we read her laborious scales as a synecdoche of the woman's role, imposed on and resisted by Bridie, or as pleasure and culture abandoned for her political will, and signifying little for her beside another music, the singing of the 'blackhaired angel of a girleen' of her father's story? The picture of the bride in the bedroom on which her attention is fixed must suggest her destiny as daughter (we can hardly be unaware of the similarities between 'Bridie' and 'bride') to pass from a father to a son/father, a destiny which she is beginning at least half to want but which is also signified in the minatory creaking that takes her attention away from the picture. The hotel sign depicting St George draws in not only yet another patriarchal figure, but the emblem of the enemy England, and another sexual association (which we may link with her growing feelings for the English officer, David) of the mounted saint thrusting into the dragon's body. Finally there is the disposal of Miller's body, which also solves the narrative enigma, left from the previous scene, of what has happened to it. Here the suspenseful night atmospherics of Bridie's journey with the corpse through the streets of Winbridge are transformed into images of semi-expressionist intensity: the dying Miller lit from below in his chair, Bridie in longshot wheeling him along the cliff top, a dizzying quasi subjective view of the drop below, Bridie shot from a low angle dominatingly above Miller, then the impossibly situated view (from below, on what would be the cliff face) of Miller hurtling out of the chair. The wheelchair belongs to another more elderly patriarch, the grandfather of the family running the hotel (who is joked about by the soldiers for his supposed interest in Bridie, and who expresses at one point highly patriarchal views of the female's role – 'That's right. Don't mind me. Clear up the bar. Powder your face. Darn a few stockings. I can wait'), and whose senility Bridie exploits as a cover for her wheelchair expedition.

When Bridie throws Miller over the cliff she is carrying out his orders, disposing of his body so that he won't be found in her room. Though the sexual interest she showed in him at their first meeting is never reactivated, and in any overt sense never reciprocated by Miller, a displaced element of it remains as the suave, powerful figure assumes control of her body and sexuality when he instructs her to prostitute herself with David to distract him while Pryce is rescued. When she reproachfully replies with the unspoken allusion 'like a ... [whore]' , he sternly says, 'It matters little, my dear, what you like or dislike'. (Verbally the text suggests that Bridie sleeps with David; visually it is much more reticent, simply an alfresco cuddle.) However, her placing of Miller in the older man's wheelchair, his now impotent corpse doubly marginalized, his power parodied by his declension to the grandfather, and the intensity of the imagery surrounding the disposal, with Bridie looming so powerfully above him, suggest a carrying out of the order that is at the same time almost a murder, an active killing of the father figure, a violent attempt to free herself from the chain of patriarchs to whom she is ironically bound in her attempts to rival the 'little blackhaired angel of a girleen' credited by her father with starting the revolution. This leads, though, to the return of Miller's hat, tumbling out of the chimney as his body tumbles down the cliff, an image of the seeming inescapability of the various strands of Bridie's fate.

This brief but compelling flurry of images lasting only 7 shots and 25 seconds (the whole sequence, dream and predream, lasting 24 shots and 120 seconds) can be seen as a kind of unconscious to the rest of the film, binding the political and personal, the sexual and the national, wishfulfilment and the operations of fate. It is symptomatically, apart from the opening, the only sequence of the film wholly without comedy, in which comedy and suspense/drama are not mixed in the narrative's characteristic mode, as if it provided the unmediated material on which the narrative makes its highly modulated variations.

## Cromwell's arms

The shot that marks the move from main narrative to epilogue through the coming of peace is, to say the least, downbeat – a drab scene of London crowds outside shops such as Walton's the Fruiterers and the unexotically named MacFisheries. The logic here, in refusing the expected VE celebration shot, could be to signify that while one war is over, other problematics, other local wars remain – i.e. that the rather complex figure of Michael Callaghan presented in the film, embodying revolutionary heroism passed into statesmanship, a voice approved both by Dublin and London (even if London was angry with Irish neutrality in the war), is too optimistic in its belief that goodwill and reasonableness will solve the continuing crisis caused by partition. The minor-key parody of 'Rule Britannia' that accompanies the shot might be taken to chime in with this.

This is the immediate context for the dissolve to the shot of the honeymooners coming to their room at the hotel. The scene takes place at night, which, in the simplest sense, helps to make more credible their not noticing the name of the hotel, on which the finale's punch line/sign depends. However this and the conventional collocation love–honeymoon–night should not hide the significance that as a night scene it is one of a chain of many, in a film predominantly set at night. (Chronologically: the scene where the young Bridie listens to her father's tale; Bridie's twenty-first birthday party; her meeting Miller on the night train to Dublin; her date with Harry Harris and passing the information prised from him to Miller; the intercut scenes of her date with David and Pryce's attempted escape; Miller's death in her room; her disposal of Miller's body; her nightmare; the attempted burglary of her room in Liverpool; the docks at Douglas where she and David are kidnapped and imprisoned on the boat; the scene in the border pub in Northern Ireland.) Even some of the daylight scenes, for instance the spies' holding up of the rural office and the interior of the carriage carrying the hero, heroine and the spies in the funeral procession, are lit so as to create shadowy sub-noir effects during a daytime action.

The shot in which the newly marrieds enter their hotel room is a highly elaborate setup, with the camera placed outside the windows of the room shooting through a pattern of diamond-shaped panes of glass and the central upright of the windows. Their medium longshot entry into the room, both dressed in suits, his darker, hers white with darker accoutrements, gloves and a muff, is preceded by a hotel employee. As David tips him Bridie moves into the foreground and opens the windows, looking very briefly outside, David moving to her as the employee exits after being tipped. As they stand there an elaborate pattern of shadows largely caused by the diamond-shaped panes plays on them, and Bridie is actually split almost like a comic-book sign of schizophrenia by the shadow of the vertical window frame. They briefly converse (BRIDIE: Darling, I am glad we stopped here instead of going on to Hereford. DAVID: Did you notice my hand trembling when I wrote Mr and Mrs Baines?), then turn to each other and kiss, after which David announces that he will go and put the car away, giving Bridie a chin chuck and a peculiar little backwards salute. Bridie stands for a moment, then, with the passage of time concentrated, in the scene's second shot, hearing the car outside, she looks out of the window. After a moment she sees something (undisclosed) that makes her angry, so that she shakes her head and utters the words 'Well, of all the ... !' as she turns to the camera, mouth pursed. (The opening notes of the revolutionary song from the Ballygarry pub burble comically, providing an aural clue.) Shot 3 cuts to a flight of stairs which David climbs and then stands outside the room, hesitating for a moment before going in. Shot 4, where David looks around the room for her and calls out her name, is taken from the same elaborate setup as shot 1. Alerted by the sound of footsteps outside, he looks out of the window, initiating the pattern of shots for the rest of the scene: Bridie seen outside from his p.o.v. (5, 7), David seen at the window from hers (6, 8, though not in perfect p.o.v. since, although seen from her angle of vision, he is in closeup not in realistic perspective as she is). In the shot/reverse shot sequence an animatedly angry conversation takes place (DAVID: Bridie, what the hell are you up to? BRIDIE: I won't stop in this place, no, I won't; not if the sky itself were to fall down on the top of me head, no I won't stop in it! the sky was to fall on the top of my head!). In the last shot as, seen from David's point of view, Bridie walks angrily away clutching her travelling bag, an alteration in camera angle reveals the hotel sign she is passing under as The Cromwell Arms.

Clearly this joke, with its elaborate setups, involves two crucial aspects of the film: the question of Anglo-Irish relations which have been idyllically realigned in the marriage of Bridie and David, and the question of the transgressive heroine which has been negotiated in the same event. The fight between the couple, resulting in Bridie's storming out of the bedroom before consummation (we now presumably aren't meant to feel that she slept with David in the course of her spying), is treated comically. It would be a deviant viewer who didn't feel (or feel that one was meant to feel) that David would pursue her, that they would find a bedroom in another more appropriately named hotel an hour or two on, but also that there might be occasions in the future when a similar fight might break out again. Like most at least relatively complicated jokes, especially ones placed at the end of complex narratives, there are various ways of reading what happens. Thus, in no particular order of ascendancy:

1 The comic spat makes us feel that the disagreements between Britain and Ireland can be solved as easily as their quarrel will be solved.

2 Oppositely, through the joke's playing on the obdurate presence of 'Oliver Mister Cromwell', the meaning is smuggled

in that the old diagreements cannot be solved as simply as the
international marriage plot suggests.

3 The bringing in of a note of disagreement is a form of what
radical theorists used to call 'inoculation', i.e. a little bit of
critical reality given to us which enables us to take the optimistic solution almost wholesale.

4 Bridie's temper shows her and Irishness in a childish light,
with both needing to be indulgently fathered.

5 Bridie's temper has positive connotations since it suggests
that, even if David is a kind of father figure, she stands up to
him, and the relationship thus suggests equality.

6 Such connotations extend to the political relationship.

7 The same again, but following the principle of inoculation.

The list is not exhaustive. The preferred meanings – the meanings
that most of the audience took and take – and, one suspects, those
the authors would have held to – are strongly built into the text. In
terms of Bridie's trajectory as a transgressive heroine, the last
scene with its honeymoon site fulfils the destiny (positive, negative, neutral, take your pick) suggested both by her name and by her
interest in the picture of the bride, and also by the semi-oneiric way
in which, in the frantic funeral procession scene, she goes through
metamorphoses of male ownership that are variants of the dimin-
utive that constitutes her name. Here, first of all, she becomes a
supposed female corpse, the chief mourner's sister, Bridgie, who
is supposedly in the coffin, and then his daughter, Biddie. (This is
how she and David are rather obscurely rescued from the spies;
she's presumed to be the daughter and grabbed in the chaos as the
smugglers flee, and David follows.) As Bridgie, the sister, she
turns out to be a coffin full of German alarm clocks, among other
contraband. As Biddie the daughter she needs to be rescued.

Such patriarchal aspects are mitigated by the fact that David – if
we interpret the relationship within its pleasantness as a double
instance of 'colonization' – is a pretty unpatriarchal patriarch who
has spent most of the film trying to keep up with Bridie, rather
than controlling what she is doing, who exudes an air of quiet
bewilderment a lot of the time, and who is remarkably unjudg-

mental about her actions as a spy. (His admission that his hand trembled while writing 'Mr and Mrs David Baines' could also be interpreted less as a romanticization of the power ceded to him than as a reflex reaction to what he's taken on!) It is also, inasmuch as Trevor Howard can be dull, a rather dull part that he plays, which consciously or unconsciously makes sure that Bridie, rather than the couple, is the real centre of the narrative. Similarly these suggestions work positively on the political allegory of the marriage – the spat, readable as a sign that Bridie may love David, but isn't dominated by him, can also be read as a healthy sign that the politically powerful (Britain) can't just dominate the less powerful (Ireland).

And yet, as demonstrated above, the scene is labile – most of the ways of interpreting it can be reversed without strain, which suggests a text balanced in ambiguity even as it plays out the preferred meanings. This is done, it should be said, in quite a different mode from its sibling film. *The Rake's Progress* advertises its ambiguity, places it at the front of the stage, declares itself enigmatic, whereas *I See a Dark Stranger* tends to disclaim it, the comic mechanisms allowing contesting meanings which are, however, disarmed by the comedy. (Hence the different reaction a demonstration of the ambiguity of each text elicits. With *The Rake's Progress* – yes, this is really what I thought, but didn't articulate. With *I See a Dark Stranger* – yes, I perhaps didn't think of this, but now that I do a lot of things about the film are illuminated.) Various elements of the mise en scène and other details of the shooting, more or less neutrally described above, carry suggestions that support the ambivalence without insisting on it: e.g. the oddity of the 'PEACE' shot already noted; the night-time setting; the curiously distanced positioning of the camera in shots 1 and 4, with the intricate barrier the windows produce and then which their shadows throw over the pair at their happiest moment; Bridie's opening of the window which fails to match the powerful symbolism of release in such moments in other films of the early postwar period – e.g. *Perfect Strangers* (Alexander Korda, 1945) and Lean's *Great Expectations* (1946), where end-of-narrative views from windows or windows allowed to let in the sun suggest future postwar optimism.

## Notes

1 Gilliat's own shooting script with his annotations and sketches is held by the British Film Institute Library.

2 Lant, 'The Female Spy', pp. 173–99.

3 Ibid., especially pp. 190, 192.

4 MacDonald, 'Interview with Sidney Gilliat', p. 144.

5 Brown, *Launder and Gilliat*, pp. 115–16.

6 MacDonald, 'Interview with Sidney Gilliat', pp. 144–6.

7 Landy, *British Genres*, pp. 282–3.

8 MacDonald, 'Interview with Sidney Gilliat', pp. 144–6.

9 Alexander Walker, *Fatal Charm: The Life of Rex Harrison* (Weidenfeld & Nicolson, London, 1986), p. 110.

10 Brown, 'Interview with Sidney Gilliat', p. 115.

11 Warwick Mannon, *The Rake's Progress* [Book of the Film] (World Film Publications, London, 1946), p. 11.

12 Brown, 'Interview with Sidney Gilliat', p. 116.

13 Pam Cook, 'Melodrama and the Women's Picture', in Sue Aspinall and Robert Murphy (eds), *Gainsborough Melodrama* (BFI, London, 1983), p. 18.

14 Landy, *British Genres*, p. 283.

15 Ibid., pp. 249–59.

16 MacDonald, 'Interview with Sidney Gilliat', p. 142.

17 John Hill in Kevin Rockett, Luke Gibbons and John Hill, *Cinema and Ireland* (Croom Helm, London, 1987).

18 India became independent on 15 August 1947, but of course the matter, and Gandhi, were in the public consciousness long before that. *Captain Boycott*'s first public showing was on 31 August and it went on general release on 27 October.

19 See Jympson Harman, 'Naughty Deborah Aids the Nazis', *Evening News*, July 1946. For instances stressing the film as good fun, see Joan Lester, *Reynold's News*, 7 July 1946 and Patrick Kirwan, *Evening Standard*, 5 July 1946. The *Daily Telegraph* review (8 July 1946) is the one that seems most worried. 'Whether espionage for Germany should be treated as a girlish indiscretion I leave others to judge.'

20 Actually it is not clear that either she or Bridie would have been executed. The release of recent classified wartime material suggests that females guilty of spying or treason were not executed. See, for instance, *Times*, 10 November 2000, 'MI5 Knew Haw-Haw's Wife Was Also Traitor'.

21 Lant, 'The Female Spy', *passim*, but especially p. 177.

22 The *Daily Herald* (6 July 1946) claimed that Launder and Gilliat 'leave themselves, by sheer carelessness, wide open to critical punches'. The *Observer* (7 July 1946) asserted that the spectator 'doesn't give a rap how the film stops so long as it does stop'.

# '**Happy days**': *The Blue Lagoon,*
*The Happiest Days of Your Life,*
*The Belles of St Trinians,* etc.

In 1949 and 1950 Launder and Gilliat released two very successful
films, *The Blue Lagoon* (18 April 1949) and *The Happiest Days of
Your Life* (10 April 1950), with almost antithetical reputations fifty
years later. *Happiest Days* is a much-loved classic (think of that
Terence Davies allusion mentioned in Chapter 1), but the earlier
film, famous in its own time, Launder and Gilliat's biggest box-
office success and Rank's second biggest (after *The Red Shoes*),[1] is
almost forgotten. Unreleased on video and unshown on British
television since 1980, it is only viewable in the National Film
Archive. It is thus, of all the central Launder and Gilliat films
discussed in this book, the one most readers are unlikely to have
seen. This fall into obscurity is intimately connected with Columbia's
suppression of it to smooth the way for the uninspiring 1980
Hollywood remake with Brooke Shields and Christopher Atkins.

The two films are in many ways highly unalike, *Happiest Days*
firmly generic, *The Blue Lagoon* ambivalently cross-generic –
romance? adventure story? melodrama? – with hints of relation to
the exotic Empire film of the late 1940s and early 1950s? Largely
filmed on location in the Fiji islands, it was Launder and Gilliat's
first colour film. With Jean Simmons's quickly rising reputation –
she had been Olivier's Ophelia in the 1948 *Hamlet* – it's not quite
true to say that the film starred totally inexperienced unknowns
(she was a hot enough property for her *Blue Lagoon Diary* to be
published),[2] but its stars were young and Donald Houston, making
his début, was wholly unknown. If *The Blue Lagoon* is, among

other things, a fantasy of escape (with ties that turn out to be umbilical) from late 1940s England – again and again the reviews dwell on the viewing of its tropical world in the depths of an English winter – *Happiest Days* is, by contrast, as close to home as could be, its cast of comfily eccentric familiars, Alastair Sim, Margaret Rutherford, Joyce Grenfell, Guy Middleton, Richard Wattis, and others, inhabiting in familiar monochrome, in pastoral Hampshire, the halls and corridors and playing fields of that British institution, the public school, in its most minor and dubious variety. Curiously the two films' very different couples (the one young and sexualized, the other elderly and extraordinarily asexualized) pass each other in off-screen implication on their inverse sea routes at the films' ends, Houston and Simmons returning from the South Pacific to England in order for Emmeline to have their son educated (at Nutborne?), while Sim and Rutherford, defeated and disgraced, indomitably decide to emigrate to seek out new educational pastures in colonial Tanganyika.

What binds the very different films together in unlikely but significant relation is their emphasis on childhood, education, authority figures, sexuality and gender, and an unresolved love–hate relationship with the Britain of the still austere late 1940s, as embodied in the complex ambivalences, considered singly or in comparison, of the two films' immigration/emigration endings.

## The Blue Lagoon

### Novel and film

The Irish writer H. de Vere Stacpoole's once famous novel, *The Blue Lagoon* (1908),[3] reprinted twenty-three times in the twelve years following publication, was well enough known for one of the less literate characters in *The Pure Hell of St Trinian's* (1961) plausibly to remember it. (The writer of this book certainly remembers from a New Zealand childhood, circa 1954, bottles of 'Flavatru' milkshake flavouring exotically called 'Blue Lagoon', presumably a residue of the novel's and film's fame.) *Pure Hell*'s playful but modest intertextuality (it is the novel rather than the film that is briefly foregrounded) comes when in some plot dislocation or other George Cole (Flash Harry), Joyce Grenfell (Ruby Gates in her plainclothes policewoman role) and Cecil Parker (in a head-masterly inflection) are cast adrift and find a desert island. Flash Harry, with a certain amount of innuendo, remarks that it is like the situation in that novel, '*The Blue Lacoon*' (as he pronounces it), where 'two kids who landed on a desert island, 'ad a baby and didn't know 'ow it 'appened'. The novel, certainly still well known in the late 1930s, was advertised around 1939, as Edward Black at Gainsborough looked for vehicles to exploit the romantic-couple success of Margaret Lockwood and Michael Redgrave in *The Lady Vanishes*, as the source of a coming project starring the two, though common sense suggests they were both too old for the adolescent roles. Launder and Gilliat would have been aware of these plans, and might even have been envisaged as the scriptwriters. Whether so or not, it was a project they took up ten years later.

The novel's exotic South Seas setting, the pervasive but decorous sexuality of the story, and its interest in compelling questions of nature and nurture were major reasons for its popularity, along with Stacpoole's expert cultivation of a persona of much travelled, ocean-wise knowledge (he had been a ship's doctor) which lends authority to the many descriptions and observations which take primacy over dramatic action. In his novel two young American cousins are separated from their father/uncle (L'Estrange) in a shipboard fire that casts them adrift in mid South Pacific. The children, Dick and Emmeline, accompanied by an Irish sailor, Paddy Button, land on an uninhabited island. Paddy dies after an alcoholic binge, leaving the children to grow up to sexual maturity alone. As Flash Harry remembered, they have a child without realizing, at first, anyway, where it comes from. Meanwhile, their father, having also survived the shipwreck and returned to civiliza-tion, looks obsessively for evidence of the lost children's survival, and, eventually finding it, embarks on a search for them. Dick, Emmeline and their child, while moving from one part of the island to another, accidentally drift out to sea where they are seen by L'Estrange and the ship's captain who have just been debating the rights or wrongs of transplanting the children back to civilization if they have been brought up as happy savages. The novel ends with them about to be rescued.

As this précis suggests, the narrative, more of a romance than a novel, is sparing of action (and indeed of dialogue), most of its events being generated by natural forces and dangers (battles with a giant squid and an ancient shark, the fear of destructive hurricanes), the skill of the novelist residing in the aura of knowledge (geographic, botanical, anthropological, natural-theological) with which he explores the events that make up the romance.

Reworking the novel, Launder and Gilliat made numerous major changes.

1  The children (the boy's name changed to Michael) become English rather than American.
2  The rescuing father, L'Estrange, is removed from the narrative along with the children's close family relationship.
3  This allows the children to be effectively orphaned as the film begins, with Michael attending his father's shipboard funeral (a mother is never mentioned), while Emmeline, as she explains to Michael, has as good as lost both parents also, her mother having left her to live in Scotland (the implication is with a lover more wealthy than her husband), while her father is too ill, and perhaps unwilling, to look after her, and has put her in charge of an aunt who is travelling with her to New Zealand.
4  This contributes to a pattern of malign or weak father figures and absent mother figures not in the novel. Michael's father has cruelly beaten him, Emmeline's aunt seems distant in the little we see of her, and Paddy Button (Noel Purcell), the rough, kindhearted Irish sailor, who becomes for a while their only link with the adult world, is a character both negative and positive – positive, to some degree, in providing through his Celtic whimsies and superstitition, a bridge between the English world and the island, but negative in his weakness for alcohol, which eventually causes his death.
5  The children are slightly older in the film than in the novel. This is a crucial change since it means that they are always

further from reverting to the more primitive state of the children in the novel. 'Children soon forget,' Stacpoole writes,[4] but Launder and Gilliat's children remember more than his. Emmeline on first seeing the island beach is reminded of Torquay! Dick retains memories of poetry from school, and such connections with the world they have left are strengthened, in a narrow but highly defined way, by the etiquette book *A Guide to Behaviour 1901* that Emmeline takes from the ship and constantly consults, which acts as an extension of memory with its extraordinary collection of cultural regulations of the English upper classes. Everything to do with this book is the film's invention.

6  Launder and Gilliat's reworking omits most of Stacpoole's interest in natural religion, in the metaphysics of the primitive mind. Indubitably these are among the main concerns and most interesting parts of the novel (e.g. 'to Dick, who had not been broken into the idea of death, who had not learned to associate it with graves and funerals, sorrow, eternity and hell, the thing spoke as it never could have spoken to you or me').[5] It might be true to say that part of Launder and Gilliat's representative Englishness is their relative immunity to religious feeling. (It's hard to think of any moments where it has much importance in their films – Sim's priest in *Captain Boycott* is a figure of social cohesion, not spiritual insight, and this is true of his sympathetically burlesqued padre in *Folly to be Wise*.) When they find Paddy dead, the children hold a funeral service for him, but this is very much regulated by Michael's memory of his father's shipboard funeral ('Men and women don't have very long to live. They just grow up and get cut down like flowers do. They're always moving like shadows and not stopping in the same place'.)

7  The novel's interest in primitive metaphyics is replaced by an emphasis on inherited roles and dispositions that even the accident of being marooned cannot completely obliterate. At times this is a source of rather surprising comedy not just in Emmeline's *Guide to Behaviour*-fed dreams of Edwardian/ Georgian England, but in the way the children adopt roles

and attitudes more in keeping with Horsham than east of the Marquesas.

8   The film's largest plot invention is the children's encounter with the two corrupt Englishmen, Dr Edgar Murdoch (James Hayter) and James Carter (Cyril Cusack), who invade the island and the children's almost self-contained world. Besides exposing the children to the greed and corrupt sexuality of the outer world – both are after the 'beads' (pearls) Michael dives for; Carter has his eye on Emmeline as a sexual trophy – and ironizing Emmeline's idealization of the civilized social world (seen when she looks at a copy of the *Illustrated London News* on their boat), this entry of these serpents into Paradise seems to hasten the sexual maturity of the children, for it is straight after Emmeline's escape from their ship that the children first make love. Untheological though Launder and Gilliat usually are, it seems almost as if they connect sexuality with the entry of the serpent(s) into Eden.

9   The endings are similar in effect but different in process. In the novel the children's drifting out to sea is a complete accident, happening as they move to another part of the island after the hurricane. In the film, however, their leaving is deliberate, Emmeline's decision that her child should be educated in the 'savwoy faire' of a 'gentleman', a turning of their backs on the island (though Michael is reluctant to leave) for the Britain of 1917.

## Torquay at Viti Levu

The impulse of pastoral is urban: the sophisticated imagining – knowing that one belongs irrevocably to the metropoles – of simpler, better times and places; alternative, more innocent structures of life and society. This is true of Theocritus, Horace and Virgil, of Byron's Don Juan and Haidee in *Don Juan*, or Nicholas Roeg's *Walkabout* (1970) and *Castaway* (1987), in the latter of which two urban malcontents (Amanda Donohoe and Oliver Reed) play out an adult return to the world of *The Blue Lagoon*. Launder and Gilliat's film slightly updates the Edwardian context of the novel, so that when the children are to return to Britain it is 1917, still deep in the carnage of World War I, making the contrast between the island and civilization even more poignant. Like any historical film, *The Blue Lagoon* crosses the time its story is set in with the time of its own making and reception, Britain of the late 40s, still in the shadow of World War II. Whereas the opening of *Castaway* shows Reed and Donohoe in a febrile but alienating 1980s London, seemingly awash with chic objects expressing a commodified yearning for the tropical pastoral, and with the arrest of the York-shire Ripper vying for television coverage with assorted disasters, *The Blue Lagoon* begins in mid-Pacific, though exterior shots are rigorously limited, making the vessel seem like a claustrophobic apartment block (reproducing, with its social stratifications between the advantaged decks and the dangerous world of 'steerage', the social distinctions of the old world) from which Michael complains at one point that he can't see the sea. Now with long-haul holiday-ing and colour location shooting commonplace it is difficult to register how refulgently exotic *The Blue Lagoon* locations must have seemed in 1949 – it, *The Red Shoes* and *Black Narcissus* con-stituting together a late-1940s explosion of British exotica. Review after review highlights this (to the degree where one feels the implicit complaint against the climate becomes a metaphor for many other things). 'South Seas Comes to Wintry Britain' (*Daily Graphic*, 23 January 1949); a cartoon of a bronzed Donald Houston and Jean Simmons entitled 'Aloha There' (*News Chronicle*, 7 March 1949); 'the film is full of beauty and sunshine. Go bask in it' (*Graphic*, 4 February 1949); 'Actual tropical Pacific island settings are welcome after so much snow and ice in British films' (*Daily Herald*, 4 March 1949); 'It is photographed in colour against Fijian backgrounds that seemed even lovelier as one stepped out of the cinema into the bleakness of Leicester-Square in March' (*Daily Telegraph*, 7 March 1949), and so on.

Though the overt meditative-philosophical voice of Stacpoole's novel is played down in the film, the shipwreck fantasy presumes in its audience two topics of fascination. First, how would children grow up outside the ideological structures of education and class that control us? And, secondly, how would one imagine a sexuality structured in a natural environment outside the governing codes and practices of postwar Britain? Here it is important to note that in neither novel nor film is the experiment of placing the children in a primitive environment a pure one – i.e. the impossible fantasy of newborn children being placed on the island and somehow surviving to answer our questions of what language they would devise, what natural religion they would follow, whether they would evolve patriarchal or matriarchal structures, etc. Instead, since the children are already highly socialized, the experiment is necessarily impure. This is even more so in the film, where the children are older than in the source, therefore carrying more permanent memories with them. Michael, for instance, says he has read two books, the Bible and *Robinson Crusoe*, and remembers, implausibly, as we shall see below, a poem by John Donne. Though references in the script to Emmeline having read *Alice* and Michael *Grimm's Fairytales* are dropped, the children never lose their literacy.

The children's experience of parents suggests that their effective orphaning may be a blessing in disguise. For a short while they have a kind of foster father in the third castaway, the Irish sailor Paddy Button, who both replicates the rules of the society they have left and deviates from them in his Celtic superstition and sentimentality, but also suffers from alcoholism which causes his death, and is identified by Michael with a pattern of adult violence embracing his father, Paddy Button, and the invaders of the island, 'Doc' Murdoch and James.

With neither Stacpoole's meditative commentary, nor the extraordinary visual troping of Roeg in *Castaway* or *Walkabout*, *The Blue Lagoon* can appear to a casual glance naive and simplistic. Apart from the dangers of the hurricane and the giant octopus, the island may seem unreally idyllic, with no trace of the persistent infections and bugs that plagued the Fijian filming, according to Launder's account,[6] an unparadisic reality that found no late inscription in the film, though the shooting script left space for additions suggested by the location.[7] There is little of the alienness of nature that is so striking in *Walkabout* (confirming that the exotic is not Launder and Gilliat's natural terrain), or the harshness of the tropics that impinges in *Castaway*, or (except for the single moment of Michael's breakdown when Emmeline disappears) of the fear and privation either from external or internal psychic sources that can haunt solitude, as in Buñuel's *Robinson Crusoe*. Further, all overt corruption seems to be placed with the invaders Doc and James.

But in two ways this softening idealization is rendered sophisticated rather than naive. First, broad patterns become less simple the closer they are looked at. Second, the fantasy idyll of the island (which only the strange facelike appearance of the cliff occasionally threatens), a dream of paradise with little irruption of reality in the shape of the rigours of the tropics (at a time when the Far East and Pacific wars would have been in people's minds), gives the narrative a semi-oneiric quality which suggests that what is dramatized is the pastoral audience's dream of a different life, not an investigation of its actualities. The thematic with which the film-makers replace Stacpoole's primary interests is the tension between the way the children's new surroundings strip away aspects of their civilized surface, and the profound resistance to change of some of their inherited and very English middle-class characteristics.

Though effectively orphaned, the children are, from the moment we first see them on board ship, culturally formed beings, epitomes of middle-class childhood, the boy dressed in that emblem of a highly mediated relation to nature, the sailor suit, the girl in an ornate frock, imitating with her miniature tea-set a grownups' tea party where she is the 'H-o-s-t-e-s-s' – a word she isn't sure how to pronounce – so spells it out to her mispronounced 'jests'. Emmeline, talking to her doll Esmerelda as if she were real, may seem straight out of Freud's parallels between the infant and savage minds in *Totem and Taboo*, but their relationship seems more civilized than animist, the doll dressed as a miniature version of the girl. The relationship the girl has with Esmerelda, and the 'little man' role that Michael takes on when helping her to rescue the doll in the shipboard fire (asking 'Why do men always have to get girls out of trouble?') illustrate how the natural laboratory set up by the narrative does not work on a tabula rasa but on qualities (whether natural or induced) that already exist in a heightened state. Stacpoole's children, are, by contrast, after even a short stay on the island, claimed to be more different from, than like, the reader – as in the passage where Dick finds Paddy's body and 'the thing spoke as it could never have spoken to you and me'.

Not only do things tend to speak to Launder's pair as they would to 'you and me', but the couple themselves speak like their more middle-class viewers, producing unexpected comedy where their verbal interactions resemble those of suburban couples seen through a satiric lens. This was commented on by some early reviews as if it was the product of the film-makers' ineptitude. ('Here they are together in a soft, warm paradise, and what do you get – passionate, surging young love? More often an argument because the dinner is getting cold,' *Daily Express*, 4 March 1949; or the *Daily Worker*, 5 March 1949, complaining of Jean Simmons's 'keeping home exactly as if she lived at Tooting'). However, while we might think that Launder and Gilliat are not writers/film-makers equipped to invent a linguistic style that somehow reflects the children's isolation (a problem Stacpoole evaded through a paring down of dialogue), at the same time they are sophisticated scenarists, and there is no way in which the slightly parodic overtones of suburban coupled life can be accidental. (By this are meant moments like Emmeline's complaint to Michael, 'you haven't even looked at my new dress'; their argument when she calls him in to dinner: 'Can't you see I'm busy?' 'Oh, come on now, you never eat when it's ready'; his shouting at her that she keeps on at him 'till I'm sick of the sight of you', and the comic climax of him hammering his thumb in his anger.) Here the limitations of Donald Houston, who, unlike Jean Simmons, can be a rather awkward, unpleasing actor, with his stiffness and his slightly wan, spoiled public schoolboy's expression contrasting with his bronzed body, in curious ways adumbrate the contradictory motifs being played out.

As the lifeboat drifts islandwards, Emmeline, waking up, seems released into a greater naturalness and physicality, announcing the presence of the unseen island, which she has sensed through smelling its unglimpsed flowers – smell, the more primitive faculty, predominating over sight. However, as the boat lands on the deserted beach, her categorization of its new reality is absolutely (and bathetically) in terms of the known. Despite the coral and tropical fish, she compares the island to ... Torquay! (In the novel she asks 'Mr Button, where are we?'[8]) This twin motion – the movement towards a more primitive sensuous self and the counter movement back towards inherited categories – encapsulates a doubleness which is one of the primary interests of the film.

Half of the film's motion then is celebration of escape into the innocence and physicality of life on the island, with Donald Houston a bronze-skinned hunter gatherer and primitive technologist, and Jean Simmons, cultivating the domestic arts, trying on clothes she has made in the water's mirror like Eve in *Paradise Lost*. Both are seen swimming and diving discreetly semi-naked (a flashforward to the shots of the children swimming in the rockpool in *Walk-about*). The scene late in the film where they make love on the beach merges them with exotic romantic nature, sea, beach, forest and sunset. But the other half, the film's contradictory drama-tization of the children's desire to escape back to the world of civilization, is equally pronounced. This contradictory motion is never expressed in simple unison, i.e. with both Michael and Emmeline first against, then for, going, but always in a more complicated divided form in which, as the one takes the first position the other takes the second, so that there is always the tension of debate. Early on, Emmeline, identified more with the body and sensuous nature, wants to stay, while Michael, identified with exploration, knowledge, the mind, wants to leave. He is ashamed of only having read two books, and when Emmeline admonishes him in one of those slightly suburban remarks both make, 'You're always thinking nowadays. I don't think because I don't remember anything to think about,' his reply is, 'Well, that's nothing to be proud of, is it?' When she shows him the clothes she's made for herself, he only thinks that she could apply those skills to making sails. Later, however, after the birth of their child, Paddy, their positions reverse and she becomes more and more obsessed with her etiquette book and the idea of educating her child to be 'a gentleman', possessing what she pronounces as 'savwoy faire', while Michael, no longer discontented with the island, and losing interest in building boats, wants to stay. When she argues that it will be terrible for Paddy to be left alone when they die, he suggests having more children to keep him company.

Emmeline's desire for culture for her child leads to an obsessive and at times grotesquely comic reliance on her book, the advice of which (proper modes of greeting acquaintances in punts, rules 'on leaving visiting cards', 'personal conversation with Royalty and rank', 'riding in the park', etc.) is exposed as comically distanced not just from life on the island but from any life that they might conceivably live in England, even if, as she plans, they sell the pearls they have gathered in order to buy a house. By the time they leave the island her desires for the child ('I want him to go to school and learn to know about everything. I want him to be a gentleman') are ironized by her apparently literally believing that the streets of London are paved with gold and that when they return to England they will live in the upper-class world of her book, in which the Boat Race plays a large part as she even fantasizes the son watching his father win it! Even her experiences with the invaders, 'Doc' and James, who embody in a kind of simplified schematic form the material and sexual corruptions of the world the children have left, seem not to affect her idealization of the world she wishes to return to – creating an intense irony whereby she reverses the audience's pastoral fantasies of the South Seas with her own pastoral fantasy of an England that never existed except perhaps for the privileged upper classes.

## Sex and gender

Sitting in the grass by the doorway, sheltered by the breadfruit shade, yet with the hot rays of the afternoon sun just touching her naked feet, was a girl. A girl of fifteen or sixteen, naked, except for a kilt of gaily-striped material reaching from her waist to her knees. [...]

It was a marriage according to Nature, without feast or guest, consummated with accidental cynicism under the shadow of a religion a thousand years dead. [...]

> Her breasts, her shoulders, her knees, her little feet, every bit of
> her, he would examine and play with and kiss ... And this used to
> go on in the broad light of day, under the shadow of the artu leaves,
> with no one to watch except the brighteyed birds in the leaves up
> above.[9]

These three brief passages from Stacpoole's novel illuminate
areas of the film's treatment of sexuality, which was full of
difficulties since part of the meaning and expectation of a film of
*The Blue Lagoon* was the pictorialization of innocent sexual love in
idyllic natural surroundings in the mode of the famous verbal text.
British cinema was by no means as sexless as much stereotyping
of the 1940s suggests, but the rendition of the body, of physicality,
is something that is missing in British films of the period, whose
most erotic moments are verbal (as in *Kind Hearts and Coronets*),
sophisticated and worldly (as in the scenes with Vivian, Sandy and
Jill in *The Rake's Progress* that the American censors didn't like) or
emanate from the dramatization of hysteria bursting out of
repression (as in *Black Narcissus*).

The first excerpt above is the one most easily within the
capabilities of the film, which stages similar moments – though
Jean Simmons is less naked than in the book in one of her 'natty
twopieces' made of bark that the *Daily Worker* critic scathingly
observed – their idyllicness, however, often complicated by the
makers' social interests. The second is more difficult than one
might expect, perhaps for three reasons. First, the film text doesn't
want to shock (particularly the American censors) by the suggestion
of established religion (the reference in the novel is to an ancient
stone idol) ironically subverted by desire that is readable into the
passage. Secondly, as mentioned, Launder and Gilliat's films tend
to exhibit not so much religious or anti-religious attitudes as a lack
of interest in religion except in its social role. And thirdly, possibly
again for the American censors, the couple's first lovemaking is
followed in the film by their extemporizing a marriage ceremony
from Emmeline's etiquette book. (Though this ceremony lacks
deep religious feeling, thus allowing the film's makers to stay
close to their social emphases while offering a sop to the censors.)
As for the third passage, there is no way in which a film of the

period, and especially film-makers of Launder and Gilliat's not immensely physical interests, could really find ways of gaining the effects of Stacpoole's prose. The scene of the lovemaking on the beach is handled with the requisite natural beauty and rather more physicality than one might have expected, and would have had more impact in 1949 than it could possibly have today. But the problematics of the representation of uncivilized sexuality are quickly abandoned as the lovers almost immediately become the core of a small nuclear family with Paddy's birth. Perhaps where the representation of sexuality becomes most interesting is the way in which the killing of the giant octopus by Michael and Emmeline becomes a kind of displaced trope of sexuality, with both repeatedly thrusting at it, and an extraordinary shot of Emmeline (which becomes a metaphor of sexual initiation) seen through the blood darkening the water.

Given the film's problems with the representation of sexuality, it gravitates towards questions of gender roles, in keeping with the social emphases that have already been noted. In the novel the children have forgotten enough about the gendered apportionment of names to call their son 'Hannah' after a remembered nurse. In the film he is called 'Paddy' after Paddy Button. Despite their confusing of the naming system, Stacpoole's characters' deeper regression seems to suggest that some bedrock of sexual nature, of essential masculinity and femininity, is reached in Dick's practicality ('life was all business to him'[10]) – and in Emmeline's dreamy aestheticism described in terms like 'mysterious', 'secretive' 'submerged'.[11]

In the film the antithesis resolves into a slightly more conventional one of practicality/technology versus domesticity, which is presented as the force of nature, though the narrative can't be absolutely sure of this, since the children are already formed by nature and/or nurture when they arrive. Emmeline, already identified as nurturer with her doll and her tea set, is Paddy's choice for the island's cook, while he makes a model of an outrigger canoe for Michael, who insists on going exploring on his own the minute he lands on the island. Though both become dissatisfied with the island, Michael is driven by desire for knowledge while

Emmeline is motivated by the desire to better her child, an extension of her nurturing role. Yet, simultaneously, in ways comparable with the comic stabilization/destabilization play on accepted characteristics in *Happiest Days*, *The Blue Lagoon* complicates this. In Michael's battle with the octopus Emmeline is as active as he is, or even more so, and if we read the moment as a displaced figure of sexuality, her phallic thrusting is more marked, more obviously masculine, than his. Later Michael seems to become more of a lotus eater, his passive surrender to the physicality of the island marked by his change from trousers to sarongs.

If Emmeline seems more unchanging in the epiphenomena of her sexuality, Michael seems more precarious in his, the film perhaps marking a transition from the problem of femininity in the cinema to the problem of masculinity. His self-conscious assumption of the masculine role of protecting the female (his remark on the ship about men having to look after girls) is continued when Emmeline is griefstricken after Paddy's death, and he comforts her by telling her that he will look after her, but adds 'you'll have to do what I say, though'. The rider seems to suggest a hectoring anxiety that overflows containment when he collapses under the strain of her brief absence, fantasizing his death alone and frantically calling, 'Don't leave me here alone. Not for years and years and years and years and years!', while the camera echoes his hysteria by quick slides down the trees on which he has carved the passing of every day, till it rests on the imagined epigraph 'Michael Reynolds Died 1972'. It is as if Michael's masculine role, or how he conceives of it, is cast in doubt by the island solitude, so that it becomes redolent of performance, a constant assertion – as where he insists, against ocular evidence, that he alone killed the octopus: 'I settled him didn't I! I finished him off all right!' – liable to collapse.

## Pastoral self-consciousness

Whatever is revealed here, either about civilization and the island, or about the nature of the sexes, is extremely ambivalent, since there is no tabula rasa on which the test of the narrative operates.

As in all pastoral, the real subject is the audience's complex state, civilized but dreaming of release into innocence, a release, however, complicated by the immitigable actualities of their sophistication, constituted as much by 'Doc' (who, speaking of the children as 'the rude clay of humanity', certainly has his floridly cynical appeal) and James, with his promise to teach Emmeline things that she won't find in her book, as by Michael and Emmeline.

This overarching self-consciousness has several rather striking manifestations which it is worth briefly considering. The first is Paddy Button's favourite song, 'Come Back Paddy Reilly to Bally James Duff', in which the narrative voice is of an old man remembering his distant childhood:

> The baby's a man now, he's toilworn and rough,
> Still the whispers come over the sea,
> Come back, Paddy Reilly, to Bally James Duff,
> Come back Paddy Reilly to me.

This hyperbole, uttered by the Irishman in exile in England, America, or wherever, remembers a childhood in a place so paradisic that, instead of crying like a normal infant on being born, he 'let out one crow of delight'. Paddy's song of exile from the pastoral of childhood, in which the village of Bally James Duff is quite as extraordinary as any blue lagoon, is an instance where the character, beneath his specificities, mirrors the authorial and audience positions as regards what the narrative is playing out. Paddy himself is the least impressed of the three castaways with the island. ('Doc' and James have only the most exploitative, 'imperialist' relationship to it, so only see it in those terms.) He expresses the wish on arriving that he'd come with 'two ladies' rather than two children, and drinks himself to a premature death when he discovers the cask of rum. His blue lagoon is emerald green and somewhere in the distant past, underlining the point that the island is the concrete contemporary instance of pastoral loci that take many different shapes.

Such mirroring of authorial and audience self-consciousness is varied, after the lovemaking on the beach, when Michael, wishing that he could find words for his love for Emmeline, remembers a poem from school. This turns out not to be 'I remember, I remember / The house where I was born' or 'Lars Porsena of Clusium', but – quite extraordinarily – the opening of Donne's *The Goodmorrow* ('I wonder by my troth what thou and I / Did till we lov'd? Were we not wean'd till then / But suck'd on country pleasures childishly?'). It's not too pedantic to point out how much of a minority taste Donne was before the 1950s, making it totally implausible that an 8-year-old boy would be taught his poems in 1949, let alone circa 1910 – especially this poem, which begins with a rather outrageous image of breast feeding.[12] The unlikely quotation serves an ancillary function in constituting yet another ironic complexity in the civilization–pastoral interaction, through its burlesque of pastoral innocence, seen in the poem as a kind of barrier to love, rather than, as in the film, its occasion – though even this is complicated by the fact that it seems to take the entry of the serpents, 'Doc' and James, into Paradise to bring about the young couple's sexual initiation. However, more obviously, the absolute implausibility of Michael's literary memory again suggests that character and character's voice are being used to allow an intentionally thinly disguised authorial voice, speaking on behalf of the audience, to enact a highly self-conscious relationship with the pastoral (here, at the very point where unmediated uncivilized love is most affirmed, quoting lines of courtly sophistication denigrating the pastoral impulse).

Finally there are the film's closing images, which also cultivate a high degree of ambiguity. In the novel, shortly before the children are seen, L'Estrange and the ship's captain have a conversation about the rightness or wrongness of rescuing the children if it were found that they had reverted to happy 'savages' (the word in Stacpoole is complexly not simply negatively used).[13] This conversation is omitted from the film which, however, has a scene in which a man and a woman, observing Michael and Emmeline on the island from a yacht, decide not to rescue them because they mistake them for (pejorative) 'savages' because of their clothes, when in fact they are dressed in complex garments they have made, which reflect more than any of the other costumes in the film an intricate, highly cultivated relationship with nature rather than a separation from it. Though the conversation is omitted from the film (L'Estrange, it will be remembered, is dropped from the adaptation), its implications are everywhere, and the film's end certainly hinges on the same question, should we be happy for or regret Michael's, Emmeline's and Paddy's rescue? The closing shot of the small family in their raft starts from the deckboard watchers' p.o.v. and then cranes down over the boat so that the exhausted pair (the baby is awake) lie under the eyes of an audience placed visually as well as psychologically in a parental attitude towards them. The film, like the novel, ostentatiously refuses to dramatize the moment of their being rescued, lifted onto the ship, etc. The ambiguity created by this refusal is not the obvious one of whether they will be picked up or not, since they obviously will be, but a deliberate mirroring of the suspension between relief and regret at their rescue on which the whole narrative is founded. The script is very bare of interpretation except for the baby crying, which may strike us as more than a naturalistic detail when the song 'Come Back Paddy Reilly' is remembered: 'Camera moves slowly in towards it until we are shooting down right into the boat where we see Michael and Emmeline lying completely inert. The baby, with a blanket wrapped round him, is crying.'[14] The process of filming largely reflects what seems to be a desire to present the moment without either overt positive or negative commentary, even to the point where, in the finished film, the baby doesn't cry. As the camera looks down at them, only the micro-gestures of the unconscious Michael and Emmeline register, but these, though minute and resisting absolute codification, seem more negative than positive: Michael's head rolling as he touches her, and his slightly fraught expression.

The other curiosity of the ending is the subjective view and interior voice given to Emmeline, in the penultimate shot, which repeats her final view of the island as they left it earlier. This shot is most obviously interpreted as her mental image, her dream memory of the island as she last saw it. As the view appears again, she speaks: 'That's the way I want to remember it always.' Again the moment is a highly self-conscious one, in which she becomes (as she is about to rejoin the audience) the voicer of its thoughts rather than the object of its fantasies. Her idea of preserving the memory of the island in perfect form in her mind for when she returns to England links her closely to the audience, as she becomes like them, the (future) metropolitan dweller who keeps some pastoral fantasy of innocence and more peaceful, sensual life in their consciousnesses, even though she has chosen to leave its actuality. It has a parallel in the ending of the later *Castaway* where Jenny Agutter, years after, married, in the kitchen of her townhouse, and talking to her husband, remembers the outback while an authorial voice speaks Housman's poem about 'the blue remembered hills' of the childhood 'land of lost content'.[15]

### *The Happiest Days of Your Life* (1950)

#### Plot

The famous plot of *The Happiest Days of Your Life* builds its growingly intricate farce out of three ascending sets of complication.

*Initial situation.* Nutborne College, a very minor boys' public school in rural Hampshire, on the skids academically, plummeting sportswise, economically in hock, regathers after the summer hols. Wetherby Pond, its headmaster (Alastair Sim), announces to his staff that he is in the running for the headship of Harlingham. The sports master, Hyde-Brown (Guy Middleton), with his involuntary 'But, that's a decent school!' points the contrast with Nutborne, but one that is hardly necessary given our view of the slothful and/or terminally eccentric inhabitants of the common room. The staff agree tacitly to support Pond, obviously keen to see him go.

*Complication 1.* As a result of a Ministry of Education 'Devacuation' order (reminiscent of schools, including some major public schools, being moved to other sites during the war) Pond and Nutborne find themselves facing the arrival of 217 pupils from another school, St Swithin's, presumed, of course, to be male.

*Complication 2.* The advance guard of the St Swithin's staff arrives at Nutborne, triggering the revelation that St Swithin's is a girls' school billeted at a boys' school, a state of affairs equally displeasing, indeed panic-provoking, to both firmly single-sex institutions. After a brief war of the sexes in which the women come out on top, an uneasy truce prevails with the two schools coexisting in the same space while they wait for the ministry to sort things out.

*Complication 3.* (A) Miss Whitchurch is suddenly reminded of the impending, potentially scandalous visit of some of her girls' parents. (B) Pond's glee at her predicament ends when the governors of Harlingham drop by for a surprise inspection. (C) Whitchurch and Pond join forces in an attempt (i) to keep both sets of visitors apart and unaware of each other's presence, and (ii) to manoeuvre the male and female pupils in such a way as to present each group of visitors with the illusion of a normally running boys' or girls' school. By wit, agility and luck Pond and Whitchurch manage this for a while, but anomalies mount up, explanations become more strained, improvisations more desperate, and eventually the whole pretence collapses and their subterfuges are exposed. As the Ministry bureaucrats repair their mistake with an even worse one, the billeting at Nutborne of a *coeducational* and *lower-class* school, Pond and Whitchurch, united in adversity, agree to emigrate in search of more traditional educational opportunities in Tanganyika.

Fifty years after its release *Happiest Days* is as paradoxically archaic and yet seemingly infinitely revivable as the late 1940s, early 1950s Ealing comedies with which it shares some of its cast and many of its values. In one sense it may seem even more distanced from the contemporary, not so much over the educational question (the public schools show no sign of dying as they cater for new influxes into the monied middle class) as the sexual one. Ealing's much-noted suppression of sexuality was an implicit value, but in *The Happiest Days of Your Life* it is articulated at the centre of the narrative, where two comic monsters, elderly celibates, not only attempt to perpetuate a system of education (portrayed at its most arbitrary and archaic) based on class and sex division into totally separate spheres, but also to discourage any signs of sexuality in their charges, with (unless I read the film wholly aberrantly) more than a little comic sympathy and a lot of licence from the audience. (Satires are seldom as popular and well loved as *Happiest Days* unless they are of the kind typed as 'fond', i.e. marked by a complex love/hate ambivalence towards the object of criticism.) Thus I speculate that the terrestrial television audience for the latest of the film's many replays (ITV, 29 April 2000), even those too young to know much of the film's historical context, still in the shadow of World War II, will have reacted ambivalently, the satirical impulse ('Did people ever really think like that? Let's watch them be punished for their presumptions') tempered by fugitive identifications with Pond and Whitchurch as they are plagued by bureaucracy and inspected by governors and parents, even their archaic insistence upon the separate spheres of male and female (and Pond's distinctly un-p.c. gender attitudes) insinuating guilty pleasures of slippage from the puritanical rigours of contemporary gender sensitivities.

Like *The Blue Lagoon*, *The Happiest Days of Your Life* was adapted from a well-known source, John Dighton's highly successful stage play of 1948 which ran for over 600 performances in London, with Margaret Rutherford as Miss Whitchurch.[16] But like the former it is a metamorphosis rather than a simple version of the original, and its new status as film rather than photocopied play is underlined by joking allusions to two major recent British films, as well as the J. Arthur Rank gag already referred to in Chapter 1. In the first, when Miss Whitchurch's home economics girls are allowed to practise by making breakfast, a frail schoolboy, echoing John Howard Davies in David Lean's *Oliver Twist* (1948), varies his pathetic request with 'Please sir, I *don't* want any more, no sir'. In the second, when Pond is displaced from his quarters by the women, he sleeps in the bath and then, getting up, wanders disconsolately round in a dressing gown, a fag hanging from his mouth, extradiegetically accompanied by the famous zither music of 'The Harry Lime Theme' from Carol Reed's *The Third Man* (also 1948). Though aficionados of the play might mourn certain omissions – e.g. Gossage's relentless cricketing enthusiasms which she attempts to force onto Billings in her pursuit of him; the Sowters' (visiting parents) grim determination that not an iota

of feminization will infect their son, a moment in the compli-
cating farce where it becomes necessary to claim that Pond and
Whitchurch are married! – in almost every respect, in the sharpness of wit, development of complications, and drawing out of
significances latent in the dramatic text, the film, rewritten by
Launder with the play's original author, John Dighton (who also co-
authored with Launder the finely wrought and Sim-dominated
script of *Folly to be Wise*), is superior. In the play, for instance, the
part of Wetherby Pond (profilmically merely Godfrey) is distinctly
underwritten, and Billings is really the more foregrounded character. In order to provide a leading part for Alastair Sim the role of
Pond is significantly increased.

One instance here must serve for many. In the play Pond's first
appearance (as 'an insignificant looking man of about fifty') is
quite unremarkable; he just enters, exchanges a few words, mostly
with Tassell, who is returning to teaching from the war. He has
already read the message from the Ministry which he is holding,
so is resigned to the arrival of the pupils from St Swithin's, thus
precluding any suspense. In the film, however, his entrance is
carefully prepared as he is gossiped about by the staff, Billings in
particular, culminating in Billings's reply to the suggestion that
Pond's aberrant behaviour may be explained by a clandestine
marriage: 'The day Pond exchanges a smile with a woman I'll
dance all night naked in the village green!' Pond's entrance takes
place unseen, except by the audience, during this conversation,
which he overhears, but then theatrically pretends not to have
heard, as he sweeps forward essaying one of Sim's asthmatically
mirthless and slightly minatory laughs. Then during afternoon tea
he relentlessly revenges himself on Billings by pushing him into
the feminine role of teamaker, sugar provider and plate carrier. As
he picks on the other masters as well (for instance suggesting that
Hyde-Brown might spend more time fulfilling his duties as rugby
coach and less at The Coach and Horses), the scene establishes
him as the major presence and underlines his histrionic and
controlling aspects, both of which are to be complexly developed in
what follows. His imparting of the news of his possible 'translation
to a higher sphere' (Harlingham) is the trigger for a virtuosic

rhetorical performance of exemplary hollowness on themes of educational service, responsibility and idealism, not a word of which he, the masters or the audience believe. Finally, the scene is also superior in terms of comic suspense. Pond reads the letter for the first time, responds to the shock it imparts by denying it with a too facile rejection of the power of the bureaucracy which will increasingly plague him ('Paper, man, mere paper'), and then has to face its reality when Rainbow reports the concrete presence of 217 suitcases in the school drive, the first of many reversals to torture him.

## Sim and Rutherford

Although many of the pleasures of *Happiest Days* stem from the ensemble interaction of a cast as near perfection as possible in a very English comic mode (e.g. Guy Middleton's innocently lubricious sports master, Joyce Grenfell's corporeally embarrassed Miss Gossage, down to small-scale cameos like Lawrence Naismith as the rugby-mad governor, Dr Collet, whose desire to see the fifteen at play causes many problems for Pond), bestriding the film's centre are two great English comic performers, Alastair Sim and Margaret Rutherford, as the headmaster of Nutborne school for boys and the principal of St Swithin's school for girls, at first locked in combat (literally as they wrestle for possession of Pond's phone) and then joined in unlikely alliance. If for nothing else *Happiest Days* would be memorable for this conjunction, the only time they appeared together, just as, in the Hollywood cinema, *My Little Chickadee* is remembered for bringing Mae West and W. C. Fields into collision.

Both Sim and Rutherford specialized in playing authority figures with a funny-peculiar as well as funny-ha-ha inflection – Sim a patriarchal rollcall of doctors, lords, lairds, policemen and priests, Rutherford a dotty gallery of expert-enthusiasts such as Madame Arcati the spiritualist in *Blithe Spirit*, Professor Hatton Jones in *Passport to Pimlico* and the petshop owner in *An Alligator Named Daisy* who converses with animals in a 'secret language' by blowing down their noses. The prominence of this very middle-aged pair in British cinema of the 1940s and 1950s reminds one that the American sociologists Wolfenstein and Leites described a pattern of idealized parental figures (particularly fathers) in British films of the 1940s, as distinct from American ones where they were less important,[17] but their rather literal-minded approach has no place for the kind of doubleness, the simultaneous assert-ing and destabilizing of authority that the pair act out.

Writing in pre-video days, Raymond Durgnat made an interest-ing slip of memory when he wrote of Sim playing a 'crooked doctor' in *Waterloo Road*.[18] In fact (although, like most of Sim's characters, he has odd disturbing aspects) Dr Montgomery clearly isn't crooked, but the mistake is interesting in bearing testimony to the slightly dubious aura Sim, even at his least suspect, may give off, as if aspects of his first great stage role, his 1930 Iago to Robeson's Othello, were in constant danger of leakage into the last, his 1962 Prospero (which I imagine as rather like the headmaster of the Blue Lagoon Academy). In a minority of films the crooked-ness becomes dominant (Professor Potter's 'Oneupmanship' in *School for Scoundrels* (Hamer, 1960)), fake spiritualist and preyer on lonely hearts in *London Belongs to Me*, jovial assassin in *The Green Man*, ruthless Nazi agent, it seems, in the first half of Asquith's *Cottage to Let* (1941), but usually it is an undertone, as where that familiar playful sadism, so much to the fore where he persecutes Billings and the other masters, is a component even of his gravest role of all, the quasi-supernatural visitor in *An Inspector Calls* (Hamilton, 1954). This underlying jolly eccentric/not quite so jolly, verging on sinister, ambivalence is physically actualized in the comic conceit in *The Belles of St Trinian's* of a doubled Sim confronting through split-screen techniques one self (Millicent Fritton, headmistress of St Trinian's) with another (Clarence Fritton, her black-sheep bookmaker brother).

By extreme contrast Margaret Rutherford's persona is wholly characterized by singleminded straightforwardness, with not a breath of deviancy or role-playing. This is self-reflexively under-lined when she replies, as much for her total persona as for Jane Marple in *Murder Ahoy!* (1967), to the chief inspector's condes-cending suggestion that she is not quite herself, with a magisterial

'I am always myself!' This self's eccentric irreduceability is wonderfully commented on by Penelope Dudley Ward in *The Demi-Paradise* (Asquith, 1943) when she introduces Miss Rowena Ventnor doing the rounds on Daisy Day, and, attempting to describe her, ends up able to do no more than laugh as she is unable to find any other terms for her but 'She's ... well, you've seen for yourself!' Rutherford's most famous stage role was Mrs Malaprop, and though she played the sinister Mrs Danvers in the stage *Rebecca*, it is difficult to imagine her – at least the film actress – doing it wholly satisfactorily, since deviousness is so much a contradiction with her. This last is what the makers so exploit in *Happiest Days* when vertiginous circumstance in the end forces Miss Whitchurch into immorality and she becomes very quickly a virtuosic talespinner.

Sim's usual and Rutherford's absolute sexless, celibate status makes them ideal casting for the senexes of *Happiest Days*, and every implication of their personae is brilliantly exploited by the revamping of the play. On the one hand there are the strands of dubiety within Sim's bachelordom (the latent misogyny in the bluff clubbability, the hint of grotesque sexuality in his susceptibility to femininity as Sergeant Bingham in the *Inspector Hornleigh* films, the mossy charm with which he woos the elderly female string trio in *The Green Man*), as if one suddenly discovered that one's favourite uncle's holidays in the Lochs had actually been spent in Amsterdam. Doing what? one might ask, given the extraordinary language which he uses about the females in *Happiest Days* – his near shrieking description of the girls' presence as 'an apalling sexual aberration' and of Miss Whitchurch like some biblical she-beast 'spawning her progeny'. On the other hand, there is the absolute imperviousness to the nonsense of sex that Rutherford's characters typically exhibit – so that when Nurse Carey in *Miranda* (Annakin, 1947), breaks the pattern of spinsterhood by announcing that she has been married, she qualifies the information by saying that she is glad her husband is dead, men being such fickle creatures! This absolute expulsion of angst, this seamless translation of the potentially baleful or neurotic into loveable oddity, is the only way in which one is able to square performance with Rutherford's now well-known tragic history and constant fear of madness.[19] The resolute oldfashionedness of Sim's and Rutherford's personae also suits the film. In Asquith's *The VIPs* (1963) there is a moment when, searching for her passport, Rutherford, here the financially sinking Duchess of Brighton, draws from the depths of her bag a 1943 ration book; and the Laird in *Geordie* is generic Sim when he complains of taxes and says, 'The whole world's gone to pot', while his reaction to the 'progress' of lady shot-putters taking part in the Olympic Games is something to behold.

Placed in positions of authority over the young this pair cannot but burlesque the serious thematics of the public school as synecdoche for the nation struggling for redefinition in the face of social change that is central to two films immediately either side of *Happiest Days*, the Boulting Brothers' *The Guinea Pig* (1948) and *Tom Brown's Schooldays* (Parry, 1951). The earlier film pursues its meanings through a contemporary plot about the trials and tribulations and eventual triumphs of a working-class boy sent to a public school experimenting with broadening intake beyond the privileged (as recommended in the Fleming Report of 1944). As has been pointed out, the film's radical intentions are slightly vitiated by the fact that the boy, played by Richard Attenborough, is shown really to be from the conservative petit bourgeoisie, thus limiting the film's reforming range.[20] The later film, adapted from Thomas Hughes's famous novel, replays the mid-nineteenth century reform and revitalization of the public schools through Thomas Arnold's headmastership at Rugby, not just as ancient history but as costumed morality drama for the present. Both films stage battles for reform between masters committed to an ossified tradition in which moral force and aspiration have been displaced by mere social conformism and prejudice, and those committed to change. While in *The Guinea Pig* the central issue is class, in *Tom Brown's Schooldays*, fascinatingly in the light of *Happiest Days*, Dr Arnold's (Robert Newton's) crusade, with its moral and religious resonances, also constantly invokes the benevolent feminization of the overmasculine world of ruling-class education. Arnold's struggle for reform is supported, even in many senses defined, by Mrs Arnold, who along with Mrs Brown and Mrs Arthur, make up a trio of young maternal females who push his manly ethics towards what is at the least a complementary feminization and maternality, so that Brown's acting as a 'pater' to George Arthur is reworked into a kind of 'pater-mater'. In a key scene where Arnold has the fatherless George Arthur to tea, George sits between the headmaster's two little daughters who offer him strawberries, while motherhood is so crucial in the narrative that Tom's friend East's cynicism and refusal of religious belief are attributed to his mother's abandoning him (or having to abandon him) when she leaves her marriage. In the earlier *The Guinea Pig* too the influence of the female in the male education system is valorized; the headmaster's daughter supports Lorraine in his reformism, the headmaster's wife Mrs Hartley is cheered by the boys ('they cheered you my dear because to them you've been a mother and a friend'), and the reforming young master, Nigel Lorraine, bears a curiously feminine surname.

Placing *The Happiest Days of Your Life* beside these films one can easily see how antithetical its comedy is – how class problematics are figured, for Nutborne and St Swithin's, in the descent of the vandals of the coeducational and lower-class school on Nutborne at the end. (The play named it 'The Meadowvale Academy for Backward Boys and Forward Girls'; the film leaves it anonymous, relying on visual implications.) At Nutborne the only class interrelationships are the implied sexual one between Hyde-Brown and Millie, the pert maid, and the school porter, Rainbow's (Edward Rigby), necessary servant role to the school. Any influence of the other sex is completely excised, except for Mrs Hampstead the doughty housekeeper (Gladys Henson). Much is made (five mentions of the most patriarchal of monarchs) of the school being in a house Henry VIII built for Ann Boleyn, but which she never occupied because of her execution! As we shall see, matters of educational reform, the moving of women into the public sphere and the motif of maternality invading the male world are irreverently played upon by *Happiest Days*, and Launder's skills as a scriptwriter are given great licence in his and Dighton's brilliant devising of languages for both Rutherford and Sim that embody different burlesquings of these values. Rutherford's was probably suggested by the language Coward gave Madame Arcati in *Blithe Spirit* ('Great Scott, I said, I believe I've been barking up the wrong tree!' 'In a moment of crisis I threw up the sponge instead of throwing down the gauntlet!'). In *Happiest Days* she moves to an endless brisk measure of energetically uttered clichés devoted to tying the devil's hands with a plethora of healthy tasks (e.g. 'shipshape and Bristol fashion', 'not on their toes', 'don't shilly shally', 'don't loiter', 'Fiddle dee dee', 'Haver about', 'show their paces', 'no dawdling', 'it's all going swimmingly now', 'brouhaha', 'let us face this squarely', 'keep on the qui vive', 'well, we must don our thinking caps', etc., etc.). Sim's distinctive rhetoric, which goes through more vicissitudes as hysteria tempts him in the later part of the narrative, is more complex, heavily marked by banteringly authoritarian irony and playful sadism and by a mastery of the automatic rhetoric of educational service and paternalistic responsibility: 'the call of duty', 'a tremendous wrench', 'bonds of trust', 'you'll find us a very happy family here', 'seeds of knowledge', 'ever more fertile fields', etc., etc.

Though Pond and Whitchurch begin as antithetical principles (principals) – Pond identified with deviousness, Whitchurch with straightforwardness; Pond shiftily allied to the past, Whitchurch bracingly to the future (criticizing Nutborne when she first sees it as 'an ancient mausoleum') – the ironies of the narrative draw them into unlikely cooperation, and at the end into a kind of non-sexual marriage of minds as they decide to go to Tanganyika where the spheres of separate influence presumably still operate and traditional English education is prized. Though each in doing this is protecting his or her own world, their interests and characteristics, at first wholly opposed, begin to merge. First the shiftiness/straightness difference closes as Whitchurch develops a startling ability to lie virtuosically – culminating in her delicious improvisation in explaining the sudden revelation of Hyde-Brown's immodest pinups: 'Well, this is Janice Hackett who won the 220 yards breaststroke in 1946, and this is Evelyn Forbes who won the 100 yards freestyle in 1947, and this is Freda Harris, our champion morris dancer caught in mid action'. Second, despite Whitchurch's apparent no-nonsense connection to the future, she and Pond are revealed as growingly alike in their essential regressiveness. They may be divided on the superiority of the sexes, but they are in strict accord, as Whitchurch puts it, that 'Never the twain shall meet'. As the narrative proceeds we realize that Whitchurch's feminism is of a particular late-ninteenth-century kind, predicated on the superiority of the female, introjecting the highest of patriarchal culture (her school is named for a male saint and all the houses after male poets, Browning, Tennyson, etc.), but with absolutely no interest in the merging of male and female worlds (though of course the irony is that the education she provides educates girls for wives). She not only views the class changes produced by the war and the interfering bureaucracies as balefully as Pond does, but has no more desire for a dismantling of the barriers between the sexes in the realm of education and elsewhere than her opposite number.

## Monstrous regiments

Set (as no doubt the prospectus stressed) in a timewarp in deepest Hampshire, Nutborne College might be seen as a local, single-sex, version of the island of *The Blue Lagoon*, about to be invaded, not by the corrupt equivalent of 'Doc' and James, but by the monstrous regiments of socialism, feminism and bureaucracy (Flash Harry's 'flamin' bureautocracy'). 'A first blast of the trumpet against the monstrous regiment of women' is the sentence that Pond tendentiously selects to parse for his sixth-form grammar class. John Knox's misogynistic fierceness is applauded by the boys as Pond orates it, but once under way the class suffers a succession of debilitating interruptions acting as exemplary punishment for his pretensions. Two nubile girls go up the stairs to gym class, drawing the boys' attention; Miss Whitchurch passes through berating a smaller girl; a female political candidate at the door pesters Pond; Rainbow and Edwin carry a large iron bed frame up the same stairs until, kicked by Whitchurch's delinquent pupil, it collapses with cacophonously distracting results; and finally a horde of boys and a pack of girls, going in their different directions, collide on the staircase, leading to the chaotic abandonment of the class.

The first part of Pond's sentence (the trumpet blast) is increasingly mimicked on the second half of the film's soundtrack by a seemingly constant blast of whistles summoning the quick changes needed to keep the complicated deceit going, and culminating in a sort of charivari played and danced around Pond and Whitchurch by the lower-class children at the end of the film, one prominently blowing a bugle. The second part of the quotation, with its 'monstrous regiment of women', in Knox's original was specifically an attack on the rule of women, as exemplified by Mary Tudor, the Catholic monarch from whose England the Calvinist Knox had fled. Pond presumably has a fellow feeling with the puritan, seeing Whitchurch as a kind of Mary Tudor. However, in the modern instance the phrase must particularly evoke World War II and the 'mobile women' of Launder and Gilliat's home front trilogy, as well those films like *The Gentle Sex*, *Perfect Strangers* and *Colonel Blimp* where women are seen prominently in uniform.

In *Happiest Days* the first view of the advance party of St Swithin's staff sees them briskly marching along, certainly mobile, and a bit militaristic, while the later view of the main body of girls has them marching in a 'croc', crossing the Knoxian echoes with other Scottish ones that suit Sim's origins, Barrie's *Peter Pan*, with Pond as Captain Hook and the female 'croc' having interesting mutilatory implications.

In *The Belles of St Trinian's*, as Geoff Brown pointed out, the headmistress Millicent Fritton (Alastair Sim in drag) briefly rehearsed the history of the school, its idealistic beginnings and later decline, to her black-sheep brother (also played by Sim). There she stressed its origins in the General Strike of 1926 – i.e. as, implicitly, a middle-class bastion against perceived social chaos – and its decline as dating from the social mobility created by the war.[21] *Happiest Days* doesn't mention the General Strike, but the war, and by extension the prewar, are constant points of implicit reference, not least in the implications surrounding the huge trophy fish that adorns the wall of Pond's study, bearing the title 'Wetherby Pond, 1939'. When Miss Whitchurch inspects this she misinterprets Pond's name as a place, a confusion significant in conflating Pond with a geographic pastoral, and, more complicatedly, with the psychic pastoral (at least viewed from circa 1950) of the prewar era, bringing into focus the year 1939 as the defining moment of (unwelcome) change.

The complexity of the motif of World War II here – very self-referentially playing on the meanings of the social changes at the heart of *Millions Like Us* and *Two Thousand Women* – is, as we shall see, double edged. On the one hand the war stands as a comic-ironic marker of disorder, as having at the very least accelerated socialism in the election of 1945, bureaucracy in the state central-ization typical of the war years, and feminism in the incursion of women into male worlds. On the other hand it is also invoked, again comically-ironically, in terms of group memory, the 'finest hour' stand against Hitler replayed in Pond and Whitchurch's battle against the forces that assail them. Dighton's original play (1948) was written nearer the war than the film and seems to be set almost immediately postwar. The film, on the contrary, is pre-cisely dated at the beginning of the new school year, September 1949. Its jokes about nationalization, and other indicators of dis-content with the ailing Attlee government, could not function without the contemporary context. But, even so, the war still seems very close, as in the early detail when Billings, meeting Tassell, the new master, at the station, immediately asks 'Ex-service?' to which Tassell replies 'Army', while Hyde-Brown's courting of the 'Senior Botany' with tales of RAF prangs and derringdo also suggests time only just past. Similarly memories of wartime exigencies are relived in the letter-censoring scene where the children's letters home are vetted for references to the mixed-sex scandal; by the date of the action, September 1949, exactly ten years on from the outbreak of the war in September 1939; and, even more exactly, with the letter from the Department of Resettlement at the Ministry of Education dated 15 September, in the popular mind the day in 1940 of the turning point of the Battle of Britain, something likely to be remembered in 1949. Most precisely of all there is the language of the Ministry document with its termin-ology of 'revacuation' – the significance of which Pond underlines by repeating it in shocked wonder three times. 'Revacuation' clearly plays on the memory of mass evacuations, particularly of children, in World War II, as well as the moving of schools, some of them much more prestigious than Nutborne, to other locations (for instance, Malvern to Blenheim Palace, St Paul's out of London, with Cheltenham and Shrewsbury and Dulwich and Tonbridge doubling up).[22] (This last is glanced at in the story Launder wrote for *Inspector Hornleigh Goes to It* (1940), which has Gordon Harker and Alastair Sim arriving at what they expect to be a fishing holiday hotel, only to find that it is now a school moved from Muswell Hill.) Given all these reminders, other details like Whitchurch synchronizing watches with Pond before their combined operation irresistibly recall the war.

The narrative events don't, however, just recall the war. They – or some of the characters – see the austerity of life in late-1940s Britain as an extension of the siege conditions of the war years. At the film's beginning comments by Billings and Hyde-Brown about Rainbow's ways of getting round rationing and scarcity by recourse to the black market emphasize the overhang of war. It must be remembered that clothing rationing only ended in 1949, petrol rationing in 1951 and the five-shilling ceiling on restaurant prices in 1950. 'Times is hard, sir,' is Rainbow's laconic summary. The increase in bureaucratic centralization, culminating in nationalization, accelerated by the war bears down early on Pond, who blames the nationalization of the railways (1947) for the mountain of luggage in the drive. The billeting of another school with Nutborne may be a bureaucratic mistake, but the parapraxis seems to have a subtext of reforming malice behind its attack on masculine separateness, at least when viewed from the torpor of the Nutborne common room. The comedy often seems to reflect the waning popularity (especially with middle-class voters) of the reforming Labour government of the immediate postwar, blamed for economic conditions beyond its control and no doubt increasingly considered overdemanding in its rhetoric of continued sacrifice.

The joke at the end of the film when Whitchurch suggests to Pond emigrating to Tanganyika *where she has a brother who grows groundnuts* is a sly reference to one of the government's most embarrassing failures. From 1946 East Africa was a target for Colonial Office schemes to develop overseas territories and at the same time provide Britain with raw materials. A large-scale attempt to grow groundnuts in Tanganyika was abandoned after failing embarrassingly in 1949.[23] At other times, as when a call can't be got through to the ministry, and Whitchurch suggests the minister is out playing golf, the satire seems more traditionally anti-Tory. And at yet other times the target seems the self-perpetuation and imperviousness of bureaucracies outside of any question of who administers them, as in the mordant little scene where Matthews, the deputy head, reports from the phone to Pond, 'It's still Arkwright, but he's trying to put us on to a Mr Tripp. Apparently a Mr Bullock got the papers from a Mr Forrester. He passed them on to Mr Arkwright. Who passed them on to Mr Tripp'. When Pond finally gets through to Tripp's desk, the camera slowly passes along IN and OUT trays full of debris, a PENDING tray full of documents, a tray marked FOR IMMEDIATE ATTENTION equally full, but clearly untouched, with a cup and saucer sitting on it. When Tripp closes his conversation with Pond by telling him 'I'll do everything to expedite matters, you may rest assured,' he then places the file in a tray marked FOR THE ATTENTION OF MR ARKWRIGHT. Dissolve to a closeup of it being placed in Mr Bullock's tray. Dissolve to a closeup of it being placed in Mr Forrester's tray, a circular motion back towards square one.

The sympathies generated for Pond and Whitchurch and other 'blocking' characters such as the cynical maths master Billings (Richard Wattis), whose only interest is the football pools, as they react against the forces assailing them, are so surrounded by layers of irony, comic indirection and the combination of satire with roguish complicity, that they aren't simply paraphrasable or reducible to a simple strategy – say, of the authors saying something that would otherwise be thought reactionary, except for the comic disguise. Once again, even if we might think that Launder and Gilliat exhibit a middle-class drift away from the optimism of 1945, the more impersonal barometric image adopted throughout this book is the one that least simplifies, in keeping with the comic artist's unideologized desire for the thickest, most multilayered and textured situation possible.

This is true of questions of class as well. Nutborne, like St Swithin's, is a firmly middle-class institution, with not a single Guinea Pig's accent to be heard. Though for most of the film implicit social questions remain only that – very implicit, sidelined by the emphasis on sex and gender – the constant presence of Rainbow, the school porter, keeps them at least in side view. Rainbow, like his younger working companion Edwin, is a servant figure, devious and extremely conservative (particularly resenting taking Miss Whitchurch's orders), and yet the school clearly depends on him. It is at the end that these questions suddenly erupt. Whereas the original play ended with staff, parents and children barricading themselves in against the invasion of the enemy, at the close of the film the invasion actually does take place, busloads of out-of-control children, co-educational and clearly lower class, with a bearded master failing to make much impact – clearly the kind who teaches at the sort of school where 'the kids throw inkpots' as Tassell remarks to Miss Harper. The film's terminating image, after Pond's and Whitchurch's exposure and decision to leave for Tanganyika, comically privileges Rainbow and Edwin. The camera, after lifting to the skies, descends to the playing fields to find Rainbow and Edwin collapsed, even comatose, under the felled rugby posts, an image full of potential but opaquely unsteady meanings. Do we see the working class sleeping, about to wake, to adopt one of Whitchurch's phrases, 'like a giant refreshed', or a working class collapsed in the regimented torpor of postwar Britain?

### 'A certain amount of hugger-mugger'

Pursued with a notable ingenuity of polite but suggestive euphemism throughout the text, the inevitable subject of sexuality rears its unwanted head, despite Pond's and Whitchurch's best efforts to suppress it. Though others too make unconscious *double entendres* – as when Miss Harper innocently asks Hyde-Brown, 'how many mistresses do you [the school] have?' – the most ingenious reminders of the debt to nature come from the principals themselves, occasionally visually (as in the ornament in

Pond's navally themed office of a sailor bestriding a phallic cannon) but usually verbally. Asked by one of the parents how things are going with the new school, Whitchurch innocently replies 'Well, we are bedding down quite nicely', which mildly eroticizes her gardening image, but she follows it with 'considering a certain amount of hugger-mugger', where the memory of *Hamlet* not only suggests one of her extraordinary euphemisms for sexuality (of which 'poodletaking' is the most mysterious) but has rhyming associations with worse, especially considering Pond's propensity for 'arse' jokes ('passing around'/'[p]arseing around', 'They don't know their LMS from their Southern Region'). Whitchurch too, with both senexes following Freud's notation of children's confusion of erotic and scatalogical zones, has a variation on this in her portentous question to Hyde Brown, 'What are you doing with my Senior Botany?', followed by her insistence that Biology lessons be cancelled. Elsewhere, when asked if she has 'grasped the dangers of adolescence', she replies, 'Oh, firmly in both hands, if I may say so'. Most memorable is her commentary on the school butterfly collection, which suggests both tumescent male energies and a rather minatory female response: 'Priscilla Johnson was romping in a haystack when that Bastard Purple alighted. But she had him in the killing bottle in a flash.' Such verbal nuances, depending with Whitchurch on an absolute innocence of utterance – Pond often suggests that he might well know what is being alluded to – echo the broader verbal and visual ironies of the impossible effort to keep the sexes apart, e.g. Jessica James's forbidden reading of *The Memoirs of Casanova*, the scene where the boys and girls alternately occupy the same beds for different sick-bay inspections, and the comedy of the later part of the film where to keep the sexes apart they actually have to work in intimate rapport (again a sort of burlesque of the war situation).

While dominantly the jokes are structured by the most basic male/female polarity, some of them drift towards the polymorphous perverse – Pond's 'arse' jokes, covert reference to dormitory homosexuality where Billings suggests to Pond sleeping the boys two to a bed, and Barbara's same-sex pash for Miss Harper which surfaces in the *Romeo and Juliet* lesson. Whereas a more conventional comedy with comparable material, the Boultings' 1960 film *A French Mistress* (nubile young teacher causes havoc in all-male institution), works basically on the one joke, in *Happiest Days* the multilayered obliquity of the comedy makes simple paraphrase difficult. Miss Harper (the English Rose equivalent of the French mistress in the Boultings' film) causes a few immediate flutters even in the flaccid Nutborne common room, but these die away, leaving her just with Tassell, and consigning both to the margins, the 'new comedy' couple of scant interest compared with the asexual blocking figures who command the centre. (This is recapitulated at the end of the film where, before the closing shot of Rainbow and Edwin, Tassell and Miss Harper kiss, but then give way to the primary couple, Pond and Whitchurch.) *Happiest Days* thrives on the paradox that its most absolute representatives of 'masculinity' and 'femininity' are in the ordinary sense completely sexless, and further, that from conventional viewpoints Whitchurch is far more 'masculine' – brisk, bluff, organizing, insensitive, action oriented – than the 'feminine' Pond – vain, histrionic, preening, growingly hysterical. These inclinations (shown early when Pond takes on a secretarial role as Whitchurch plans their campaign) reach a peak late in the film where, trying to explain away the presence of *crêpe de chine* underwear in the boys' desks, Pond floats into a display of arch campness, while in Whitchurch's parallel moment, when a rugby ball (booted adjacently in a different shot by Pond) suddenly rears at her she catches it with at least the aplomb of a second fifteen prop.

Two parallel comic sequences (the second taking up most of the second half of the film) are specifically structured around sexual difference – its absoluteness, its stereotypical recognizability for both dramatic characters and audience, and yet at the same time its mutability, its tenuousness. In the first sequence, Whitchurch's staff arrives at Nutborne, thinking it is a girls' school. Exploring it, they are confronted by markers of unregenerate bachelor occupation – dirt and dust, erotic literature, boxing, gambling, smoking, shootin', huntin' and fishin' instead of the expected signs of a girls' school (cleanliness, neatness, culture, etc.). The second layer of comedy, building on these incongruities, comes when, instead of reinterpreting them as male signs, the women reinterpret them as female, though to do so they have to strain the binary division masculine/feminine to produce as explanation a separate category of deviant, manly, uncouth, pugilistic, hunting, gambling, billiard playing (which Gossage actually betrays herself to be), Pepys, Casanova and Boccaccio enjoying hybrids.

In the later major sequence, where Pond and Whitchurch attempt to sustain the fiction of a boys' school for Harlingham's governors and a girls' school for St Swithin's parents, numerous breakdowns present anomalies which either Pond or Whitchurch have to explain away, this time with deliberately false explanations which become more and more heightened in their ingenuity and implausibility. This acceleratingly frenzied sequence is built around sets of stereotypically binary sex/gender indicators – rugby balls/netballs, rugby posts/lacrosse goals, broken male voices/soprano female voices, male songs ('Billy boy')/female songs ('Nymphs and shepherds'), science–analytical grammar–algebra/mime, drama, eurhythmics (which actually infect with dancing rhythms the wasted algebra master's writing of signs), naval cadets/needlework, etc. As anomalies present themselves Pond and Whitchurch struggle to recast them within the binary divides – girls' singing as boy trebles, rugby balls and *Men Only* as mistaken deliveries for netballs and *Woman's Own*, etc., until, with plausibility stretched to breaking point Pond attempts to justify the *crêpe de chine* underwear in the boys' desks (arguing that the navy has asked that boys be taught to repair their clothes) in a way so effete (when his questioner expostulates 'But it's *crêpe de chine* underwear!' his reply is the feyest: 'And lucky to get it!') that the categories can stretch no further, heralding the collapse of the deceit. This great comic sequence, like the shorter one, has no palpable design on the audience; it can't really with plausibility be read as a purposive assault upon sex and gender certainties, but at the same time, in typical Launder and Gilliat fashion, it gravitates to the densest, most fundamentally structuring material of the film and exploits its manifold possibilities, equally interested in the conservative comedy of deviance from the norm and the destabilizations potential in the stablest positions.

### The belles go down: the St Trinian's cycle (1954–78)

Essentially a minor byproduct of *Happiest Days*, *The Belles of St Trinian's* – its title parodying the great sentiment-filled *The Bells of St Mary's* (McCarey, 1945) – became the best known of all Launder and Gilliat's films and the begetter of a line of repeats running from the mid-1950s to the late 1970s. The box-office success of the series is in itself significant, arguing that British audiences over that twenty-year period of sex and gender transition/confusion were fascinated by harmlessly comic versions of the female sex out of control, the mobile woman gone wrong, and the male enforcers and protectors of the social order (educational bureau-crats, police, the legal system, even the army) in panicking retreat. The logic of the title pun is revealing: church bells – school bells – middle-class young ladies out of control, susceptible neither to the traditional disciplines of religion and morality nor education, the lower-form girls strange, violently unsocialized troglodytes, the upper-form belles dressed as the gymslip fantasies of ageing punters seeking discipline (with starlets famed for their material-ism like Belinda Lee and the once celebrated Sabrina playing minor parts).

The central conceit beneath the plot (flimsy even in the first film of the cycle) concerns an Arab princess sent to St Trinian's to escape the sexual encroachments of American servicemen, and associated ruses involving Arab and English racehorses. The pronounced Arab element reflects the Near East post-imperial problems plaguing Britain and reminds viewers of Britain's diminished status, a political parallel to the secondarization of the males in the film. Her own view of the decline is summed up in Millicent Fritton's words to her black-sheep brother Clarrie (both played by Alastair Sim in an antic mixed-sex version of Bette Davis's and Olivia De Havilland's melodramatic good and evil siblings). Set up as 'a gay arcadia of happy girlhood', once the war has abolished 'such things as good manners and good taste', St Trinian's now educates for success in a changed world: 'You see in other schools girls are sent out quite unprepared into a merciless world, but when our girls leave here it's the merciless world which has to be prepared.' If the resolute old-fashionedness of the Frittons and Flash Harry (George Cole, given the genesis of a 12-year-old bootboy hired by Miss Fritton during the war and now grown into the archetypal wideboy and engineer of the films' plots), provides a historic link with the war and guarantees for the audience – importantly – the harmlessness of what goes on, it is at the same time the key to the films' disappointments. The films display a world-upside-down where changes are burlesqued in a form as stripped of tendentiousness as possible, but the very suppression of tendentiousness, which probably guaranteed the films' success, leaves them tame for later viewers.

The later films of the *St Trinian's* cycle – *Blue Murder at* (1958), *The Pure Hell of* (1961), *The Great St Trinian's Train Robbery* (1966), *The Wildcats of* (1980) – much more Launder's projects than Gilliat's, justified themselves by their box-office success in difficult times for British cinema, but long before the end the joke wears thin. The spasmodic pleasures of the films are revuelike. This is seen in the characters, as with Raymond Huntley's sexually corruptible Justice Slender in *Pure Hell*; Superintendent Kemp Byrd's (Larry Lamble's) interminable engagement to Police Sergeant Ruby Gates (Joyce Grenfell), ever doomed to undercover work trying to expose the school; Terry-Thomas as the caddish Captain Carlton-Ricketts wooing Joyce Grenfell for what her granny has put aside for her in *Blue Murder*; Lionel Jeffries in reluctant drag impersonating the headmistress Dame Maude Hackshaw in the same; Maureen Lipman as a professional co-respondent ('Correspondent?' 'No co-respondent') put out of work by changes in the divorce laws in *The Wildcats*. Revue-like too are the witty allusions to topical circumstances: a schoolgirl in court giving her name as 'Lolita Chatterley, Peignton Place, Brighton' (where it's the less obvious detail of 'Peignton Place' that really makes the joke); or in the same film that wonderful marker of the decline of imperial Britain, the elderly Arab who announces himself 'representative of Her Majesty's Government, ICI and Hotpoint washing machines'. Certainly the films comically encapsulate references that show the moving of the times: Marks (Marx) and Spencer, closed-shop union practices, European Union closing in as the school gets a trip to the Continent as a result of illicitly winning a Unesco competition, and by the end, in *The Wildcats*, the *Sun*, sloganized t-shirts ('Wigan is for Lovers') and a separate Ministry for Female Education.

But the finely calibrated farce of *Happiest Days* has dwindled to a series of turns and one-liners, and the central weakness of the conceit behind the whole series – hardly concealed in the first film – that the comic problematics of the release of the postwar 'monstrous regiment of women' are not able to be satisfactorily registered in plots as oldfashionedly centred on 'gees', illicit stills, smoking fags, big girls in little gym slips, as these are, is increasingly exposed. Just once in *The Wildcats* a schoolgirl speaks in a harder, more contemporarily jaundiced sneer which suddenly exposes what surrounds it as a 1940s image of the 1970s. By contrast the true antique of *The Happiest Days* gets younger every year.

## Notes

1 Brown, *Launder and Gilliat*, p. 124.
2 *Jean Simmons' Blue Lagoon Diary* (World Film Publications, 1949). Held in the British Library.
3 H. de Vere Stacpoole, *The Blue Lagoon* (George Newnes, London, 1918).
4 Stacpoole, *The Blue Lagoon*, p. 95.
5 Ibid., p. 168, also pp. 132–4.
6 Brown, *Launder and Gilliat*, p. 124.
7 The draft script, dated 23 October 1947, is held in the British Film Institute Library.
8 Stacpoole, *The Blue Lagoon*, p. 74.
9 Ibid., pp. 139, 180, 183.
10 Ibid., p.143.
11 Ibid., pp. 143–4.
12 The Grierson edition of Donne was not published until 1933. His earlier anthology of the metaphysical poets was reviewed by Eliot in 1923. Leavis's celebration of Donne in 'The Line of Wit' in *Revaluations* was in 1936.
13 Stacpoole, *The Blue Lagoon*, pp. 249–52.
14 Draft script, page 97, shot 483.

15 A. E. Housman, 'Into my heart an air that kills', *A Shropshire Lad*, Poem XL.

16 John Dighton, *The Happiest Days of Your Life: A Farce in Three Acts* (Samuel French, London, 1951).

17 Martha Wolfenstein and Nathan Leites, *Movies: A Psychological Study* (Free Press of Glencoe, Glencoe, 1950).

18 Durgnat, *A Mirror for England*, p. 51. Here Montgomery/Sim is also misremembered as helping Ted rather than Jim.

19 See *New York Times*, 18 March 1984; *Daily Telegraph*, 13 April 1990; and *Independent on Sunday*, 10 May 1992.

20 Noted by Julian Petley in Burton, O'Sullivan and Wells (eds), *The Family Way*, pp. 20–1.

21 Brown, *Launder and Gilliat*, p. 19.

22 Susan Briggs, *Keep Smiling Through: The Home Front 1939–45* (Weidenfeld & Nicolson, 1975), p. 28.

23 A full account of the groundnut débâcle is found in Alan Wood, *The Groundnut Affair* (Bodley Head, London, 1950). Thanks to Ron Guariento for drawing my attention to the significance of Miss Whitchurch's words, and to Keith Syers for agricultural amplification.

## 5

# Authors and genres: thrillers and comedies

## Preliminaries

The consequence of writing at length on a limited number of the films is that others worth detailed discussion can only receive curtailed treatment in which generalizing patterns will predominate. As its title indicates, this chapter is organized around the two broad multifaceted modes which Launder and Gilliat favoured, the thriller and comedy. Discussion of the thrillers pushes back briefly into the 1930s, but its main focus is from *Green for Danger* (1947) to *Endless Night* (1972). The section on comedies moves from *Lady Godiva Rides Again* (1952) to *Only Two Can Play* (1962), subdividing them into three dominant types, more easily categorizable than the intricate cross-fertilizations that the thrillers undergo.

## The thrillers

### Overview

Any account of Launder and Gilliat's significant thrillers – stretching from the early 1930s (Gilliat's script for Forde's *Rome Express*) to the early 1970s (Gilliat's *Endless Night*) – is complicated by two factors. The first is that their later thrillers are overshadowed by two celebrated works where their contribution was limited to the screenplays, *The Lady Vanishes* and *Night Train to*

*Munich*, directed by Alfred Hitchcock and Carol Reed respectively. The second is that Launder and Gilliat's characteristic mode, the comedy–thriller–romance, is predominantly associated with the most celebrated of British directors, Hitchcock, with the triple consequence not just of an undervaluation of their contribution to the works cited above, and to a characteristic mode of 1930s and early 1940s British cinema, but also of a tendency to see their later thrillers merely as unsuccessful attempts to reproduce earlier 'Hitchcockian' patterns rather than in their own terms.

While I have no intention of claiming either that the Hitchcock or Reed films are more the writers' than the directors', or that Launder and Gilliat's role in the development of the thriller–comedy–romance was greater than Hitchcock's, still, matters of ascription are far from simple. The screenplays of both films are highly structured prototypes for the directors, marked indelibly by the wit and ethos of the writers. Who else, to echo Brown,[1] would have Caldicott on an eve of war German train, recognize from Balliol days Dickie Randall in his disguise as Major Kruger, or then have him debate with Charters Dickie's patriotism by reference to his playing cricket for the Gentlemen? Who else would have constructed the suspense of trying to communicate the breaking of his disguise by the Nazis around a memory unsure whether it was rock cakes or doughnuts that Dickie Randall used to have sent up to his rooms? But it is not just matter of a few memorable situations or verbal felicities (Miss Froy's 'Harriman's Herbal Tea drunk by a Million Mexicans', or Iris's characterizing herself to her girlfriends as 'a slightly sunburnt offering on an altar in Hanover Square') but of intricate narrative structures underpinning the whole of the films. Even such definitively 'Hitchcockian' elements as the oneiric episodes unleashed by the flowerpot falling on Iris's head are present in the scenario,[2] even if we feel that Hitchcock worked them, and the implications of the romantic relationship, in ways that were highly characteristic.

In the MacDonald interview Gilliat both articulates a resentment at Hitchcock's refusal to state publicly what he admitted privately, the screenwriters' importance to *The Lady Vanishes*, and contests the idea that Hitchcock singlehandedly defined the thriller–comedy–romance mode. His tracing of sources back to earlier German cinema may have elements of a desire to bypass Hitchcock, but the point is still a powerful one.[3] Hitchcock's dominance is hardly in doubt, but the subgenre's history is one of multiple borrowings and influences on all sides, and Launder and Gilliat's earlier screenplays for *Rome Express* (Gilliat's) and *Seven Sinners* (the pair's) are important milestones, as well as their work in the two later films.

Launder and Gilliat's relationship with Hitchcock, stretching beyond their collaboration on and bad feeling over *The Lady Vanishes* to the larger inevitable marginalization caused by Hitchcock's predominance, was a complex, lingering one, involving mutual debts and borrowings. For instance, in *Seven Sinners* (1936) the clue leading to the police chief's unmasking is a version of the revelation of the Professor as arch criminal in *The Thirty-nine Steps* (1935), the policeman's characteristic hand gesture when he smokes echoing the Professor's showing of his mutilated finger, but with his cigar providing an extra rather than a missing digit. Thirty-six years later in *Frenzy* (1972) Hitchcock borrowed the opening aerial shot moving down the Thames from *London Belongs to Me* (1948). It will be argued below that the relationship persisted postwar on Launder and Gilliat's side, not in the form of further borrowings (though they were obviously aware of using of Hitchcock's composer, Bernard Herrmann, in *Endless Night*) but in attempts to free their films of Hitchcock's shadow.

Seen outside the 'Hitchcockian' framework, the series takes on different meanings with only *State Secret* (1950) fulfilling the most dominant Hitchcock prototype of the hero pursued, the chase intricately connected to a romantic relationship. The earliest, *Green for Danger* (1947), deploys a ratiocinative detective framework – mysterious crimes, closed atmospheric environment, multiple suspects, and an authoritarian detective. *Fortune is a Woman* (1957), is influenced by film noir narrative structures combined with anglicized aspects of the genre's paranoid heroes. Launder's script (with Peter Barnes) for *Ring of Spies* (Tronson, 1963) reworks the documentary elements latent in the quirky realism of the earlier thrillers into a treatment of the recent Portland spy scandal.

Finally, Gilliat's last film, *Endless Night*, is an extreme instance of unreliable subjective narration by a criminal protagonist. Three of the five films replace the chase structure with variants of the 'whodunnit' plot. Gilliat a number of times refers to 'that unfortunate whodunnit' element in the thrillers,[4] but the film-makers return to it enough to suggest that in providing an alternative structure it functions more than negatively.

This perspective enables other patterns, suggesting experiment rather than repetition, to be seen.

1  *Variations on the flawed hero/protagonist*. In *Green for Danger* Inspector Cockrill's dramaturgical arrogance leads to Esther Sanson's death. In *State Secret* Marlowe's naivety is intriguingly developed. In *Fortune is a Woman* Oliver Bramwell's class inferiority and sexual suspicions make him a clouded protagonist. In *Ring of Spies* Harry Houghton betrays his country, and in *Endless Night* Michael Rogers murders his wife for her fortune.

2  *Variations on/subversions of the couple*. The only obviously 'Hitchcockian' instance is *State Secret* where Lisa, the young Vosnian woman, at first refuses to help Marlowe, but eventually becomes involved, his attempt to escape becoming hers. In *Green for Danger* the couple, or couples – with Freddi moving between Barney and Eden – are not at the centre of the narrative, and, though Freddi and Barney are eventually reconciled, they cannot but seem an unstable pair. The couple in *Fortune is a Woman* is also undermined by distrust, the hero believing that his ex-girlfriend committed fraud and murder. In *Ring of Spies* the couple are traitors, and their relationship is deceptive, 'Bunty' for Harry being primarily a means of getting at the naval secrets. Imbalance in the couple is intensified in *Endless Night* where the protagonist and his mistress are found, retrospectively, to have murdered his wife. More broadly, the series can be seen through two other perspectives. The first reveals

3  *A movement towards contemporary settings*, away from the brilliantly deployed wartime context of *Green for Danger*, to

ones where, if the war functions at all, it as a memory-trace, a past determining the present (at least in the characters' minds) of Tracey Moreton in *Fortune is a Woman* and Harry Houghton in *Ring of Spies*.

4  *Movements towards later modes and styles.* Attempts to push their thrillers into the contemporary mainstream, given the realization that the *The Lady Vanishes* and *Night Train to Munich* belong to an irrecoverable history (social and filmic) that cannot simply be revived postwar.

## From *Green for Danger* to *Endless Night*

*Green for Danger*, like four of the five films (*Ring of Spies* is the exception), uses elements of subjective narration, elaborating the tendencies of *The Rake's Progress* and *I See a Dark Stranger*. The film begins with Inspector Cockrill (Alastair Sim) retrospectively typing his account of the case. All four films are interested in the terms in which the character-narrator tells his story, and in ironies connected with the telling. Here Cockrill's overvoice intermittently and lugubriously accents failure even as he strides through the narrative with histrionic command. Stage-managing semi-sadistic scenarios throughout, Cockrill at one point transforms the hospital grounds into a site of Shakespearean comedy. Here, hidden by the darkness as Eden (Leo Genn) courts Freddi (Sally Gray) with Lorenzo's love speech from *The Merchant of Venice*, 'On such a night as this ...', he sardonically breaks in with Jessica's reply, 'In such a night / Did young Lorenzo swear he loved her well / Stealing her heart with many vows of faith, / And ne'er a true one'.[5] Then, after insouciantly signing off with 'Good night, Dr Eden', he hooks his brolly round a bush to expose the jealous Barney (Trevor Howard) spying on them and adds a further 'Good night Dr Barnes'. This directorial panache dominates the detective story's climax, where he uncovers the guilt of Esther Sanson (Rosamund John), brilliantly deducing her method of murder. However, when he sees Eden attempting to give her an injection, he prevents him, only for Eden deflatingly to tell him that he was about to inject her with the antidote to the poison with which she has just committed suicide, a self-destruction which a crestfallen Cockrill has inadvertently allowed.

*Green for Danger*, made during 1946, is, though not a military uniform is seen, situated in the war, its action placed against the whine and sinister silence of the buzzbombs of August 1944. The murderess has gone insane with guilt at failing to save her mother, immolated in an air raid, and one of the suspects has a sister whose voice (mistaken for hers) is heard making Nazi broadcasts from Germany. The hospital-staff dance sequence replays with difference the dance in *Millions Like Us*, embodying the tension between postwar production and wartime setting. In *Millions* Charlie and Jennifer snub each other during the 'Paul Jones', that most characteristic World War II dance, its structure a microcosm of the wartime interaction of the sexes. In it the women form one line, the men another, mirroring the segregation of the armed forces as well as the primacy of the communal. The lines move past each other to jolly music. When the music stops men and women are left opposite each other as arbitrary partners for a couple dance, which is then broken up by the communal dance, which in turn gives way to a new chance selection of couples – mirroring the arbitrariness of contact in wartime.

Though in *Millions Like Us* the dance is the site of a skirmish between Jennifer and Charlie, their quarrel is contained within the huge communal celebration. In *Green for Danger*'s reworking, Freddi, dancing with Eden, sees Barney, from whom she has broken off her engagement, looking down at her from the balcony. She goes to him and they converse tensely. Nurse Woods (Megs Jenkins) appears on the balcony announcing the 'Paul Jones'. Barney and Freddi are separated, Barney pulled away by the men, Freddi by the women. (In *Millions* as the Englishman and Canadian quarrel over Jennifer the 'Paul Jones' starts, and their fight forgotten, they drag her into the dance.) When the communal music stops, Barney forces his way to Freddi to continue their discordant conversation, with Freddi distractedly watching Eden, to whom she is attracted, dancing with someone else. When the communal dance restarts, Barney moves over to Sister Bates (Judy Campbell) who is gloomily spectating. She talks to him about her obsessive love for Eden, and then sadistically tells him she saw Eden and Freddi kissing. Rushing back to the communal dance she then finds herself coupled with her ex-lover Eden, aggressively ignoring his attempts to soothe her. Suddenly, she breaks away to the balcony, sweeps the needle off the record, and announces, with barely checked hysteria, that she has the solution to the murder. Then she rushes out of the room. This impeccable sequence generates much of its force from the friction of the later version, dominated wholly by the characters' individual problems, against the values encapsulated in the dance scene in *Millions* where, though some characters are caught up in individual problems, they are dominated by the communal context. The moment where the enraged, degraded Marian Bates ('He's sick of me and I'm sick of myself!') breaks off the music in a frenzy of private rage is unthinkable in a film made in the war. Clearly, though, the retrospective war setting was not infinitely repeatable and Launder and Gilliat, though there is a case to be made for *Green for Danger* as the most perfectly executed of their later thrillers, had to look in other directions.

*State Secret* updates to circa 1950 and a setting alluding to iron-curtain Europe, while ambiguous enough to suggest rightwing Spain as much as leftwing Yugoslavia.[6] The film, however, was a renovated prewar project, which explains its staying with the chase-romance plot. The casting of the American Douglas Fairbanks Jr as Marlowe was dictated by American box-office considerations.[7] It does, however, complicate the film, adding a significant layer of subtext. His opposite, the Vosnian Colonel Galcon (whose well-mannered ruthlessness and cynical pragmatism descend from Paul Lukas's Dr Hartz in *The Lady Vanishes*, and prior to that from Conrad Veidt's sophisticated killer, Zurta, in *Rome Express*) is played by that inalienably English actor, Jack Hawkins, so that beneath the America:Democracy versus Vosnia:Totalitarianism antithesis they act out there are also glimpses of a postwar American/British dialectic.

Marlowe is classified above as a flawed hero, whose naivety resides in his unwillingness to believe that medicine can be put to the service of ideology. ('They tell me that in some parts of the world musicians are finding it increasingly difficult to compose non-political music, so it's very gratifying to think that a doctor can still perform a non-political operation.') This doesn't prevent him from fulfilling his heroic role, but, through his relationship with Colonel Galcon/Hawkins, the literal as well as metaphorical son of 'His Majesty the American' is subjected to subtle scrutiny. Symbiotically linked through crucial sections of the film, the two become the most important pairing, rather eclipsing Marlowe's relationship with Lisa (Glynis Johns) in interest.

This romance follows in outline the most typical 'Hitchcockian' formula. Initially hostile, Lisa, even when reluctantly helping, remains highly suspicious (lacing Marlowe's drink with sleeping pills to inhibit sexual assault and then holding him at gunpoint when she finds Theodor's documents in his pockets). Endangered by aiding him, she eventually has no option but to try to escape with him. On the plane to London, her repeated insistence that they will part immediately they get to England gives way to intimations of their being permanently together. The unconventional final curtain twist on this is that she then suddenly announces that she is going to be sick, sending Marlowe scrabbling for a paper bag. This ending suggests an attempt to work at least spasmodically against the grain of expectation with the couple.

Galcon, ironic *homo politicus* incarnate (dealing with the possibility of falling from power by contemplating a Chair of Political Science in America), is parallelled by Herbert Lom's Theodor, a smoothly charming but dangerous black marketeer, with whom the couple become involved through Marlowe's accidental appropriation of his jacket. Their encounter leads to an apparently simple opposition – sympathetic good couple versus nasty but charismatic crook – which, however, is complicated when the fugitives adopt his tactics (threats and blackmail) in order to force him to help them, suggesting that Marlowe's original view of the world is less than adequate to the realities he encounters and that his parapraxis in putting on the crook's jacket in the barber's shop is more than a simple plot mechanism. Lom's insidious charm (offering his toast 'To me', quipping about 'the survival of the unfittest') is, as ever, Middle European, but

Hawkins is, even with a slight European accent, always English, which leads to the undertext of the naive American versus the more worldly and pragmatic Englishman – the latter defeated (gracefully) in the plot but victor in some sense in the debates, a way of both recognizing American postwar dominance and ironizing it. This explains the otherwise ludicrous moment when Marlowe, trying to get to the American embassy, hails a cab, driven by Danny Green, playing a Vosnian who in the three years he says he lived in New York has attained an impossibly flawless demotic accent with not a trace of European origins.

If *State Secret* ironizes the American hero, the reverse could be posited – American film noir's subversion of an English icon – as Hawkins becomes the protagonist in *Fortune is a Woman* (1957), which adeptly emphasizes the frayed edges of that stoical but also febrile and slightly deceptive persona. The film opens with a magnificent sequence in which a car is driven through a stormy night from an unknown subjective viewpoint, till it reaches a country house, whereupon the unseen protagonist walks up to a landscape painting of a country house through the door of which he uncannily enters, to find, in a sinister mise en scène, a dead body. This sequence is revealed as the nightmare of Oliver Bramwell (Jack Hawkins), an insurance investigator who then relates in flashback the events of the film. Deceptively set at the beginning of the film, his nightmare, we realize later, is actually situated post flashback narrative. This being so, its apparent portending of future events, which invests the more mundane narrative (Bramwell's investigations into the decaying upper-class Tracey Moreton's/ Dennis Price's house-burning insurance fraud, complicated by the fact that his ex-girlfriend, Sarah/Arlene Dahl, is now married to Moreton) with a quasi-supernatural aura, might seem over-wrought. Viewed however as a metaphor for Bramwell's emotional insecurities with his ex-girlfriend, whom he marries after Moreton's death, and his uneasy class relations with her late husband, the financially embarrassed upper-class snob (bitterly imagining the family's property being turned in the democratic postware dispensation into 'a home for retired boilermakers'), it makes perfect sense.

After Tracey's death in a second fire, Bramwell suspects Sarah of having tricked him, murdered Tracey, and prosecuted an art fraud involving some of the paintings in Lowes Manor, Tracey's house. His suspicions allayed, they marry, and a new phase of the plot begins as they are blackmailed and persecuted in ways that suggest Tracey is still alive and behind it all. After a false resolution where the blackmailer proves to be only a minor player, Sarah suddenly leaves to visit Tracey's mansion. Bramwell, following her, finds her talking to someone who is obscured from the audience by Sarah's body. As Sarah moves aside, Tracey's mother (who has played a small but memorable part earlier) is uncovered, and then further revealed as the persecutor of the newly married pair. While the mother's confession of having punished Sarah for her disloyalty to Tracey in marrying Oliver shows her son to be the real criminal, this discovery of her is the last of a chain of criminalizing displacements of Sarah – first to the marvellously invented figure of the hyper-promiscuous Vera Litchen (Greta Gynt), a blonde with a generic likeness to Sarah, then to Ambrosine, the strawberry blonde who paints the art forgeries and is misidentified as Sarah, and, lastly to the mother.

The sexually voracious Vera Litchen is a memorable character, whom Bramwell, despite resisting her seductions when he first meets her, later visits twice more, arrivals she interprets as his inappropriately timed consent (the third coinciding with her marriage reception). Her naive, cuckolded American fiancé becomes a heightened representative of Bramwell's own insecurities. In another dream visit to Lowes Manor, Bramwell enters the painting to find himself looking down a long table at an unsettlingly smirking Sarah. Such fears of female treachery intertwine with the self-made Bramwell's social inferiority, giving Hawkins's familiar postwar meritocrat a more than usual unease, shadowed as he is by the asthmatic, declining, yet ineffably superior upper-class Moreton. Two elements add to the irresolutions of the close. First, after Bramwell has honourably resigned his job because of his various minor deceits, he lets himself be talked round, an action readable as either a very shifty aspect of the new pragmatic sector he represents, or as a reasonable jettisoning of archaic concerns. At the conclusion Bramwell's overvoiced question 'And, well, there couldn't be any harm in just discussing it, could there?' seems more addressed to his peers in the audience than to anyone else. The other disturbing element is that the nightmare at the beginning of the film must date from after the events recounted, thus suggesting that they continue to haunt him.

The pair's last thrillers, Launder's script (with Peter Barnes) for *Ring of Spies* (1963), and *Endless Night* (1972), writtten and directed by Gilliat, push to extremes opposite tendencies in the oeuvre – the former reviving documentary impulses, the latter advancing the fragmentary subjective narration of other films into sustained primacy. (That pivotal text *The Green Man* (1956), where a thriller plot, rather than following the thriller–comedy–romance model of balanced elements, is radically comedicized, is briefly at one with the later thrillers' interest in subjective narration, beginning with Hawkins's/Sim's relation of events up till the entry of William Blake/George Cole, but then abruptly dropping it.) *Endless Night*'s source, Agatha Christie's late (1967) novel, is an exception to her usual clue-puzzle detective stories, a deceptive first-person narrative in which the narrator turns out to be the murderer of his wife. The film, like the novel, narrated by Michael Rogers (Hywel Bennett), has the narrative task of finding cinematic equivalents of the novel's clues to reveal restrospectively the concealed core of Michael and Greta's (Britt Ekland's) plan for Michael to marry and murder an heiress. This deceptive presentation is prefigured in *Green for Danger*, where Esther Sanson's guilt is suggested when she visualizes Sister Bates facing her murderer. However, what retrospectively appears a sign of guilt, is likely to be discounted at first viewing as the frightened imaginings of a hypersensitive character.

Michael's poor-boy-meets-rich-girl narrative of marrying Ellie (Hayley Mills) and then suffering her sudden death – only revealed as artfully suppressive near the film's end – is shaded with omens and auguries, not sufficient to deconstruct the narrative but enough to destabilize it unsettlingly. A simple instance is Uncle Andrew's (George Sanders) ironic scepticism about Michael's claims not to have known Greta in the past, finally made concrete in his photograph of the pair in Amsterdam, but which until that point functions as an unspecific omen-puzzle (part rationalizable as Sanders's usual superciliousness). More complex is the strange crunch of gravel when Michael looks at Rembrandt's *The Syndics* in the Rijksmuseum near the narrative's beginning. This is eventually explicable as Greta's footsteps (we see the part of the Rijksmuseum scene suppressed in Michael's account, his first meeting with Greta, much later) subjectively filtered by Michael through the sound of gravel as he and Dr Philpotts walk in the grounds of the asylum Michael has been committed to, in the opening moments of the narrative (a location only clarified at the end of the film).Without the later information it creates an air of oddity, a warning of subjectivity about the telling, but there is simply not enough evidence for it to register more particularly – something true of many other vaguely unsettling elements in Michael's narrative.

Michael's meditation, when recalling the portrait of the Syndics, on the self-assurance of the Stallmeesters' faces and their ability to read his thoughts, surrounds the narrative with ominous mystery, but also cannot be fully understood until the end, when, having killed Greta, he sits listening to the tape of Ellie singing Blake's poem, and then looks up to find his accusers watching him, grouped in the exact portrait attitudes of the painting he was observing at the moment he met Greta. The skilful interweaving of visual motifs binds into the scene another of the film's primary motifs of scrutiny, the painted motto of the eye of God, 'God Thou Seest Me', which haunts Michael through his narrative, by having him look up at his observers through his hands, which expose only a single eye in an echo of the sign.

While the later Agatha Christie film cycle (e.g. *Murder on the Orient Express*, 1974) developed, in concert with the retro television appropriation of her works, a mini-genre based around nostalgia, elements of the heritage film, bravura impersonations of Poirot, and, in the case of the films, multiple star cameos, *Endless Night* is the only film to find sustained cinematic correlatives for the detective novelist's intricacies, while also being, of the pair's late works, the one that most pronouncedly attempts a contemporary stylistic transformation, with the clue-setting, mystery-provoking, double-text requirements of the narrative releasing a cascade of 1960s and 1970s traits – near subliminal memory interruptions of Michael's monologue, scenes suppressively fragmented into multiple parts, pronounced displacements of visuals and sound track, and scenes in which fantasy melds with actuality (for instance where Mike's listening to the financial advisor becomes confused with Ellie's funeral sermon).

*Endless Night* presents the most excessive in a chain of more or less flawed heroes and defective couples, with Michael murdering both his wife and his mistress (and going insane by the end). However, as the deconstructions fall into place, the narrative, cleared of ambivalence at one level, becomes increasingly ambivalent at another, as the sympathy generated for Michael by his telling, even as it is exposed by the narrative's unreeling, is paradoxically reinstated. Details in the novel suggesting a psycopathic edge to Michael are removed. A scene later revealed as consummate acting, in which, leaving Ellie on the day he will kill her, he rushes back to kiss her soulfully, suggests the post-deconstructive possibility that the kiss is genuine beneath the acting. Michael's journey to the death bed of his moral father figure, the architect Santonix (Per Oscarsson), even his killing of Greta as the catalyst of his own tendencies to depart from 'joy and light' for 'endless night' – the polarities of the Blake poem that Ellie sings – reinterpret him from psychopath to near-tragic figure.

In contrast *Ring of Spies* is distanced and unsubjective as it documents the real-life Portland spy scandal, concentrating on Harry Houghton's (Bernard Lee's) dismissal for drunkenness from the British embassy in Warsaw, his unwise redeployment in the Portland naval secrets establishment, his recruitment by the Soviets with threats of blackmail, his use of his mistress Elizabeth Gee (Margaret Tyzack) to 'borrow' documents, the arousal of suspicion through his mildly ostentatious spending, the surveillance, then entrapment of the pair and their contact Gordon Lonsdale and his colleagues Peter and Helen Kroger (though that of the Krogers is not dramatized). The prologue and epilogue framing the narrative have the obvious function of giving hortatory urgency to what is very cool storytelling, but also move self-consciously through a number of documentary modes in a way reminiscent of the brief play with varieties of narration at the beginning of *Millions Like Us*. The prologue shifts from mocking antique stage and silent film representations of spying to displaying the mid-century reality of electronic espionage and fragments of newsreels featuring the spy sensations of the day, Harry Goldman, Colonel Abel, Klaus Fuchs and the Rosenbergs, while the epilogue warns that a spy may be sitting in the same row as you even as you watch the film in the cinema! But in the narrative the urgent drama of the newreels and the hortatory commentary are downplayed in a way as systematically disciplined as the plotting of the textual doublenesses of *Endless Night*, with irony replacing them as the dominant narrative mode.

The spies use the advanced technology foregrounded in the newsreels, but the narrative seems most interested in its ironic and incongruous intersections with unlikely contexts: contacts made on the roof garden of Derry and Toms; the fusty bibliophile Kroger (David Kossoff) placing a microdot in the punctuation of Blake's 'Infant Joy'; the newly recruited spies treated by Lonsdale to a 'Crazy Gang' concert in London; another spy, Blake,[8] at the margins of the narrative, being observed making contact with a Russian embassy official in the pavilion at Lord's. Though there are two sequences where the narrative, rather than following Houghton and Gee, follows Lonsdale as he photographs classified material and visits the homely Krogers in Ruislip to transmit it, the presumably ideologically driven spies never discuss politics. This means that the narrative's central interest is in the motivations of the English pair, stuck at the bottom of the minor civil service culture, and in the mundane resentments and apolitical material desires that make them susceptible to temptation. Though Houghton is initially blackmailed into espionage, he never uses this to excuse himself, presumably aware that his resistance has been minimal and that he has essentially welcomed the opportunity. While Bunty has simple fantasies of a lifestyle she has never known, dreaming of owning shares and a small yacht, Houghton's materialism intersects with motivations exposed in the opening scenes, where he disgraces himself at the Warsaw embassy garden party and then drunkenly soliloquizes to his Polish mistress over his soured resentment at a stunted naval career, a mediocre war and the lack of social tone that has held him down, leading us to see (an effect furthered by his anti-establishment monologues for the pub audiences he flashes his newfound wealth on) that revenge on an establishment that has snubbed him drives him almost as much as swapping his poky mobile home for a real house. Robert Murphy's observation that 'The story ... comes to seem like a warning less of the corrupting power of Communism than of the dangers awaiting those who shed the bonds of conventional morality and assume the amoral attitudes of the classless, materialistic, affluent society'[9] is particularly meaningful when the difference between narrative and frames is considered.

The narrative remains close to Houghton and Gee even when it widens to follow the gathering investigation, in which they are officially observed, bugged, tailed, and finally arrested. The film takes great care to maintain a distance, sometimes ironic, from the investigators, so that Houghton and Gee remain at the film's centre, not given sympathy, exactly, but certainly understanding of a kind. They are, however, never sentimentalized. Ironically, beside the apparent domestic happiness of the Krogers and Lonsdale's fidelity to his absent wife (we see him getting rid of an attractive girl who wants to stay the night), the relationship between Harry and Bunty is illusory on her side and pragmatic on his – both his Polish mistress and the girl in the office he makes a play for before her are younger and more attractive – and the further deceit he practises on her, telling her, in order to soothe moral qualms, that the secrets are for the Americans, not the Russians, is never rectified, even when on their last contact journey to London she starts fantasizing about being granted American citizenship for services rendered. By this point she has deceived herself into believing what she knew not to be true (as shown in her initial intensely sceptical reaction), and Houghton has even forgotten for a moment what she is talking about. We are a long way from the world of *Night Train to Munich* and *Millions Like Us*.

## The comedies

Launder and Gilliat's later comedies basically fall into three categories, different from their prewar predominantly 'comedian comedies'. First, there are Gilliat's sophisticated sex comedies, *The Constant Husband* (1954) and *Only Two Can Play* (1962), the former, with its redeployment of Rex Harrison, pointing to their derivation from the more hybrid *The Rake's Progress*. Second, there are what are called here 'State of England' films, *Lady Godiva Rides Again* (Launder, 1952), *Folly to be Wise* (Launder, 1953) and *Left Right and Centre* (Gilliat, 1959), as well as, though they are discussed elsewhere, *Happiest Days*, the *St Trinian's* cycle and *Joey Boy*, all marked by dystopian leanings expressed through satiric comic realism alternating with mildly surreal farce. Third, there are the Scottish pastoral comedies *Geordie* (1955) and *The Bridal Path* (1959). Again, as one surveys the terrain, Launder and Gilliat's famous versatility has to be remarked. In Category 1 one looks for comparison with films such as *Miranda* (Annakin, 1947) and *Kind Hearts and Coronets* (Hamer, 1949). Category 2 pushes into the satiric territories dominated by the Boultings in the late 1950s and early 1960s. Category 3 invokes more the world of Ealing.

### Rakes' regress

*The Rake's Progress*, *The Constant Husband* and *Only Two Can Play* all centre on philandering male protagonists, though differently placed chronologically, circumstantially and ethically. Vivian in *The Rake's Progress* is unrepentant over his relations with women. *The Constant Husband* has Harrison committing multiple bigamies (for financial more than sexual reasons, in a way alien to his predecessor, whose single marriage of convenience was initiated by Rikki). While Vivian suffers a breakdown near the narrative's end, *The Constant Husband*'s protagonist suffers a loss of memory before its beginning. Whereas Vivian displays a cool moral amnesia, the later rake, confronted with his past, is morally shocked. *Only Two Can Play* descends socially to John Lewis (Peter

Sellers) an impoverished semi-intellectual, trapped in lower-middle-class near-poverty, burdened with a young family (whereas both the other protagonists are notably unreproductive), tempted by an affair with the glamorous, socially superior Mrs Gryffyd Williams (Mai Zetterling). In *The Rake's Progress* negative attitudes towards the hero's actions are given exterior expression by other characters. In *The Constant Husband* conflict is dramatized through, but not within, the hero, by means of his pre- and post-amnesic difference, his present 'moral' and past 'immoral' selves. In *Only Two Can Play* the conflict is given interior dramatization in the protagonist's present consciousness: knowing that he shouldn't, but very much wanting to. Thus each of the films, while fascinated by the transgressive hero, places him differently, refusing in different ways to allow his actions to go uninterrogated, though in no easily calculable terms. But similar interrogation also extends to the narratives' females, and all three films reflect complexly on male and female psychological characteristics, their differences and their mutability.

In *The Constant Husband* 'Mr X' wakes up in a hotel in coastal North Wales without any memory of his past. Helped by Professor Llewellyn (Cecil Parker) he attempts to reconstruct from scattered clues (a knowledge of Bentley cars, his reply of 'zabaglione' in a word association test, etc.), his lost life. Gradually the truth is revealed. A wife, Monica (Kay Kendall), is discovered and the pair resume their marriage, but 'Mr X' (otherwise variously 'Charles', 'William' or 'Peter') is then kidnapped by the Italian family of a second wife, Lola (Nicole Maurey), and forced to resume his marriage with her. Through all this his memory remains lost. As a bevy of other wives is discovered, Harrison is 'overcome by horror and disgust' to discover he has been 'a professional bigamist. An exploiter of women. A monster'. Worse, his motivations have been primarily economic. Arrested, and refusing to offer a defence, he has a barrister forced on him, a fait accompli subsidized by his wronged but loving wives. His defence counsel is a woman, Miss Chesterman (Margaret Leighton), who offers a philosophical plea of innocence, claiming that 'the physical man is not the mental man', i.e. that the accused, disgusted by his unremembered actions, is not the entity who committted them. But the accused rejects Miss Chesterman's virtuosic defence, pleads guilty despite her tears, and is sent to jail. On his release, seeing his wives waiting for him, he takes the back exit, only to be followed by Miss Chesterman who orders him into her car until he obeys her.

The film's intricately staged opening suggests its interest in the destabilization of motive and identity. Built around Harrison's puzzled subjectivity as he amnesically wakes in what seems a Mediterranean setting but resolves into a Welsh one,[10] it has him peering at himself interrogatively in a mirror, an action repeated throughout the narrative. If Vivian in *The Rake's Progress* is constituted as an enigma, here Harrison is the subject of a trial to decide who and what he is, the darker possibilities of which assail him, as when he finds a lost property ticket from Charing Cross station and claims a huge trunk, which in the traditions of the English domestic murder he obviously thinks contains a female body. The sequence ends in comic relaxation when he finds inside it a set of upper-class costume changes, much decorated army *and* naval uniforms, Eton *and* Harrow ties, markers of his shifting, but not of any essential, identity.

In *The Constant Husband* the male protagonist is radically split into desiring amoral (past) and condemning moral (present) selves. Such fissures and contradictions, though, are not limited to the hero. Like the women in *The Rake's Progress*, the women here both condemn and adore him. Different though they are, both the coolly aloof Monica and the sensuous Italian Lola prove to be, like all the rest (except for Monica's sceptical mother), willing victims, insisting when cross-examined that they would take him back. As Marcia Landy notes, Harrison is treated here in 'terms more often associated with women. He is presented as the object of desire, subject to the gaze of females, gazing at himself, fragmented in his many identitites, divided between mind and body, and seeking to escape the possessiveness and sexual desires of his pursuers'.[11] But the women too exhibit extreme instability, not just in simultaneously condemning and desiring the hero, but in being caught almost equally in paradoxes of contradictory 'maleness' and 'femaleness'. While the hero is conventionally hyper-'female' (in the time's most conventional sense) in his wish to be economically kept by his women instead of supporting them, the women too transgress the conventional binaries, Monica by her antithetical hyper-'masculine' insistence on being a 'career girl' and her self-flagellation for becoming 'emotionally dependent', and Lola by her extreme physical aggression. (Aptly enough, Lola – who is otherwise more associated with an almost claustrophobic sexual-domestic world – has a circus act which associates her with a phallic cannon.)

These cross-gendering ambiguities come to a head in Miss Chesterman's version of Monica's career priorities. Margaret Leighton, whose character's name sounds obvious sex-gender ambiguities, is a performer distinguished by somewhat harsh vocal and visual semiotics, here underlined by her 1950s version of power dressing, in which even the four rows of pearls arranged on her pale grey suit are rather minatory. These are abetted by her air of almost military authority, one manifestation of which is addressing Harrison by his surname ('Egerton' in the circumstances) in the male institutional style. His immediate response is 'sir', corrected to 'ma'am'. Although she constantly asserts his unworthiness, and refers to his victims scornfully ('this case is a monument to the inestimable folly of womankind'), she succumbs as quickly as the others, using her interview with him to complain wooingly about the difficulties of being a professional woman and cooing, 'Oh, how kind, thank you' when he merely hands her her bag. Her defence of him – though its arguments function beyond her motivations for using them – is an inversion of the familiar representation of the male judge swayed by a beautiful female defendant (cf. Raymond Huntley in *The Pure Hell of St Trinians*). Finally, she follows him as he leaves the prison, orders him into her car, and, presumably, is about to make him marry her. These final moments bring together, as well as the tensions around sex and morality which run through the film, the motifs of the irresistible but feminized male and the predatory masculinized female, in a particularly ironic and coolly puzzling variation.

*Only Two Can Play* (adapted from Kingsley Amis's novel *That*

*Uncertain Feeling*) combines an astringent version of romantic comedy with more various satire than in *The Constant Husband*, particularly of claustrophobic Welsh small-town life (an anti-pastoral to *Geordie* and *The Bridal Path*), parodic Welsh types and literary society. But at its centre is John Lewis's sexual–moral problematic, a conscience-troubled would-be rake, lying in bed surveying the stags on the wallpaper, designating himself 'a stag at bay'. The film is particularly rich, for a director modest about his visual abilities, in finding expressive correlatives for Lewis's entrapment: the narrow hall and stairway of the house; the three rooms the four Lewises live in; the shared malodorous bathroom.[12] Spatial combines with erotic claustrophobia, with the library prologue catching Lewis variously trapped and framed behind the barriers of bookcases as desirable women approach. Soon after, Mrs Gryffd Williams's visit to the library finds Lewis haunted by his grotesque doppelgänger, the appropriately named Mr Hyman (Graham Stark) with his 'eggstained' copies of the books most nearly approaching erotica in the Aberdarcy library, whom Lewis jostles aside in order to get a view of Elizabeth arriving. In another variation on the framing entrapment of those early images, Lewis is stationed behind a wall and wire netting voyeuristically watching a couple of nubile girls playing tennis. Entering and leaving his rented house, he has to squeeze around the courting couple at the gate. Yet another highly composed variation has Lewis with Ieuan (Kenneth Griffiths) in an overcrowded bus in extreme tantalizing proximity to a tarty blonde girl, unable to move his arms for fear of touching her. These images of constrained desire embody both his sense of entrapment and his split psyche, his desire and his simultaneous attempt not to be 'immoral'. The accidents that prevent the consummation of his desire for Elizabeth (Mai Zetterling), first the unexpected return of husband and colleagues, then the cow invading the car when parked in a field, have that half sense of being somehow psychically called up by his 'moral' while cursed by his 'immoral' self.

One may well agree with Roger Lewis's analysis of the extra-ordinariness of Sellers at the centre of the film, and of the way the intuitive depths of his performance actually recover elements of the novel dropped from the film.[13] However, this performance is enabled in all sorts of ways by narrative and visual devices. This can be illustrated throughout the sequence where Elizabeth drives him home and they go to bed, only to be interrupted by her husband's return. From the beginning, with her driving her car to her house, and the whole enterprise proceeding according to her plan, Lewis is secondarized, his masculinity impugned. This secondarization is increased by his social inferiority in the grand upper-middle-class surroundings of the adultery to be. Ordered to follow her upstairs with drinks, he then is made to wait, while she changes, in the bathroom with its extension of Vernon, her husband's, gymnasium. These sites of the body, where Elizabeth seems to want to have sex (and which are given comically threatening inflections first in Sellers's mishap with the rowing machine, then in her joking remark suggesting that she bought it to hasten her husband's death), might seem particularly in tune with Lewis's rakehell self-image, but he finds them distressing because his own predatoriness needs a veil of romanticism. When he and Elizabeth smoke a precoital cigarette, Lewis lights two simultaneously, while talking about his memory of Paul Henreid doing it for Bette Davis in *Now Voyager*. She replies by remembering it being done for her by a Major in midwinter in Rhyll during the war. In her version the cold freezes the cigarettes to his lips, resulting in a lot of bleeding. The scene subtly adds to Lewis's discomfort by rewriting his romantic Hollywood image with one less romantic, indeed minatory in its tearing of the male figure's mouth. Finally she makes her confession (putting Lewis's self-vaunting amorality in the shade) that she 'loved the war' and cried the day it ended. On Vernon's return to the house the ensuing farce is replete with telling details: Elizabeth's impatient kicking of Lewis as he scrambles for the cigarettes, her commanding use of the phrase 'buzz off', and Lewis, who performs impersonations throughout the film for others' and his own applause, burlesquing his social inferiority and his position in the relationship with Elizabeth, as, in order to escape, he impersonates a butler, then a plumber.

Various connections (thematics of desire, morality, the hero's divided self, parallel female divisions spread across his wife, Jean/

Virginia Maskell, and Elizabeth, female aggression and dominance, masculine fragmentation and imprisonment) can be traced between the last of the series and its predecessors. The primary critique made of the film (by Amis, who otherwise commended it) was its fudging of the issue of 'the fuck' which, evaded through accidents in the film, happened in the novel, becoming the catalyst for complex observations relating to the hero's view of himself.[14] The film's shortcoming in this respect was due, no doubt, to romantic comic conventions of the time, which preferred a hero less compromised in his moral stance at the end. However, at another level, the ending (Gilliat's revision of Bryan Forbes's script)[15] pursues ambiguities relating to the hero's desire and reform. The film's coda finds Lewis, after he has refused the job that goes hand in hand with being Elizabeth's lover, less because of his wife, Jean, than because of Elizabeth's dominating control of him, working in a mobile library van, rejecting the approach of a forward borrower. As the encounter ends, it turns out that he is not alone. Jean enters the scene from below, and they discuss his progress in rejecting propositions. The film closes with the couple driving home in the L-plate-sporting mobile library. Significantly, this last scene, though granting a (slightly provisional) conventional happy ending, takes place in a highly constricted space, as does the previous moment of Lewis's reconciliation with Jean, on their knees, picking up cigarettes, hemmed in by furniture. The implications of a situation where the hero's virtue is guaranteed by his not being in any location long enough to transgress, and where his progress is monitored by the unremitting presence of his wife, leave Lewis's crisis of desire and morality unresolved.

## Boulting via Ealing

Three films, *Lady Godiva Rides Again* (Launder, 1952), *Folly to be Wise* (Launder, 1953) and *Left, Right and Centre* (Gilliat, 1959), comprise a trilogy of satiric social comedies which gain definition against the most characteristic tendencies of the best-known comedy producers of the early postwar period, Ealing Studios and the Boulting Brothers. To type the former as wholly affirmative (extracting that strand Barr defines as a '"daydream" – of universal benevolence')[16] and the latter as wholly satirical is to oversimplify, but the exaggeration indicates significant tendencies. If the Launder and Gilliat comedies fall between, this is not because they are luke-warmly neither one thing nor the other, but rather, at their best, register a tension between Ealingesque communality, optimistic but growingly nostalgic, and a contrary, and in the end stronger, pull towards the harsher world of the major Boulting comedies (*I'm All Right Jack* and *Heavens Above*). Less able to assert optimism than Ealing, they are less eager to take the jaundiced view than the Boultings, but find themselves unable to do otherwise.

*Folly to be Wise* is the richest of the three, its satire complicated by complicit familiarity with the insufficiencies of the high-middle-class hegemony whose intimations of breakdown it dramatizes. The Reverend Paris (another key role for Sim) is that most secular of religious figures the army padre. As entertainments officer he is also responsible for the cultural uplift of a garrison more interested in beer than culture. After numerous ill-attended con-certs, he decides to mimic the famous BBC programme 'Any Questions' ('The Brains Trust'), with himself in the controlling position of questionmaster. Beginning in 1941, the show was an institution of wartime broadcasting (gaining Sunday and Tuesday audiences of over 6 million and over 5 million respectively),[17] with panel members who became household names – C. E. M. Joad, Julian Huxley, Commander Campbell. Its remit, according to Howard Thomas, its inventor, was 'to present useful knowledge in its lightest form and to gain the interest of the more thoughtful members of HM Forces'.[18] The film keeps, even in its postwar setting, the army camp background of its source, James Bridie's drama, bringing into play connotations of (1) a very male-controlled institution, (2) an institution hierarchically divided into lower-class ranks presided over by middle-class officers, and (3) an institution not given to self-questioning of its hierarchies. All these elements continue in the postwar setting, except that, as sometimes in Launder and Gilliat, the army context also has echoes of (4) the radicalism associated with the war and the 'mobile woman', since it is a young servicewoman, Jessie Killigrew (Janet

Brown), whose question throws the panel into disarray: 'Is marriage a good idea and, if it is, what's the best way to choose a partner?'

When Paris chooses the panel he symptomatically largely follows the recommendations of the local aristocrat, Lady Dodds (Martita Hunt) whose only interests are canine–conservative. The visit to the locality of Professor J. F. X. Mutch (Colin Gordon) provides one panel member. His friends, the children's writer Angela Prout (Elizabeth Allan) and her husband George Prout (Roland Culver), an artist, add two more, though the fact that Mutch and Angela are hovering on the brink of an adulterous affair will create major complications later. The panel is completed by Lady Dodds, a deaf elderly gentlemanly general practitioner (Miles Malleson) – a burlesque of the real-life show's 'eminent physician' (Lord Moran) – and the local Labour MP (Edward Chapman), whose presence reflects postwar changes.

Paralleling the vetting of religious and political questions on the real-life show, Paris censors the questions submitted, omitting any touching on religion, politics or 'smut'.[19] Complications arise when Jessie (Janet Brown), Paris's assistant, and engaged to a gormless soldier, Walter, worrying about her lack of education and her forthcoming marriage to a man clearly her intellectual inferior, smuggles her question about marriage into the performance. This catalyses the panel's tensions (particularly those of Mutch and the Prouts) into uninhibited confessional and near violence, much to the audience's joy and the horror of Paris, faced with an out of control debate about love and marriage. Torn between liberal niceness and authoritarian desires to close the debate down, swinging between attempts to soothe and propensities to panic, Paris/Sim virtuosically embodies the last attempt of the old-style liberal-authoritarian dispensation to hand down knowledge and control society. As the debate rages he attempts ineffectually to stem the flow, trying to enforce judgements like the inappropriateness of 'Holy Matrimony' being discussed in front of 'mixed audiences', appealing to phrases like 'play the game', at one point actually driven to physically assaulting one of the panellists, and finally, face buried in hands, turned away from them and the audience in catastrophic defeat. (At the film's beginning the thinness of his commitment to the intellect and the arts is marvellously exposed by the way that, though he mugs bodily rapture to the quartet's rhythms, first waving a pencil, then jerking a bony knee, finally convulsively beating time with a sheet of paper, he keeps mistaking pauses for the end, rising to applaud prematurely).

The narrative patches together an ending out of disorder. Mutch and Angela run off together; George drives off, to commit suicide everyone mistakenly thinks; and the chaos that ensues resolves when Mutch gets cold feet about commitment, the Prouts are reunited, Jessie decides she does love Walter, and Sim returns chastened to concerts by the May Savitt Qualthrope Quartet. The closure hardly pretends to resolve the problems raised, and in particular Jessie's decision to marry the drippy Walter, brought on by her pride in his being stirred to a long speech crystallizing his opinions about 'blokes' and 'judies', registers uneasily.

If the complexity of *Folly to be Wise* is encapsulated in Paris/ Sim's unsuccessful attempt to impose Ealing on Boulting, the other two 'state of the nation' films, *Lady Godiva Rides Again* (set during the 1951 Festival of Britain) and the later *Left, Right and Centre*, move to the Boulting pole, without attempting to resurrect vanished certainties, but also without any sense of alternative positive routes available, which creates an air of regret not found in the Boultings' exhilarating nihilism. (Paris's visions of a higher culture are highly compromised and comically exposed, but at least they are inept gestures beyond consumerism.) The more rewarding of the two films, *Lady Godiva Rides Again*, while never as biting as *I'm All Right, Jack* and *Heavens Above*, in fact invents what later becomes a trademark of Boulting satire, in its opening montage of a claustrophobic, cultureless British life enclosed by the horrors of a wet old-style British Sunday, later varied in *Left, Right and Centre*'s parody of the apathetic by-election voters. *Lady Godiva*'s only postwar equivalent of the female mobility of *Millions Like Us*, for Marjorie Clark/Pauline Stroud (a minimally talented, only faintly pretty girl, unkindly juxtaposed with Kay Kendall, Dagmar Wynter and Diana Dors) is via a beauty contest which she accidentally wins, becoming 'Miss Fascination Soap' and gaining a worthless place at a parody of the Rank Charm School. Predictably she fails to make the screen, but unlike Jessie in *Folly to be Wise* she manages, accidentally, to get rid of her lower-class boyfriend (George Cole) and escape to a life as mother and housewife with John McCallum in Queensland. (This was the high period of emigration to Australia.) The portrait of English lower-middle-class/working-class life ten years on from *Millions Like Us* is discouraging. The petit bourgeois restrictiveness of her newsagent parents' (Gladys Henson, Stanley Holloway) homelife; her more vivacious americanophile sister, Kay Kendall's, resentment at her lot (the first sound in the narrative is her husband belching); the tackiness of the beauty-contest world that seems to offer Marjorie a way out of routine entrapment; the portrait of a failing film industry; the old-style nude revue 'L'Amour the Merrier' in which the heroine is reduced to reprising her Lady Godiva role – all these make her eventual escape to Australia a relief.

*Left, Right and Centre*'s epigraph 'A plague o' both your houses' feels less like a searching parody of both left and right than statutory equal airtime for the 1959 general election which it attempted to exploit, balancing the mildest satirical points emerging from the complications that ensue when the by-election's male Tory and female Labour candidates fall in love. The tensions of this situation are abandoned rather than resolved when the Tory, Robert Wilton (Ian Carmichael), having defeated his wife to be, who is clearly the more capable political figure, is prevented from taking his seat by inheriting his uncle's title. Where a more perceptive critique comes into play is in the film's focusing on the growing mediatization of politics as Carmichael (reprising his Boulting middle-class innocent abroad) is made a candidate solely because he is a minor television personality. As in the properly more celebrated film of the same year, *I'm All Right, Jack*, real-life early television celebrities appear, and one of them, Gilbert Harding, when discussing with Robert his chances in the by-election, asks if the opposition candidate has appeared on television. When told no, he says she hasn't a chance.

If one way of looking at the three films together is through the frame of Ealing and Boulting, a second is through the young females at their centres, and a third is through the shifting roles enacted by the film-makers' paradigmatic comedian, Alastair Sim. Jessie, Margery and Stella (Patricia Bredin), the Labour candidate in *Left, Right and Centre*, exist in distant relationship to Celia in *Millions*, all three lowish-class young women attempting some kind of mobility, some bettering of their situation, Jessie by education, Marjorie through somewhat pathetic attempts at glamour, and Stella, the most highpowered and successful of them, through politics. Each is defeated – though Jessie is at least the most questioning voice of her film – whether by their own weaknesses, the postwar structures they inhabit, or, in the case of the most compromised of the films, *Left, Right and Centre*, low-level comic plot machinations that don't even grant Stella a continuing disagreement (like the one Amanda is famously allowed with Adam in *Adam's Rib*). Sim's progression/regression through the films is from the defeated centrality of *Folly to be Wise* to more marginal or compromisedly surviving figures. In *Lady Godiva* his position has shrunk to that of the British film producer Murington, too bankrupt to offer Marjorie a part in any film and quoting Walter Savage Landor elegaically (of the gas fire, but also much else) 'It sinks and I am ready to depart', while in *Left, Right and Centre* he has become the ultimate pragmatist, Lord Wilcot, whose response to a changing England is to shift himself into political neutrality and turn his stately home (the conversion of these into commercial enterprises was much in the news) into a vulgarized heritage Britain: peepshow machines with sex in 3D and a bed in which Queen Elizabeth I slept, in which visitors can also sleep, with prices advertised in dollars as well as guineas.

## Healing studios: the Scottish pastorals

Where the 'state of England' films create their comedy out of material more than tinged with the dystopic, and the sophisticated sex comedies tease certainties of morality and identity, the two Celtic Fringe Scottish comedies, *Geordie* and *The Bridal Path*, enact more utopian scenarios. The plots of both are simple, and beneath their variations play on the same complexly enfolded desires and nostalgias. In *Geordie*, a runtish highland lad, 'wee'

Geordie McTaggart (Bill Travers in his grown-up form), son of the laird's (Alastair Sim's) gamekeeper, follows a bodybuilding regime, wins a local Highland Games hammerthrowing competition, and is plucked out of obscurity to represent Britain at the 1956 Melbourne Olympics. (The film was released about a year before them.) Stricken with homesickness in the Antipodes, he seems about to fail ignominiously. But, on his final throw, translating the reality around him back to his native hills and glens, and remembering his girlfriend Jean's cry of 'Come away ma wee Geordie', he wins, immediately retires, and returns (despite amorous half-complications) to his home, semi-feudal job and sweetheart, Jean (Norah Gorsen), rejecting the advances of a statuesque Danish athlete, Helga (Doris Goddard) whose gigantism might represent femininity ominously aspiring to male equivalence.

Geordie is played by the hulkingly gentle and pleasant Bill Travers who, in the second of the films, as Ewan McEwan, is sent by the elders of his Hebridean island to find himself a wife on the Scottish mainland after the chief elder has banned marriages to cousins because of the ill effects of 'the consanguinity' – inbreeding that has led to several islanders being confined in asylums. Like Geordie he leaves behind a faithful girlfriend, his cousin, Katie (Fiona Cryne), though, even more innocent than Geordie, he seems unaware of her interest in him. Armed with a list of desirable female qualities (strong arms and legs for carrying and walking up hills, hips for childbearing) and a list of prohibitions (no English, Irish, Welsh, widows, etc.) Ewan sets out on his quest. In it he has a large number of encounters, all of which end in comic failure, is mistaken for a criminal from Glasgow (the shadow of urban Scotland/Britain/England), and is pursued and captured by the police. Escaping, he gets back to his island where a convenient plot revelation places him in the same final position as Geordie. The girl next door (or in this case sharing his own house, helping him look after children he has inherited from a dead sister) is proved not to be ultra-consanguineous by her mother's confession of a long-ago adultery, and Ewan eventually recognizes true love. (In fact the couple seem determined to ignore the dangers of consanguinity anyway.)

Like other film-makers in the British cinema attracted to the Celtic Fringe, Launder and Gilliat find Scotland a much less fraught site than Ireland. In both of Launder and Gilliat's Irish films the rural beauties of Ballygarry and County Mayo are always shadowed by violent politics, more intractable in the quiet backwaters than in cosmopolitan Dublin. Their Scotland is rural (not the undesired urban, which for an English or American audience is only another version of their own reality): in *Geordie* the Highlands, in *The Bridal Path* the Western Isles, the latter doubly removed from mainland Scotland let alone mainland England. Like other idyllic representations of Scotland in the English/British cinema it has complex, ambivalent meanings. On the one hand it is different from England. Here even the weather can be celebrated as Geordie misses the Highland rains and mists in Australia, and when Geordie insists on wearing his father's kilt in the opening procession of the Games it not only marks non-homogenized difference but the strength of traditional family ties dissipated in modern 'hot' societies. On the other hand, though, rural Scotland is also a metaphor for a pastoral England of the mind, all that England is conceived to have lost through urbanization and industrialization. In addition it is a more extreme version of what postwar England has become, or is feared to have become, a small, vestigial nation without world power and influence, but with the consolation of its own proud quiddity.

In *Geordie*, where England plays a more overt role (in *The Bridal Path* geographically the film gets no further than Oban and there is only one English character), this is self-consciously registered. As a boy Geordie, when reciting Sampson's mantra about the 'English bulldog breed', substitutes 'Scottish' for 'English'. Later, when the very Home Counties English British team selectors, Raymond Huntley and his colleague, tell Geordie that he will be throwing at Melbourne for 'England', Geordie corrects it to 'Scotland', while the laird intercedes with the median term, 'Britain'. There's a slightly harsh piece of comedy as, driving back South, the two English Olympic selectors laughingly imitate Geordie's accent. However, when the crisis over the wearing of the kilt reaches its climax, involving also the English aristocrat Lord

Paunceton (Miles Malleson), the originally stuffy English trio's role changes. As the question of whether Geordie can parade in his kilt is referred back to the British (English) Olympic Committee in London – their negative arriving only after Geordie is already marching – there is a perfect example of how the 'good' English become affiliated to the idealized Scottish, while another party becomes the 'bad' English onto whom are shifted their previously dominant overbearing, authoritarian, over-conventional qualities. Thus the representation of Scotland has, over and above nostalgia for a disappearing pastoral culture, two functions – the assertion of Scottish individuality within Britain, and the assertion of English/British individuality within the wider world.

*Geordie* was a topical film catching public interest in what was only the third postwar Olympic Games and the first in the Southern hemisphere. Its fantasy of a Briton winning the hammer throw was exceedingly unlikely. The event was massively dominated by Eastern Europeans (though an American, Harold Connolly, won in 1956), and Britain's modern record in throwing events was dismal. The fantasy here is of a society, now beginning to perceive itself as a weakling among giants, to the US and the major powers of Europe as Scotland is to England, triumphing, and in triumphing asserting its individuality, its difference, its amateurism in a growingly professional world. Geordie, when his talent is first discovered by the laird and the minister, even has to be convinced, against his intuition, of the virtues of competition.

Whereas *Geordie* cosmopolitanly moves from the Highlands to England to Melbourne and back, *The Bridal Path*'s quest takes Ewan only as far as Oban on the North West coast of Scotland. The only mention of Glasgow is of its criminals making forays into Oban, and London is completely out of sight. Ewan's quest highlights a thematic that relates to *Geordie*'s: the question of 'consanguinity', which, concretized in his hunt for a wife, relates more widely to questions of change – getting a wife from the mainland (i.e. interacting with greater entities, with the readjustments that that will force) or marrying one's cousin back on the island (i.e. staying as one has traditionally been). The placing of this conflict in the almost fairytale region of the Western Isles (a much less real site than Kirta, the island in Powell's *Edge of the World*, where the reality of depopulation is enacted, and with less danger in the fantasies than in either Powell and Pressburger's *I Know Where I'm Going* (1945) or MacKendrick's *Whisky Galore* (1948)) allows the question to be simplified, partly disavowed, pastoralized, experienced pleasurably rather than anxiously. However, both texts' simplicities are artful and barbs of reality snag the paradise. The small societies appeal in their face-to-face relations (Stanley Baxter, playing the postman, does his rounds when Geordie is a child and is still doing them twelve years later) but, on the other hand, Sim's laird in *Geordie*, even if relations with him are more personalized than those in an industrialized society, is a whimsically authoritarian feudalist; three over-con-sanguineous islanders have been removed from Ewan's island to asylums; and the marriage-enabling plot resolution of *The Bridal Path* depends on the revelation of a wife committing adultery while her husband was absent, which suggests that the pastoral idyll does not dissolve all sexual tensions. Oban, which borders on the fairytale, seems to have its full share of the sexually devious and neurotic as Ewan meets them. Further, Siona, the last woman that Ewan meets, wants to head back to Ewan's island with him, but only so that she can catch a boat to the mainland to elope with her American serviceman, a Jehovah's Witness! The prognos-tications for this relationship don't seem optimistic, but Siona's flight suggests that the Western Isles and Highlands (which are filmed in considerable muted beauty) aren't necessarily viewed as paradisically by their inhabitants as by those who imagine them.

## Notes

1 See Brown, *Launder and Gilliat*, p. 20.
2 See the discussion in Charles Barr, *English Hitchcock* (Cameron & Hollis, Moffat, 1999), pp. 190–202.
3 MacDonald, 'Interview with Sidney Gilliat', pp. 128–30 and 143–4 (*The Lady Vanishes*); pp. 138–9 (German cinema).
4 E.g. Brown, *Launder and Gilliat*, pp. 119, 155.
5 Shakespeare, *A Midsummer Night's Dream*, V.I.17–20.
6 Brown, *Launder and Gilliat*, p. 126.

7 See ibid., regarding the American release and Gilliat's work on it for Harry Cohn.

8 See Chapter 1, note 44.

9 Robert Murphy, *Sixties British Cinema* (BFI, London, 1992), pp. 221–2.

10 Cf. the opening of *Two Thousand Women*.

11 Landy, *British Genres*, p. 283.

12 See on the bathroom Roger Lewis, *The Life and Death of Peter Sellers* (Arrow Books, London, 1995), p. 738.

13 Lewis, *The Life and Death of Peter Sellers*, p. 735.

14 *The New Review Anthology*, ed. Ian Hamilton (London, 1985), p. 55.

15 Brown, *Launder and Gilliat*, pp. 147–8.

16 Barr, *Ealing Studios*, p. 83.

17 Hugh Thomas, *With an Independent Air* (Weidenfeld & Nicolson, London, 1977), p. 76.

18 Thomas, *With an Independent Air*, p. 70.

19 Ibid., pp. 82–3.

# Last words

## 6

Two brief anecdotes. When I was half way through this book, a friend, a notable figure in British film criticism asked me, in a spirit of friendly enquiry, whether I was going to prove that Launder and Gilliat were great film-makers. I mumbled something inept about feeling that *Millions Like Us* was a great film, whatever that meant, though in some ways not particularly characteristic of their work, and that a lot of their other films were, at the least, enormously interesting. On another occasion, when I had contacted another distinguished critic about some matter to do with the pair, that critic, whose detailed knowledge of the biographies of Launder and Gilliat far outstripped my own, expressed interest in the list of films that I'd chosen to highlight, noting, however, that Gilliat might have found one of the choices (*The Story of Gilbert and Sullivan*) strange. I replied, again rather ineptly, that I knew Gilliat might not have approved but that I found the film fascinating and a case of 'trust the tale and not the teller'.

Thinking about these two encounters, the second seems to me to show that the body of work produced by Launder and Gilliat is large and various enough to lead to distinct differences of interpretation and evaluation, and also that the particular films are complex enough to escape ranking exactly as their authors saw them. Both points argue a richness and variety in the output and in individual films that make them open to different approaches and different historical priorities. Part of my point about *The Story of Gilbert and Sullivan* was that Mike Leigh's reworking of it in

*Topsy-Turvy*, Geoffrey O'Brien's praise of it, and now I hope my own discussion, have created a shift of circumstances in which its virtues might reappear and be redefined. In this book changing ways of seeing are suggested as having brought certain slightly submerged films such as *Two Thousand Women*, *The Rake's Progress* and *I See a Dark Stranger* into prominence through new or revived perspectives, and as having the ability to add to the significances of better-known films such as *Millions Like Us* and *The Happiest Days of Your Life*. Such shifts – for example, the new accents of feminism, emphasis on the complications of masculinity in the cinema, the impact of placing the films within larger generic categories (as in Landy's *British Genres*) – are likely to give way to, or be supplemented by, other dominant paradigms, but what has been revealed makes it unlikely that these and some other of the films will lapse from centrality. It may be possible to imagine a time when World War II, the complex changes enacted in it and in its aftermath, and a world of familiar types and tensions given lasting comic and melodramatic expression in Launder and Gilliat's films, could lose all meaning for British audiences, but until then I find it difficult to imagine that *Millions Like Us*, *The Rake's Progress*, *The Happiest Days of Your Life* and a number of the other films discussed here could lose their interest and their power to give pleasure. I remember from childhood my father's pleasure in *Folly to be Wise* when our family saw it in the early 1950s. I am sure that his delight in it partly derived from an intimate recognition of World War II and immediate postwar experiences that I have no direct access to, and can only reconstruct and hypothesize. My own pleasure in the film now is in many ways very different from his, informed by different histories and questions, and yet the film has survived to be both *Cinéma du papa* and *Cinéma du fils*, a domestic and personal version of larger movements, discontinuities and continuities.

The question whether Launder and Gilliat were great film-makers is more likely to be uttered informally than textually, for reasons that most people reading this book will understand – on the one hand the very different frameworks within which evalua-tion takes place, on the other the suspicion that an approach basically concerned with evaluation tends to neglect analysis in favour of statements of immutable value. At the same time we do utter and answer such questions informally, and know that our own critical practice, in particular what we choose to devote our analytical energies to, is usually underpinned by implicit positive valuations. In my introduction I used carefully constructed words, meant to do justice both to the films I have treated at length in this book as well as what seem to me lesser works, and the minority I wouldn't easily bring myself to revisit: 'more than ordinary filmmakers, touched with genius in perhaps half a dozen films, and with more than common abilities in many others', and this remains for me an appropriate definition. Even if one takes the least evaluative context possible – or the most minimal and basic one – that, whatever the varying quality of its individual films, the British cinema is an object of great interest, culturally and aesthetically, it is difficult to imagine a study of its output from the 1930s to the 1960s in which Launder and Gilliat would not be important figures. To wander through Brown's filmography is to see them at the hub of British film over a long period, so much so that they seem to hold within themselves a majority of the tendencies – positive and negative – of the feature film world around them in a time which (at least through the 1940s) was one of few indubitably major periods of British film-making. Like the *Mail*'s critic of 1947 in his facetious classroom analogy quoted in Chapter 1, we may place them below a few exceptional figures (Hitchcock, Powell and Pressburger, Lean), and think of odd important movements to which they did not contribute – e.g. Gainsborough costume drama and the woman's film of the later 1940s, though they worked at Gainsborough, and their own female-centred films surely had some influence on later melodramas. But to have been central to so much, and to have made films which half a century later not only continue to intrigue and satisfy the analyst but are also constantly revived and viewed with pleasure on the great repertory of television, is epitaph enough.

# Filmography

This list includes the films from *Millions Like Us* onwards, plus eleven
key earlier films written by Launder and Gilliat, or by one of the pair.
For a full filmography see Geoff Brown, *Launder and Gilliat* (BFI,
London, 1977). The credits are based on Brown's, but are sometimes
in shortened form, especially in the case of films not foregrounded in
the text. The date given is of general release.

## Pre *Millions Like Us*

### *Rome Express* 6 February 1933, 94 mins

Director: Walter Forde
Production company: Gaumont British
Producer: Michael Balcon
Scenario/additional dialogue: Sidney Gilliat
Story: Clifford Grey
Dialogue: Frank Vosper, Ralph Stock
Photography: Gunther Krampf
Editors: Frederick Y. Smith, Ian Dalrymple
Art director: Andrew Mazzei
Costumes: Gordon Conway
Sound editors: George Gunn, S. A. Jolly
Cast: Conrad Veidt (Zurta), Harold Huth (George Grant), Gordon
    Harker (Tom Bishop), Donald Calthrop (Poole), Joan Barry (Mrs
    Maxted), Esther Ralston (Asta Marvelle), Cedric Hardwicke (Alastair
    McBane), Frank Vosper (Inspector Jolif), Hugh Williams (Tony),
    Muriel Aked (Spinster), Finlay Currie (Sam), Eliot Makeham (Mills)

## Seven Sinners 2 August 1936, 70 mins

Director: Albert de Courville
Production company: Gaumont British
Scenario: Sidney Gilliat, Frank Launder
Adaptation: L. du Garde Peach
Photography: Mutz Greenbaum
Editor: M. Gordon
Art director: Erno Metzner
Music: Bretton Byrd
Music director: Louis Levy
Sound recording: A. Birch
Wardrobe: Marianne
Costumes: Molyneux
Cast: Edmund Lowe (Harwood), Constance Cummings (Caryl Fenton), Thomy Bourdelle (Paul Tourbé), Henry Oscar (Axel Hoyte), Felix Aylmer (Sir Charles Webber), Joyce Kennedy (Elizabeth Wentworth), O. B. Clarence (Registrar), Mark Lester (Chief Constable), Allen Jeayes (Wagner), Anthony Holles (Reception Clerk), David Horne (Hotel Manager), Edwin Laurence (Guildhall Guide), James Harcourt (Vicar)

## A Yank at Oxford 5 September 1938, 105 mins

Director: Jack Conway
Production company: Metro-Goldwyn-Mayer British Pictures
Producer: Michael Balcon
Story: Sidney Gilliat, Michael Hogan
Original idea: J. Monk Saunders
Scenario: Leon Gordon, Roland Pertwee
Additional dialogue: Malcolm Stuart Boylan, Walter Ferris, George Oppenheimer
Photography: Harold Rosson, Cyril Knowles
Supervising editor: Margaret Booth
Editor: Charles Frend
Music director: Herbert Bath
Sound recording: A. W. Watkins, C. C. Stevens
Costumes: Renée Hubert
Cast: Robert Taylor (Lee Sheridan), Lionel Barrymore (Dan Sheridan), Vivien Leigh (Elsa Craddock), Maureen O'Sullivan (Molly Beaumont), Edmund Gwenn (Dean of Cardinal College), Griffith Jones

(Paul Beaumont), C. V. France (Dean Snodgrass), Edward Rigby (Scatters), Morton Selten (Elderly Passenger), Claude Gillingwater (Ben Dalton), Tully Marshall (Cephas), Robert Coote (Wavertree), Peter Croft (Ramsey), Walter Kingsford (Dean Williams), Noel Howlett (Tom Craddock), Edmond Breon (Captain Wavertree), Norah Howard (Barmaid), Ronald Shiner (Mechanic), Sid Saylor (Newspaper Printer), Doodles Weaver (Reporter at Track), Richard Wattis (Student), Jon Pertwee, Kenneth Villiers

### *The Lady Vanishes* 2 January 1939, 98 mins

Director: Alfred Hitchcock
Production company: Gainsborough Pictures
Producer: Edward Black
Based on the novel *The Wheel Spins* by Ethel Lina White
Scenario: Sidney Gilliat, Frank Launder
[Script] continuity: Alma Reville
Photography: Jack Cox
Supervising editor: R. E. Dearing
Editor: Alfred Roome
Art director: Vetchinsky
Music director: Louis Levy
Music: Cecil Milner
Sound recording: S. Wiles
Cast: Margaret Lockwood (Iris Henderson), Michael Redgrave (Gilbert), Paul Lukas (Dr Hartz), Dame May Whitty (Miss Froy), Cecil Parker (Mr Todhunter), Linden Travers ('Mrs' Todhunter), Naunton Wayne (Caldicott), Basil Radford (Charters), Mary Clare (Baroness), Emile Boreo (Hotel Manager), Googie Withers (Blanche), Sally Stewart (Julie), Philip Leaver (Signor Doppo), Zelma Vas Dias (Signora Doppo), Catherine Lacey (The Nun), Josephine Wilson (Madame Kummer), Charles Oliver (The Officer), Kathleen Tremaine (Anna)

### *Jamaica Inn* 16 October 1939, 108 mins

Director: Alfred Hitchcock
Production company: Mayflower Pictures. A Pommer-Laughton Production
Producer: Erich Pommer

Scenario: Sidney Gilliat, Joan Harrison
Based on the novel by Daphne du Maurier
Dialogue: Sidney Gilliat
Additional dialogue: J. B. Priestley
[Script] continuity: Alma Reville
Photography: Harry Stradling, Bernard Knowles
Editor: Robert Hamer
Music: Eric Fenby
Sound recording: Jack Rogerson
Costume supervisor: Yvonne Caffin
Cast: Charles Laughton (Sir Humphrey Pengallan), Maureen O'Hara
    (Mary Yellard), Robert Newton (Jem Trehearne), Leslie Banks (Joss
    Merlyn), Marie Ney (Patience Merlyn), Emlyn Williams (Harry the
    Pedlar), Wylie Watson (Salvation Watkins), Morland Graham (Sea
    Lawyer Sydney), Edwin Greenwood (Dandy), Mervyn Johns
    (Thomas), Stephen Haggard (The Boy), Horace Hodges (Chad-
    wick, Pengallan's Butler), Hay Petrie (Sam, the Groom), Frederick
    Piper (Davis, Pengallan's Agent), Herbert Lomas (Tenant), Clare
    Greet (Mrs Tremarney, Tenant), William Devlin (Tenant), Mabel
    Terry Lewis (Lady Beston), A. Bromley Davenport (Ringwood),
    George Curzon (Captain Murray), Basil Radford (Lord George)

## *Inspector Hornleigh on Holiday* 15 January 1940, 87 mins

Director: Walter Forde
Production company: Twentieth Century Productions
Producer: Edward Black
Based on the novel *Stolen Death* by Leo Grex and the radio series by
    Hans Wolfgang Priwin
Scenario: Frank Launder, Sidney Gilliat
Adaptation: J. O. C. Orton
Photography: John J. Cox
Editor: R. E. Deering
Art director: A. Vetchinsky
Music director: Louis Levy
Sound: S. G. Wiles
Cast: Gordon Harker (Inspector Hornleigh), Alastair Sim (Sergeant
    Bingham), Linden Travers (Miss Meadows), Wally Patch (Police
    Sergeant), Edward Chapman (Captain Fraser), Philip Leaver
    (Bradfield), Kynaston Reeves (Dr Manners), John Turnbull (Chief
    Constable), Wyndham Goldie (Sir George Winbeck)

### *Inspector Hornleigh Goes to It* 5 May 1940, 87 mins

Director: Walter Forde
Production company: Twentieth Century Productions
Producer: Edward Black
Story: Frank Launder
Based on the radio series by Hans Wolfgang Priwin
Photography: John J. Cox
Scenario: Val Guest, J. O. C. Orton
Supervising editor: R. E. Dearing
Editor: Alfred Roome
Art director: A. Vetchinsky
Music director: Louis Levy
Sound: S. G. Wiles
Cast: Gordon Harker (Inspector Hornleigh), Alastair Sim (Sergeant
    Bingham), Phyllis Calvert (Mrs Wilkinson), Edward Chapman (Mr
    Blenkinsop), Charles Oliver (Mr Wilkinson), Raymond Huntley
    (Dr Kerbishley), Percy Walsh (Inspector Blow), David Horne
    (Commissioner), Peter Gawthorne (Colonel), Wally Patch (Sergeant
    Major), Betty Jardine (Daisy), O. B. Clarence (Professor Mackenzie),
    John Salew (Mr Tomboy), Cyril Cusack (Night Mail Sorter)

### *Night Train to Munich* 24 June 1940, 95 mins

Director: Carol Reed
Production company: Twentieth Century Productions
Producer: Edward Black
Based on a story 'Report on a Fugitive' by Gordon Wellesley
Scenario: Sidney Gilliat, Frank Launder
Photography: Otto Kanturek
Supervising editor: R. E. Dearing
Editor: Michael Gordon
Art director: A. Vetchinsky
Music director: Louis Levy
Sound supervisor: B. C. Sewell
Cast: Margaret Lockwood (Anna Bomasch), Rex Harrison (Dickie
    Randall/'Gus Bennett'), Paul Henreid (Karl Marsen), Basil Radford
    (Charters), Naunton Wayne (Caldicott), James Harcourt (Axel Bo-
    masch), Felix Aylmer (Dr John Fredericks), Wyndham Goldie (Dryton),
    Roland Culver (Roberts), Eliot Makeham (Schwab), Raymond Huntley
    (Kampenfeldt), Austin Trevor (Captain Prada), Kenneth Kent

(Controller), C. V. France (Admiral Hassinger), Fritz Valk (Gestapo Officer), Irene Handl (Station Mistress), Billy Russell (Hitler)

## *Kipps* 30 June 1941, 108 mins

Director: Carol Reed
Production company: Twentieth Century Productions
Producer: Edward Black
Based on the novel by H. G. Wells
Scenario: Sidney Gilliat
Photography: Arthur Crabtree
Supervising editor: R. E. Dearing
Editor: Alfred Roome
Music: Charles Williams
Music director: Louis Levy
Art director: A. Vetchinsky
Costumes: Cecil Beaton
Sound: S. Wiles
Cast: Michael Redgrave (Kipps), Diana Wynyard (Helen Walsingham), Arthur Riscoe (Harry Chitterlow), Phyllis Calvert (Ann Pornick), Max Adrian (Chester Coote), Helen Haye (Mrs Walsingham), Michael Wilding (Ronnie Walsingham), Lloyd Pearson (Shalford), Edward Rigby (Buggins), Mackenzie Ward (Pearce), Hermione Baddeley (Miss Mergle), Betty Ann Davies (Flo Bates), Arthur Denton (Charshot), Betty Jardine (Doris), Frank Pettingell (Old Kipps), Beatrice Varley (Mrs Kipps), Philip Frost (Kipps as a Boy), Diana Calderwood (Ann Pornick as a Girl), George Carney (Old Pornick), Robert McCarthy (Sid Pornick), Irene Browne (Mrs Bindon-Botting), Peter Graves (Sidney Revel), Viscount Castleross (Man in Bath Chair), Kathleen Harrison, Felix Aylmer

## *Partners in Crime* June 1942, 8 mins

Directors: Frank Launder, Sidney Gilliat
Production company: Gainsborough Pictures, for the Ministry of Information
Producer: Edward Black
Scenario: Frank Launder, Sidney Gilliat
Photography: Jack Cox
Editor: Alfred Roome
Cast: Irene Handl (Mrs Wilson), Robert Morley (The Judge)

***The Young Mr Pitt*** 21 September 1942, 103 mins

Director: Carol Reed
Production company: Twentieth Century Productions (Gaumont British)
Producer: Edward Black
Scenario: Sidney Gilliat, Frank Launder
Dramatic narrative/additional dialogue: Rt Hon. Viscount Castlerosse
Photography: Frederick Young
Supervising editor: R. E. Dearing
Editor: Alfred Roome
Music: Charles Williams
Music director: Louis Levy
Art director: A. Vetchinsky
Sound editor: Eric Wood
Dress design/decor: Cecil Beaton
Costumes: Elizabeth Haffenden
Cast: Robert Donat (Earl of Chatham), Robert Morley (Charles James
    Fox), Phyllis Calvert (Eleanor Eden), John Mills (William Wilber-
    force), Raymond Lovell (George III), Max Adrian (Sheridan), Felix
    Aylmer (Lord North), Albert Lieven (Talleyrand), Stephen Haggard
    (Lord Nelson), Geoffrey Atkins (William Pitt as a Boy), Jean Cadell
    (Mrs Sparry), Agnes Lauchlan (Queen Charlotte), Ian McLean
    (Dundas), A. Bromley Davenport (Sir Evan Nepean), John Salew
    (Smith), Herbert Lom (Napoleon), Stuart Lindsell (Earl Spencer),
    Henry Hewitt (Addington), Frederick Culley (Sir William Farquhar),
    Leslie Bradley (Gentleman Jackson), Roy Emerton (Dan Mendoza),
    Hugh McDermott (Mr Melvill), Alfred Sangster (Lord Grenville),
    Leslie Dwyer (Servant), Frederick Leister (Lord Auckland), Ronald
    Shiner (Man in Stocks), Esme Cannon (Servant at Lord Auckland's
    House), Margaret Vyner (Duchess of Devonshire), Leo Genn
    (Danton), James Harcourt (Bellamy)

### *Millions Like Us* and beyond

 ***Millions Like Us*** 15 November 1943, 103 mins

Directors: Frank Launder, Sidney Gilliat
Production company: Gainsborough Pictures
Producer: Edward Black
Scenario: Frank Launder, Sidney Gilliat

Photography: Jack Cox, Roy Fogwell (2nd Unit)
Supervising editor: R. E. Dearing
Editor: Alfred Roome
Music director: Louis Levy
Art director: John Bryan
Sound supervisor: B. C. Sewell
Cast: Patricia Roc (Celia Crowson), Eric Portman (Charlie Forbes), Gordon Jackson (Fred Blake), Anne Crawford (Jennifer Knowles), Joy Shelton (Phyllis Crowson), Megs Jenkins (Gwen Price), Terry Randall (Annie Earnshaw), Basil Radford (Charters), Naunton Wayne (Caldicott), Moore Marriott (Jim Crowson), John Boxer (Tom Crowson), Valentine Dunn (Elsie Crowson), John Salew (Dr Gill), Hilda Davis (Miss Hodge), Irene Handl (Landlady), Angela Foulds (Megs), Terence Rhodes (Johnnie), Paul Drake (Handsome Young Man), Gordon Edwards (Wing Commander), John Wynn (Squadron Leader), Albert Chevalier and Frank Webster (Roof Spotters), Beatrice Varley (Miss Wells), Courtney Luck (Polish Officer), Amy Dalby (Mrs Bourne), John Schofield (George), Amy Veness (Mrs Blythe), Jack Vivyan (Sam), Arthur Denton (Ernie), Jonathan Field ('Ugly Youth'), Avis Scott (Alice), Clifford Cobbe ('Heavy Rescue'), Grace Allardyce (Mrs Hammond), Barry Steele (Percy Hoskins), Brenda Bruce (Brenda), Stanley Paskin (Warrant Officer), Hilda Davies (Labour Officer), Bertha Willmott (The Singer), John Slater (Man on Pier)

## *Two Thousand Women* 17 September 1944, 97 mins

Director: Frank Launder
Production company: Gainsborough Pictures
Producer: Edward Black
Scenario: Frank Launder
Additional dialogue: Michael Pertwee
Photography: Jack Cox
Supervising editor: R. E. Dearing
Editor: Charles Knott
Music director: Louis Levy
Incidental music: Hans May
Sound supervisor: B. C. Sewell
Art director: John Bryan
Costumes: Elizabeth Haffenden

Cast: Phyllis Calvert (Freda Thompson), Patricia Roc (Rosemary Brown), Flora Robson (Miss Manningford), Renée Houston (Maud Wright), Jean Kent (Bridie Johnson), Anne Crawford (Margaret Long), Reginald Purdell (Alec Harvey), James McKechnie (Jimmy Moore), Bob Arden (Dave Kennedy), Carl Jaffe (Sergeant Hentzner), Muriel Aked (Miss Meredith), Kathleen Boutall (Mrs Hatfield), Hilda Campbell-Russell (Mrs Hope Latimer), Christina Forbes (Frau Holweg), Thora Hird (Mrs Buttshaw), Dulcie Gray (Nellie Skinner), Betty Jardine (Teresa King), Christianne de Maurin (Annette), Guy Le Feuvre (Monsieur Boper), Joan Ingram (Mrs Tamarsh), Paul Sheridan (French Officer)

### *Waterloo Road* 12 January 1945, 76 mins

Director: Sidney Gilliat
Production company: Gainsborough Pictures
Producer: Edward Black
Scenario: Sidney Gilliat
Story: Val Valentine
Photography: Arthur Crabtree
Editor: Alfred Roome
Music director: Louis Levy
Sound supervisor: B. C. Sewell
Art director: A. Vetchinsky
Dress supervisor: Yvonne Caffin
Cast: John Mills (Jim Colter), Stewart Granger (Ted Purvis), Alastair Sim (Dr Montgomery), Joy Shelton (Tillie Colter), Beatrice Varley (Mrs Colter), Arthur Denton (Fred), Vera Francis (Vera), Leslie Bradley (Mike Duggan), Ben Williams (Corporal Lewis), George Carnet (Tom Mason), Anna Konstam (May), Dennis Harkin (Alf), Jean Kent (Toni), Johnny Schofield (Landlord), Frank Atkinson (Barman), Wylie Watson (Tattooist), Mike Johnson (Mugsy), Dave Crowley (Baked Beans), John Boxer (Policeman), George Merritt (A. R. P. Warden), Wallace Lupino (Tillie's Uncle), Amy Dalby (Tilly's Aunt), Nellie Bowman (Tillie's Mother)

## *Soldier, Sailor* 13 August 1945, 61 mins

Director: Alexander Shaw
Production company: Realist Film Unit, for the Ministry of Information
Producer: John Taylor
Scenario: Frank Launder
Film treatment: Leigh Clowes, Al Lloyd
Photography: A. E. Jeakins
Location photography: Raymond Elton
Editor: Jack Ellitt
Music: William Alwyn
Music director: Muir Mathieson
Art director: Edward Carrick
Sound recording: Jack Mary
Cast: Sergeant Ted Holliday (Bill, the Sergeant), Gun Layer Al Beres-
    ford (Mike, the Petty Officer), Engineer David Sime (David, the
    Second Engineer), Rosamund John (Rose), Jean Kent (Cigarette
    Girl), Charles Victor (Tacky), Jean Cadell (Mrs Church), George
    Carney (Mr Church), Bill Elliot (Cobber), Jimmy Plant (Captain),
    Jimmy Knight (First Officer), Neville Mapp (Second Officer), John
    Rae (Chief Engineer), Esme Lee (Oriental dancer), with Gunners of
    the Defensively Equipped Merchant Ships and Men of the New
    Zealand Expeditionary Force

## *The Rake's Progress* 31 December 1945, 124 mins

Director: Sidney Gilliat
Production company: Individual Pictures
Producers: Sidney Gilliat, Frank Launder
Story: Val Valentine
Scenario: Sidney Gilliat, Frank Launder
Photography: Wilkie Cooper
Editor: Thelma Myers
Music: William Alwyn
Production designer: David Rawnsley
Art director: Norman Arnold
Introductory drawings: Feliks Topolski
Sound supervisor: B. C. Sewell
Costumes: Yvonne Caffin
Cast: Rex Harrison (Vivian Kenway), Lilli Palmer (Rikki Krausner),
    Godfrey Tearle (Colonel Kenway), Griffith Jones (Sandy Duncan),

Margaret Johnston (Jennifer Calthrop), Guy Middleton (Fogroy), Jean Kent (Jill Duncan), Marie Lohr (Lady Angela Parks), Gary Marsh (Sir Hubert Parks), David Horne (Sir John Brockley), John Salew (Burgess), Alan Wheatley (Edwards), Brefni O'Rorke (Bromhead), Charles Victor (Old Sweat), Patrick Curwen (The Major), Joan Hickson (Miss Barker), Frank Ling (The Corporal), Joan Maude (Alice Duncan), Olga Lindo (Waitress in Palais de Danse), Patricia Laffan (Miss Fernandez), Howard Marion Crawford (Coldstream Guardsman), David Wallbridge (Vivian as a Boy), John Dodsworth (Team Manager), Emrys Jones (Bateson), Jack Vyvyan (Fred, the Mechanic), Frederick Burtwell (Magistrate), George Cross (Policeman), Kynaston Reeves (Dean), Sidney Gilliat (Voice of Pedro the Barman)

 *I See a Dark Stranger* 5 August 1946, 112 mins

Director: Frank Launder
Production company: Individual Pictures
Producers: Frank Launder, Sidney Gilliat
Story: Frank Launder, Sidney Gilliat, Wolfgang Wilhelm
Scenario: Frank Launder, Sidney Gilliat
Additional dialogue: Liam Redmond
Photography: Wilkie Cooper
Editor: Thelma Myers
Music: William Alwyn
Production designer: David Rawnsley
Art director: Norman Arnold
Sound recording: Stanley Lambourne
Wardrobe: Cathleen Moore
Cast: Deborah Kerr (Bridie Quilty), Trevor Howard (David Baynes), Raymond Huntley (Miller), W. O'Gorman (Danny Quilty), Harry Webster (Uncle Joe), Liam Redmond (Uncle Timothy), Eddie Golden (Terence Delaney), Marie Ault (Mrs O'Mara), Tony Quinn (Guide), Brefni O'Rorke (Michael Callaghan), John Salew (Man in Bookshop), James Harcourt (Grandfather), Olga Lindo (Mrs Edwards), Humphrey Heathcote (Sergeant Harry Harris), David Ward (Oscar Pryce), Kenneth Buckley (R. T. O.), David Tomlinson (Intelligence Officer), Michael Howard (Hawkins), Torin Thatcher (Policeman), Everley Gregg (First Woman on Train), Kathleen Boutall (Second Woman on Train), Katie Johnson (Old Lady on

Train), Norman Shelley (Man in Straw Hat), Kathleen Harrison (Waitress), Pat Leonard (Receptionist), Gerald Case (Colonel Dennington), Garry Marsh (Captain Goodhusband), Tom Macaulay (Lieutenant Spanswick), Dorothy Bramhall (A. T. S. Corporal), Cameron Hall (Usher in Tynewald Court), Joan Hickson (Hotel Manageress), Dorothy Percheron (Receptionist), George Woodbridge (Walter), Harry Hutchinson (Chief Mourner), Albert Sharpe (Irish Landlord), Bob Elson (Policeman), Brenda Bruce (American Girl), Eddie Byrne and Austin Meldon (Customs Officials), Leslie Dwyer (Soldier with Newspaper), Kathleen Murphy (First Irish Woman), Josephine Fitzgerald (Second Irish Woman), Ethel O'Shea (Mrs Hogan), Patricia Laffan

## *Green for Danger* 10 March 1947, 91 mins

Director: Sidney Gilliat
Production company: Individual Pictures. A Frank Launder–Sidney
    Gilliat Production
Scenario: Sidney Gilliat, Claud Gurney
Based on the novel by Christianne Brand
Photography: Wilkie Cooper
Editor: Thelma Myers
Music: William Alwyn
Music director: Muir Mathieson
Production designer: Peter Proud
Art director: W. E. Hutchinson
Wardrobe: Kathleen Moore
Sound supervisor: John S. Dennis
Cast: Sally Gray (Nurse Freddi Linley), Trevor Howard (Dr Barnes),
    Rosamund John (Nurse Sanson), Alastair Sim (Inspector Cockrill),
    Leo Genn (Dr Eden), Megs Jenkins (Nurse Woods), Judy Campbell
    (Sister Bates), Moore Marriott (Postman Joseph Higgins), Henry
    Edwards (Mr Purdy), Ronald Adam (Dr White), George Wood-
    bridge (Detective Sergeant Henricks)

*Captain Boycott* 27 October 1947, 93 mins

Director: Frank Launder
Production company: Individual Pictures. A Sidney Gilliat–Frank Launder Production
Based on the novel by Philip Rooney
Scenario: Frank Launder, Wolfgang Wilhelm
Additional dialogue: Paul Vincent Carroll, Patrick Campbell
Photography: Wilkie Cooper
Editor: Thelma Myers
Music: William Alwyn
Music director: Muir Mathieson
Art director: Edward Carrick
Sound supervisor: J. S. Dennis
Costume supervisor: John Godenian
Costumes: Sophie Harris
Cast: Stewart Granger (Hugh Davin), Kathleen Ryan (Anne Killain), Cecil Parker (Captain Boycott), Mervyn Johns (Watty Connell), Noel Purcell (Daniel McGinty), Niall McGinnis (Mark Killain), Liam Redmond (Martin Egan), Liam Gaffney (Michael Fagan), Bernadette O'Farrell (Mrs Fagan), Edward Lexy (Sergeant Dempsey), Harry Webster (Robert Hogan), Robert Donat (Charles Stewart Parnell), Eddie Golden (Harry Piggott), Harry Hutchinson (Shamus Moore), Maurice Denham (Lieutenant-Colonel Strickland), Phyllis Ryan (Bridget), Joe Linnane (Auctioneer), Ian Fleming (*Times* Correspondent), Reginald Purdell (American Reporter), Cavan Malone (Billy Killain), John Kelly (Sheriff), Anne Clery (Post Mistress), Shelagh Carty (Mary Creog), Michael Ripper (Pat Nolan), Norah O'Mahoney (Irish Villager), Bill Shine (Press Photographer), James Hayter (Music Hall Comic), Nora Finn (Farmer's Wife)

*London Belongs to Me* 13 September 1948, 112 mins

Director: Sidney Gilliat
Production company: Individual Pictures
Producers: Frank Launder, Sidney Gilliat
Based on the novel by Norman Collins
Scenario: Sidney Gilliat, J. B. Williams
Photography: Wilkie Cooper
Editor: Thelma Myers

Music: Benjamin Frankel
Music director: Muir Mathieson
Art director: Roy Oxley
Sound recording: Jack Locke
Wardrobe: Dorothy Perry
Cast: Richard Attenborough (Percy Boon), Alastair Sim (Mr Squales), Stephen Murray (Uncle Henry), Fay Compton (Mrs Josser), Susan Shaw (Doris Josser), Ivy St Helier (Connie), Wylie Watson (Mr Josser), Andrew Crawford (Detective Bill Todds), Eleanor Summerfield (Myrna), Gladys Henson (Mrs Boon), Hugh Griffith (Headlam Flynne), Arthur Howard (Mr Chinkwell), Maurice Denham (Jack Rufus), Jack McNaughton (Jimmy), Hatton Duprez (Campbell), Ivor Barnard (Judge), Kenneth Downey (Veesey Blaize), Cecil Trouncer (Wassall), Lionel Gross (Usher), Russell Waters (Clerk of the Court), Michael Kent (Pathologist), Basil Cunard (Foreman of the Jury), Cyril Chamberlain (Detective Taylor), Edward Evans (Detective Jenkins), John Salew (Barks), Henry Edwards (Superintendent), Fabia Drake (Mrs Jan Byl), Alexis France (Miss Bowker)

## *The Blue Lagoon* 18 April 1949, 93 mins

Director: Frank Launder
Production company: Individual Pictures. A Sidney Gilliat–Frank Launder Production
Based on the novel by H. de Vere Stacpoole
Scenario: Frank Launder, John Baines, Michael Hogan
Photography: Geoffrey Unsworth
Supervising editor: Thelma Myers
Editor: Joan Warwick
Art director: Edward Carrick
Music: Clifton Parker
Sound recording: Charlie Poulton, John S. Dennis
Wardrobe: John Gudenian, Dorothy Edwards
Gown designer: Liz Hennings
Cast: Jean Simmons (Emmeline Foster), Donald Houston (Michael Reynolds), Susan Stranks (Emmeline as a Child), Peter Jones (Michael as a Child), Noel Purcell (Paddy Button), James Hogan (Dr Edgar Murdoch), Cyril Cusack (James Carter), Nora Nicholson (Mrs Stannard), Maurice Denham (Captain of Cargo Ship), Philip Stainton (Mr Anstey, First Mate), Patrick Barr (Mr Bruce, Second

Mate), Lyn Evans (Trotter), Russell Waters (Craggs), John Boxer (Nick Corbett), Bill Raymond (Marsden), Kethleen Boutall (Other Woman), Gladys Boot (Woman on Yacht), Edwin Styles (Man on Yacht), Captain Gray (Knife Thrower), E. A. Kelly (Leprechaun), Anthony Verney (First Sailor on Yacht), Stuart Lindsell (Sailor), Frank Coburn (Sailor)

### *The Happiest Days of Your Life* 10 April 1950, 81 mins

Director: Frank Launder
Production company: Individual Pictures. A Sidney Gilliat–Frank Launder Production
Based on John Dighton's play, *The Happiest Days of Your Life*
Scenario: Frank Launder, John Dighton
Photography: Stan Pavey
Editor: Oswald Hafenrichter
Music: Mischa Spoliasky
Sound supervisor: G. Burgess
Title background: Ronald Searle
Dress designer: Joan Ellacott
Cast: Alastair Sim (Wetherby Pond), Margaret Rutherford (Miss Whitchurch), John Bentley (Tassell), Guy Middleton (Hyde-Brown), John Turnbull (Matthews), Richard Wattis (Billings), Edward Rigby (Rainbow), Harold Goodwin (Edwin), Percy Walsh (Monsieur Jove), Arthur Howard (Ramsden), Myrette Morven (Miss Chappell), Patience Rentoull (Miss Armstrong), Millicent Wolf (Miss Curtis), Gladys Henson (Mrs Hampstead), Muriel Aked (Miss Jezzard), Joyce Grenfell (Miss Gossage), Bernadette O'Farrell (Miss Harper), Gladys Henson (Mrs Hampstead), Kenneth Downey (Sir Angus McNalley), Lawrence Naismith (Dr Collet), Stringer Davis (Reverend Rich), Kenneth Downey (Sir Angus MacNally), Stanley Lemin (Mr Parry), Olwen Brookes (Mrs Parry), Alan Broadhurst (Mr Ibbetson), Vivienne Wood (Mrs Ibbetson), Nan Munro (Mrs Jones), Russell Waters (Mr West), George Benson (Mr Tripp), Angela Glynn (Barbara Colhone), Pat Owens (Angela Parry), Margaret Anderson (Alice), Betty Blackler (Mary), Fred Marshall (Metcalfe), John Rhodes (Cranbourne), Jim Davies (Talbot), Keith Faulkner (Unsworth), William Symons (Oliver)

***State Secret*** 11 September 1950, 97 mins

Director: Sidney Gilliat
Production company: London Films
Producers: Frank Launder, Sidney Gilliat
Scenario: Sidney Gilliat
Photography: Robert Krasker
Editor: Thelma Myers
Music: William Alwyn
Art director: Wilfrid Shingleton
Sound recording: Alan Allen
Costumes: Beatrice Dawson, Ivy Baker
Cast: Douglas Fairbanks, Jr (Dr John Marlowe), Glynis Johns (Lisa),
    Therese Van Kye (Teresa), Olga Lowe (Baba), Jack Hawkins
    (Colonel Galcon), Walter Rilla (General Niva), Karel Stepanek (Dr
    Revo), Leonard Sachs (Dr Poldoi), Herbert Lom (Theodor), Robert
    Ayres (Buckman), Howard Douglas, Martin Boddey, Russell
    Waters, Arthur Howard (Clubmen), Carl Jaffe (Janovic Prada),
    Gerard Heinz (Bendel), Leslie Linder (André), Paul Demel (Barber),
    Danny Green (Taxi Driver)

***Lady Godiva Rides Again*** 7 January 1952, 90 mins

Director: Frank Launder
Production company: London Films in association with British Lion
    Film Corporation
Scenario: Frank Launder, Val Valentine
Photography: Wilkie Cooper
Editor: Thelma Connell
Music: William Alwyn
Music director: Muir Mathieson
Sound supervisor: John Cox
Art director: Joseph Bato
Costumes: Anna Duse
Cast: Pauline Stroud (Marjorie Clark), John McCallum (Larry Burns),
    Dennis Price (Simon Abbott), Stanley Holloway (Mr Thomas
    Clark), Gladys Henson (Mrs Clark), Bernadette O'Farrell (Jane),
    Kay Kendall (Sylvia), Cyril Chamberlain (Harry), George Cole
    (Johnny West), Diana Dors (Dolores August), Eddie Byrne (Eddie
    Mooney), Lyn Evans (Vic Kennedy), Dora Bryan (Film Publicity
    Woman), Fred Berger (Mr Green), Alastair Sim (Mr Murington),

Dagmar Wynter (Myrtle Shaw), Renée Houston (Beattie), Richard Wattis (Casting Director), Sidney James (Lew Beeson), Lucille Laroche (Charlotte Mitchell), Googie Withers (Simon Abbott's Co-star in 'The Shadow of the Orient'), [Trevor Howard (at film preview)] Jimmy Young (Singer at Lady Godiva Contest), Leslie Mitchell (BBC Interviewer), Russell Waters (Shop Customer)

## Folly to be Wise 19 January 1953, 91 mins

Director: Frank Launder
Production company: London Films. A Sidney Gilliat–Frank Launder Production
Based on the play *It Depends What You Mean* by James Bridie
Scenario: Frank Launder, John Dighton
Photography: Jack Hildyard
Editor: Thelma Connell
Music: Temple Abady
Art director: Arthur Lawson
Sound recording: Peter Handford
Wardrobe: Ivy Baker
Cast: Alastair Sim (Captain Paris), Roland Culver (George Prout), Elizabeth Allan (Angela Prout), Martita Hunt (Lady Dodds), Miles Malleson (Dr McAdam), Colin Gordon (Professor Mutch), Edward Chapman (Joseph Byres, MP), Janet Brown (Jessie Killigrew), Peter Martyn (Walter), Robin Bailey (Intellectual), Clement McCallin (Colonel), Michael Ripper (Corporal), Leslie Weston (Landlord), Michael Kelly (Staff Sergeant), George Cole

## The Story of Gilbert and Sullivan September 1953, 109 mins

Director: Sidney Gilliat. A Frank Launder–Sidney Gilliat Production, for London Film Productions
Scenario: Sidney Gilliat, Leslie Baily
Photography: Christopher Challis, Edward Scaife
Production designer: Hein Heckroth
Art director: Joseph Bato
Music director/conductor: Sir Malcolm Sargent
Sound supervisor: John Cox
Costumes: Hein Heckroth, Elizabeth Haffenden
A general credit to Vincent Korda 'for his contribution to this production'

Cast: Robert Morley (W. S. Gilbert), Maurice Evans (Arthur Sullivan), Eileen Herlie (Helen Lenoir), Isabel Dean (Mrs Gilbert), Peter Finch (Richard D'Oyly Carte), Martyn Green (George Grossmith), Dinah Sheridan (Grace Marston), Muriel Aked (Queen Victoria), Wilfred Hyde-White (Mr Marston), Michael Ripper (Louis), Bernadette O'Farrell (Jessie Bond), Eric Berry (Rutland Barrington), Lloyd Lamble (Joseph Bennett), Ian Wallace (Captain), Richard Warner (Cellier), Perlita Neilson (Lettie), Charlotte Mitchell (Charlotte), Stella Riley (Millicent), Leonard Sachs (Smythe), Owen Brannigan, Anthony Snell, Muriel Brunskill, Anne Hanslip, Yvonne Marsh, Tom Round, Harold Williams, Gron Davies, John Banks, John Hughes. With the singing voices of Webster Booth, Martyn Green, Elsie Morison, Marjorie Thomas, John Cameron, Gordon Clinton, Owen Brannigan, Harold Williams, Tom Round, Muriel Brunskill, Jennifer Vyvyan, Joan Gillingham, Sidney Gilliat

## *The Constant Husband* 16 May 1954, 88 mins

Director: Sidney Gilliat
Production company: London Films for British Lion Film Productions. A Frank Launder–Sidney Gilliat Production
Scenario: Sidney Gilliat, Val Valentine
Photography: Ted Scaife
Editor: Gerald Turney-Smith
Music: Malcolm Arnold
Art director: Wilfrid Shingleton
Sound supervisor: John Cox
Costumes: Anna Duse
Cast: Rex Harrison (A Man Who Has Lost His Memory), Margaret Leighton (Miss Chesterman), Kay Kendall (Monica), Cecil Parker (Professor Llewellyn), Nicole Maurey (Lola Sopranelli), George Cole (Luigi Sopranelli), Raymond Huntley (J. F. Hassett), Michael Hordern (The Judge), Robert Coote (Jack Carter), Eric Pohlmann (Papa Sopranelli), Marie Burke (Moma Sopranelli), Eric Berry (Prosecuting Counsel), Arthur Howard (Clerk of the Court), Charles Lloyd Pack (Mr Daniels, Solicitor), Derek Sydney (Giorgio Sopranelli), Guy Deghy (Stromboli), Valerie French (Bridget), Jill Adams (Joanna Brewer), Ursula Howells (Ann Pargiter), Roma Dumville (Elizabeth), Sally Lahee (Nurse)

***The Belles of St Trinian's*** 15 November 1954, 91 mins

Director: Frank Launder
Production company: London Films, for British Lion Film Productions.
   A Sidney Gilliat–Frank Launder Production
Scenario: Frank Launder, Sidney Gilliat, Val Valentine. Inspired by
   the original drawings of the girls and staff of St Trinian's by
   Ronald Searle
Photography: Stanley Pavey
Editor: Thelma Connell
Music: Malcolm Arnold
Sound supervisor: John Cox
Costumes: Anna Duse
Wardrobe supervisor: Bridget Sellers
Cast: Alastair Sim (Miss Millicent Fritton/Clarence Fritton), Joyce
   Grenfell (Ruby Gates), George Cole (Flash Harry), Betty Ann Davies
   (Miss Waters), Hermione Baddeley (Miss Drownder), Lloyd Lamble
   (Superintendent Kemp Bird), Irene Handl (Miss Gale), Renée
   Houston (Miss Brimmer), Beryl Reid (Miss Wilson), Richard Wattis
   (Manton Bassett), Sidney James (Benny Holster), Michael Ripper
   (Albert Faning), Guy Middleton (Rowbottom-Smith), Arthur
   Howard (Woodley), Eric Pohlmann (Sultan of Makyad), Stuart
   Saunders (Police Sergeant), Mary Merrall (Miss Buckland), Joan
   Sims (Miss Dawn), Balbina (Miss De St Emilion), Jerry Verno (Alf,
   Bookmaker), Jane Henderson (Miss Holland), Jean Langston
   (Rosie), Belinda Lee (Amanda), Vivienne Wood (Miss Anderson),
   Cara Stevens (Sultan's Secretary), Jack Doyle (Assistant Trainer),
   Andrée Melly (Lucretia Baldock), Elizabeth Griffiths (Gladys
   Hunter), Vivienne Martin (Arabella), Diana Day (Jackie), Pauline
   Drewett (Celia), Jill Braidwood (Florrie), Lorna Henderson (Prin-
   cess Fatima), Annabel Covey (Maudie), Wendy Adams (Maryella),
   Gillian Gordon-Inglis (Daphne Potter), Gillian Town (Celeste
   West), Jeanne Marsh, Shirley Eaton, Ronald Searle

***Geordie*** 3 October 1955, 99 mins

Director: Frank Launder
Production company: Argonaut Films. A Sidney Gilliat–Frank Launder
   Production
Based on the novel by David Walker

Scenario: Sidney Gilliat, Frank Launder
Photography: Wilkie Cooper
Supervising editor: Thelma Connell
Music: William Alwyn
Art director: Norman Arnold
Sound supervisor: John Cox
Costumes: Anna Duse
Cast: Bill Travers (Geordie), Alastair Sim (The Laird), Norah Gorsen (Jean Donaldson), Molly Urquhart (Geordie's Mother), Jameson Clark (Geordie's Father), Francis de Wolff (Henry Samson), Alex Mackenzie (Macrimmon), Jack Radcliffe (Reverend Macnab), Brian Reece (Harley), Raymond Huntley (Bill Rawlins), Doris Goddard (Helga), Miles Malleson (Lord Paunceton), Stanley Baxter (Mr Duncan the Postman), Duncan Macrae (Schoolmaster), Paul Young (Young Geordie), Anna Ferguson (Young Jean)

## *The Green Man* 29 October 1956, 89 mins

Director: Robert Day
Supervising director: Basil Dearden
Production company: Grenadier Productions. Presented and produced by Frank Launder and Sidney Gilliat
Scenario: Sidney Gilliat, Frank Launder. Based on their play *Meet a Body*
Photography: Gerald Gibbs
Editor: Bernard Gribble
Music: Cedric Thorpe Davie
Music director: Muir Mathieson
Art director: Wilfrid Shingleton
Sound recording: Buster Ambler
Costumes: Anna Duse
Cast: Alastair Sim (Hawkins), George Cole (William Blake), Terry-Thomas (Boughtflower), Jill Adams (Ann Vincent), Avril Angers (Marigold), John Chandos (McKecknie), Dora Bryan (Lily), Colin Gordon (Reginald), Eileen Moore (Joan Wood), Raymond Huntley (Sir Gregory Upshott), Cyril Chamberlain (Sergeant Bassett), Doris Yorke (Mrs Bostock), Arthur Brough (Landlord), Maria Burke (Felicity), Vivienne Wood (Annabel), Peter Bull (General Niva), Arthur Lowe (Radio Salesman), Michael Ripper (Waiter), Leslie Weston (Porter)

### *Fortune is a Woman* 15 April 1957, 95 mins

Director: Sidney Gilliat
Production company: John Harvel Productions. A Frank Launder–
Sidney Gilliat Production
Based on the novel by Winston Graham
Scenario: Sidney Gilliat, Frank Launder
Adaptation: Val Valentine
Photography: Gerald Gibbs
Editor: Geoffrey Foot
Music: William Alwyn
Music director: Muir Mathieson
Art director: Wilfrid Shingleton
Costumes: Anthony Mendleson
Sound recording: John Aldred
Cast: Jack Hawkins (Oliver Bramwell), Arlene Dahl (Sarah Moreton),
  Dennis Price (Tracey Moreton), Violet Farebrother (Mrs Moreton),
  Ian Hunter (Clive Fisher), Malcolm Keen (Old Abercrombie),
  Geoffrey Keen (Michael Abercrombie), Patrick Holt (Fred Connor),
  John Robinson (Berkeley Reckitt), Michael Goodliffe (Sergeant
  Barnes), Martin Lane (Detective Constable Watson), Bernard Miles
  (Mr Jerome), Christopher Lee (Charles Highbury), Greta Gynt (Vera
  Litchen), John Phillips (Willis Croft), Patricia Marmont (Ambrosine)

### *Blue Murder at St Trinian's* 31 March 1958, 86 mins

Director: Frank Launder
Production company: John Harvel Productions. Produced and presented
  by Sidney Gilliat and Frank Launder, in association with British
  Lion Films
Scenario: Frank Launder, Val Valentine, Sidney Gilliat
Photography: Gerald Gibbs
Editor: Geoffrey Foot
Music: Malcolm Arnold
Art director: Allan Harris
Sound supervisor: John Cox
Costumes: Anna Duse
Cast: Terry-Thomas (Captain Romney Carlton-Ricketts), George Cole
  (Flash Harry), Joyce Grenfell (Sergeant Ruby Gates), Alastair Sim
  (Miss Fritton), Sabrina (Virginia), Lionel Jeffries (Joe Mangan),
  Lloyd Lamble (Superintendent Kemp-Bird), Raymond Rollett

(Chief Constable), Terry Scott (Police Sergeant), Ferdy Mayne (Italian Police Inspector), Thorley Walters (Major), Cyril Chamberlain (Captain), Judith Furse (Dame Maud Hackshaw), Kenneth Griffith (Charlie Bull), Eric Barker (Culpepper-Brown), Richard Wattis (Manton Bassett), Guido Lorraine (Prince Bruco), Alma Taylor (His Mother), Charles Lloyd Pack (Henry Roberts, Prison Governor), Lisa Gastoni (Myrna Mangan), Jose Read (Cynthia), Dilys Laye (Bridget), Rosalind Knight (Annabelle), Patricia Lawrence (Mavis), Vikki Hammond (Jane Osborne), Nicola Braithwaite (Daphne), Janet Bradbury (Mercia), Amanda Coxell (Tilly), Moya Francis (Bissy), Marianne Brauns (Fluffy)

## *The Bridal Path* 24 August 1959, 95 mins

Director: Frank Launder
Production company: Vale Film Productions in association with British Lion. Presented and produced by Sidney Gilliat and Frank Launder
Based on the novel by Nigel Tranter
Scenario: Frank Launder, Geoffrey Willans
Photography: Arthur Ibbetson
Editor: Geoffrey Foot
Music: Cedric Thorpe Davie
Music director: Muir Mathieson
Art director: Wilfrid Shingleton
Sound recording: Freddy Ryan
Wardrobe: Irma Birch
Cast: Bill Travers (Ewan McEwan), Alex Mackenzie (Finlay), Eric Woodburn (Archie), Jack Lambert (Hector), John Rae (Angus), Roddy McMillan (Murdo), Jefferson Clifford (Wallace), Neil Ballantyne (Jessie), Fiona Cryne (Katie), Bernadette O'Farrell (Siona), Patricia Bredin (Margaret), Dilys Laye (Isobel), Joan Fitzpatrick (Sarah), Pekoe Ainsley (Craigie), Joan Benham (Barmaid), Annette Crosbie (Grand Looking Waitress), Nancy Mitchell (Hotel Waitress), Lynda King (Bank Clerk), George Cole (Sergeant Bruce), Gordon Jackson (Constable Alec), Robert James (Inspector), Terry Scott (Constable Donald), Duncan Macrae (Sergeant), Jameson Clark (P.C. at Crossroads), John Dunbar (Sergeant Macconochie), Andrew Downie (Constable Hamish), Vincent Winter (Neal), Elizabeth Campbell (Kirstie), Myreth Morney (Mrs Macchonochie), Eddie Byrne (Mike Flanagan), Russell Waters (Bank Cashier)

### *Left, Right and Centre* 7 September 1959, 95 mins

Director: Sidney Gilliat
Production company: Vale Film Productions in association with British
 Lion
Producers: Frank Launder, Sidney Gilliat
Story: Sidney Gilliat, Val Valentine
Scenario: Sidney Gilliat
Editor: Gerald Handling
Photography: Gerald Gibbs
Supervising editor: Geoffrey Foot
Music: Humphrey Searle
Scenario artist: Ernest Smith
Sound recording: P. T. Handford
Wardrobe: Felix Evans
Cast: Ian Carmichael (Robert Wilcot), Patricia Bredin (Stella Stoker),
 Alastair Sim (Lord Wilcot), Eric Barker (Bert Gummer), Jack Hedley
 (Bill Hemingway), Leslie Dwyer (Alf Stoker), Philip Morant
 (Bulson), Russell Waters (Mr Bray), Hattie Jacques (Woman in
 Car), Richard Wattis (Harding-Pratt), Moira Fraser (Annabel),
 William Kendall (Pottle), George Benson (Egerton), Anthony Sharp
 (Peterson), Moultrie Kelsall (Grimsby-Armfield), Olwen Brookes
 (Mrs Samson), Gordon Harker (Hardy), Frederick Leister (Dr
 Rushall), John Salew (Mayor), Bill Shine (Basingstoke), Eric Chitty
 (Returning Officer), Jeremy Hawke (TV Interviewer), Redmond
 Phillips (Mr Smithson), Irene Handl (Mrs Maggs), [Sidney Gilliat
 (Sleeping Member of the Electorate)] TV Panel: Eamonn Andrews,
 Gilbert Harding, Carole Carr, Josephine Douglas

### *The Pure Hell of St Trinian's* 23 January 1961, 94 mins

Director: Frank Launder
Production company: Vale Film Productions in association with British
 Lion, Hallmark Productions and Tudor Productions
Producers: Sidney Gilliat, Frank Launder
Scenario: Frank Launder, Val Valentine, Sidney Gilliat
Photography: Gerald Gibbs
Music: Malcolm Arnold
Art director: Wilfrid Shingleton
Sound recording: H. C. Pearson, Red Law
Costumes: Honoria Plesch

Wardrobe: Bridget Sellers

Cast: Cecil Parker (Professor Canford), Joyce Grenfell (Sergeant Ruby Gates), George Cole (Flash Harry), Thorley Walters (Butters), Eric Barker (Culpepper Brown), Irene Handl (Miss Mathilda Hacker-Packer), Dennis Price (Charles Gore-Blackwood), Lloyd Lamble (Superintendent Kemp-Bird), Liz Fraser (Miss Partridge), Sidney James (Alphonse O'Reilly), Nicholas Phipps (Major), Cyril Chamberlain (Captain), Raymond Huntley (Judge), Elwyn Brook-Jones (Emir), John Le Mesurier (The Minister), Lisa Lee (Miss Daphne Brenner), Clive Morton (VIP), Harold Berens (British Consul), Julie Alexander (Rosalie Dawn), Maria Lennard (Millicent), Dawn Berret (Jane), Ann Wain (Lolita Chatterley), Gilda Emmanuelli (Minnie Henn), Sally Bulloch (Maud Birdhanger), Warren Mitchell (Mr Campbell, Tailor)

## *Only Two Can Play* 5 February 1962, 106 mins

Director: Sidney Gilliat

Production company: Vale Productions

A Frank Launder–Sidney Gilliat production in association with British Lion

Producer: Leslie Gilliat

Based on the novel *That Uncertain Feeling* by Kingsley Amis

Scenario: Bryan Forbes

Photography: John Wilcox

Editor: Thelma Connell

Music: Richard Rodney Bennett

Art director: Albert Witherick

Sound recording: Cecil Mason, Red Law

Wardrobe: Muriel Dickson

Cast: Peter Sellers (John Lewis), Mai Zetterling (Elizabeth), Virginia Maskell (Jean), Richard Attenborough (Gareth Probert), Kenneth Griffiths (Ieuan Jenkins), Sheila Manahan (Mrs Jenkins), Maudie Edwards (Mrs Davis), Frederick Piper (Mr Davies), John Arnatt (Bill), John Le Mesurier (Salter), Raymond Huntley (Vernon), David Davis (Beynon), Graham Stark (Hyman), Meredith Edwards (Clergyman on the Committee), Eynon Evans (Clerk at the Town Hall), Marjie Lawrence (Girl on Bus), Charles Lloyd Pack (Committee Member), Gerald Sim (Guest at Party)

**_Ring of Spies_** 19 March 1963, 90 mins

Director: Robert Tronson
Production company: British Lion Films
Producer: Leslie Gilliat
Scenario: Frank Launder, Peter Barnes
Photography: Arthur Lavis
Editor: Thelma Connell
Sound recording: Cecil Mason
Art director: Norman Arnold
Cast: Bernard Lee (Harry Houghton), William Sylvester (Lonsdale),
    Margaret Tyzack (Elizabeth Gee), David Kossoff (Peter Kroger),
    Nancy Nevinson (Helen Kroger), Thorley Walter (Commander
    Winter), Gillian Lewis (Marjorie Shaw), Brian Nissen (Lieutenant
    Downes), Newton Blick (Police Officer Meadows), Philip Latham
    (Captain Ray), Howard Pays (Police Officer Garton), Cyril Cham-
    berlain (Anderson), Justine Lord (Christina), Richard Marner
    (Colonel Monat), Norma Foster (Ella), Anita West (Tilly), Edwin
    Apps (Blake), Patrick Barr (Captain Warner), Garry Marsh (First
    Member at Lord's), Basil Dignam (Second Member at Lord's),
    Derek Francis (Chief Supt. Croft)

**_Joey Boy_** 4 April 1965, 91 mins

Director: Frank Launder
Production company: Tenegrance. A Sidney Gilliat–Frank Launder
    Production
Producer: Leslie Gilliat
Based on the novel by Edward Chapman
Scenario: Frank Launder, Mike Watts
Photography: Arthur Lavis
Editor: John Shirley
Music: Philip Green
Art director: George Provis
Sound recording: Buster Ambler, Robert Jones
Cast: Harry H. Corbett (Joey Boy Thompson), Stanley Baxter ('Benny
    the Kid' Lindowski), Bill Fraser (Sergeant Dobbs), Percy Herbert
    ('Mad George' Long), Lance Percival (Clarence Doubleday), Reg
    Varney ('Rabbit' Malone), John Arnatt (Brigadier Chapman), Derek
    Nimmo (Lieutenant Hope), Anna Gilchrist (Rebecca), Cyril Cham-
    berlain (R. A. Lieutenant), Lloyd Lamble (Sir John Averycorn), Eric

Pohlmann (Italian Farmer), Moira Lister (Lady Thameridge), Thorley Walters (Colonel)

## *The Great St Trinian's Train Robbery* 11 March 1966, 94 mins

Directors: Frank Launder, Sidney Gilliat
Production company: Braywild. A Frank Launder–Sidney Gilliat Presentation
Producer: Leslie Gilliat
Executive producer: Sidney Gilliat
Story: Frank Launder, Sidney Gilliat, Leslie Gilliat
Scenario: Frank Launder, Ivor Herbert
Photography: Kenneth Hodges
Editor: Geoffrey Foot
Music: Malcolm Arnold
Art director: Albert Witherick
Sound recording: Cecil Mason, Bob Jones
Costumes: Honoria Plesch
Wardrobe: Dora Lloyd
Cast: Frankie Howerd (Alphonse Askett), Reg Varney (Gilbert), Desmond Walter-Ellis (Leonard Edwards), Norman Mitchell (William), Larry Martyn (Chips), Cyril Chamberlain (Maxie), Arthur Mullard (Big Jim), Stratford Johns (The Voice), Dora Bryan (Amber Spottiswoode, Headmistress), Barbara Couper (Mabel Radnage, Deputy Head), Elspeth Duxbury (Maths Mistress), Maggie McGrath (Games Mistress), Margaret Nolan (Art Mistress), Jean St. Clair (Music Mistress), Carole Ann Ford (French Mistress), George Cole (Flash Harry), Portland Mason (Georgina), Maureen Crombie (Marcia Askett), Raymond Huntley (The Minister), Richard Wattis (Manton Bassett), Peter Gilmore (Butters), Eric Barker (Culpepper-Brown), George Benson (Gore-Blackwood), Godfrey Winn (Trulove), Lisa Lee (Miss Brenner), Colin Gordon (Noakes), Salley Geeson

## *Endless Night* 22 October 1972, 99 mins

Director: Sidney Gilliat
Production company: National Films Trustee Company in association with British Lion Films and EMI Film Productions. A Frank Launder–Sidney Gilliat Production
Executive producer: Frank Launder

Producer: Leslie Gilliat
Based on the novel by Agatha Christie
Scenario: Sidney Gilliat
Photography: Harry Waxman
Editor: Thelma Connell
Music: Bernard Herrmann
Scenario artist: Peter Wood
Sound recording: Paul Le Mare, Bill Rowe
Wardrobe: Barbara Gillett
Costumes: John Furness
Cast: Hayley Mills (Ellie), Hywel Bennett (Michael), Britt Ekland (Greta), George Sanders (Lippincott), Per Oscarsson (Santonix), Peter Bowles (Reuben), Lois Maxwell (Cora), Aubrey Richards (Philpott), Patience Collier (Miss Townsend), Madge Ryan (Michael's Mother), Walter Gotell (Constantine), Geoffrey Chater (Coroner), David Healey (Jason), Robert Keegan (Innkeeper), Robert O'Neil (Broker), Mischa de la Motte (Maynard), Leo Genn (Psychiatrist), Windsor Davies (Sergeant Keene), Ann Way (Mrs Philpott), Russell Waters (Waiter)

### *The Wildcats of St Trinian's* May 1980, 91 mins

Director: Frank Launder
Production company: Wildcat Film Productions
Producer: E. M. Smedley-Aston
Production consultant: Sidney Gilliat
Scenario: Frank Launder
Photography: Ernest Steward
Editor: Antony Gibbs
Art director: John Beard
Music: James Kenelm Clarke
Costumes: Masada Wilmot
Sound recording: John Bramall
Cast: Sheila Hancock (Olga Vandemeer), Michael Horden (Sir Charles Hackforth), Joe Melia (Flash Harry), Thorley Walters (Culpepper-Brown), Rodney Bewes (Peregrine Butters), Deborah Norton (Miss Brenner), Maureen Lipman (Katy Higgs), Julia McKenzie (Dolly Dormancott), Ambrosine Philpotts (Mrs Mowbray), Rose Hill (Miss Martingale), Diana King (Miss Mactavish), Luan Peters (Poppy Adams), Patsy Smart (Mrs Wormold), Bernadette O'Farrell

(Miss Carfax), Sandra Payne (Mrs Taylor), Frances Ruffell (Princess Roxanne), Hilda Brand (Miss Summers), Veronica Quillan (Lizzie), Miranda Honnisett (Jennie), Eileen Fletcher (Agatha), Anna McKeown (Harriet), Sarah Jane Varley (Janet), Theresa Ratcliff (Maggie), Lisa Vanderpump (Ursula), Debbie Linden (Mavis), Sandra Hall ('Big Freda'), Eliza Emery ('Butch'), Suzanna Hamilton (Matilda Harcourt), Danielle Corgan (Eva Potts), Ballard Berkeley (Humphrey Wills)

# Select bibliography

Aldgate, Anthony and Richards, Jeffrey, *Britain Can Take It: The British Cinema in the Second World War* (Basil Blackwell, Oxford, 1986).

Amis, Kingsley, *That Uncertain Feeling* (Victor Gollancz, London, 1984).

Babington, Bruce (ed.), *British Stars and Stardom* (Manchester University Press, Manchester, 2001).

Barr, Charles, *All Our Yesterdays: 90 Years of British Cinema* (BFI, London, 1986).

Barr, Charles, *Ealing Studios* (Tayleur & Cameron in assocation with David & Charles, London, 1977).

Barr, Charles, *English Hitchcock* (Cameron & Hollis, Moffat, 1999).

Brown, Geoff, *Launder and Gilliat* (BFI, London, 1977).

Brown, Geoff, *Walter Forde* (BFI, London, 1977).

Burton, Alan, O'Sullivan, Tim and Wells, Paul, *The Family Way: The Boulting Brothers and British Film Culture* (Flicks Books, Trowbridge, Wiltshire, 2000).

Calder, Angus, *The People's War: Britain 1939–1945* (Jonathan Cape, London, 1971).

Calder, Angus and Sheridan, Dorothy (eds), *Speak for Yourself: A Mass Observation Anthology, 1937–1949* (Jonathan Cape, London, 1983).

Christie, Agatha, *Endless Night* ([1967] Harper Collins, London, 1993).

Christie, Ian, *Powell, Pressburger and Others* (BFI, London, 1978).

Dighton, John, *The Happiest Days of Your Life: A Farce in Three Acts* (Samuel French, London, 1951).

Durgnat, Raymond, *A Mirror for England: British Movies from Austerity to Affluence* (Faber & Faber, London, 1970).

Dyer, Richard, *Brief Encounter* (BFI Classics, London, 1993).

Gledhill, Christine and Swanson, Gillian, 'Gender and Sexuality in Second World War Films – A Feminist Approach', in Geoff Hurd (ed.), *National Fictions: World War Two in British Films and Television* (BFI, London, 1984), pp. 56–62.

Halliwell, Leslie, *Halliwell's Film Guide* (5th edn, Grafton Books, London, 1986).

Harper, Sue, 'The Representation of Women in British Feature Films, 1939–1945', in Philip M. Taylor, *Britain and the Cinema in the Second World War* (Macmillan, Basingstoke and London, 1988), pp. 168–95.

Hennessy, Peter, *Never Again: Britain 1945–1951* (Jonathan Cape, London, 1992).

Higson, Andrew, 'Addressing the Nation: Five Films', in Geoff Hurd (ed.), *National Fictions: World War Two in British Films and Television* (BFI, London, 1984), pp. 22–6.

Higson, Andrew, *Waving the Flag: Constructing a National Cinema in Britain* (Clarendon Press, Oxford, 1995).

Hurd, Geoff (ed.), *National Fictions: World War Two in British Film and Television* (BFI, London, 1984).

Katz, Ephraim, *Macmillan International Film Encyclopedia* (Macmillan, London and Basingstoke, 1994).

Korda, Michael, *Charmed Lives: A Family Romance* (Allen Lane, London, 1980).

Kulic, Karol, *Alexander Korda: The Man Who Could Work Miracles* (W. H. Allen, London, 1975).

Landy, Marcia, *British Genres: Cinema and Society, 1930–1960* (Princeton University Press, Princeton, New Jersey, 1991).

Lant, Antonia, *Blackout: Reinventing Women for Wartime British Cinema* (Princeton University Press, Princeton, New Jersey, 1991).

Lant, Antonia, 'The Female Spy: Gender, Nationality, and War in *I See a Dark Stranger*', in Robert Sklare and Charles Musser (eds), *Resisting Images: Essays in Film and History* (Temple University Press, Philadelphia, 1990), pp. 173–99.

Low, Rachael, *The History of the British Film*, vol. VII, *1918–1929*, (Allen & Unwin, London, 1985).

MacDonald, Kevin, 'Interview with Sidney Gilliat', *Projections* 2, eds, John Boorman and Walter Donohoe (Faber & Faber, London, 1993).

McFarlane, Brian, *An Autobiography of British Cinema* (Methuen, London, 1977).

McFarlane, Brian (ed.), *Sixty Voices: Celebrities Recall the Golden Age of British Cinema* (BFI, London, 1992).

Macnab, Geoffrey, *J. Arthur Rank and the British Film Industry* (Routledge, London, 1993).

Macnab, Geoffrey, *Searching for Stars* (Cassell, London, 2000).

Mannon, Warwick, *The Rake's Progress* [Book of the Film] (World Film Publications, London, 1946).

Marwick, Arthur, *The Home Front: The British and the Second World War* (Thames & Hudson, London, 1976).

Mayer, J. P., *British Cinemas and Their Audiences: Sociological Studies* (Dobson, London, 1948).

Murphy, Robert, *Realism and Tinsel: Cinema and Society in Britain 1939–48* (Routledge, London, 1989).

O'Brien, Geoffrey, 'Stompin' at the Savoy: *Topsy-Turvy*: A Film Directed by Mike Leigh', *New York Review of Books*, 47/3 (2000), 16–19.

Richards, Jeffrey, *Films and British National Identity* (Manchester University Press, Manchester, 1997).

Richards, Jeffrey and Sheridan, Dorothy, *Mass Observation at the Movies* (Routledge & Kegan Paul, London, 1987).

Rockett, Kevin, Gibbons, Luke and Hill, John, *Cinema and Ireland* (Croom Helm, London, 1987).

Stacpoole, H. de Vere, *The Blue Lagoon* ([1908] George Newnes, London, 1918).

Taylor, A. J. P., *English History: 1914–1945* ([1965] Penguin, Harmondsworth, 1970).

Taylor, Philip (ed.), *Britain and the Cinema in the Second World War* (Macmillan, Basingstoke and London, 1988).

Walker, Alexander, *Fatal Charm: The Life of Rex Harrison* (Weidenfeld & Nicolson, London, 1986).

Walker, Alexander, *Hollywood England: The British Film Industry in the Sixties* (Michael Joseph, London, 1994).

Wells, H. G., *Kipps* in *A Quartette of Comedies by H. G. Wells* (Ernest Benn, London, 1928).

# Index

Note: page numbers in *italic* refer to illustrations

Aked, Muriel 30, 67, 68
Allen, Elizabeth 198
*Alligator Named Daisy, An* 156
Alwyn, William 11, 25
*Anna and the King of Siam*
     (1946) 100–1
Anstey, Edgar 72, 76, 97, 99
*Arms and the Man* (Lewis) 21
Archers, The (Powell and
     Pressburger) 1, 2, 94
Arnold, Malcolm 9, 11
Asquith, Anthony 17, 157, 158
Attenborough, Richard 24, 159

Barnes, Peter 176
Barr, Charles 26
*Belles of St Trinian's, The* 157,
     163, 171–2
*Bells Go Down, The* 19, 48
Bennett, Hywel 24, 185
Black, Edward 5, 45, 136
*Blackmail* 23
*Black Narcissus* 27, 94, 140, 146
*Blithe Spirit* 156, 162
*Blue Lagoon, The* (film) 11, 13, 42,
     134–52, 154
*Blue Lagoon, The* (novel) 135–9,

     141, 142, 145–7, 150, 151
*Blue Murder at St Trinian's* 172
*Body Was Well Nourished, The* 26
Bordwell, David 17
Boulting Brothers 3, 14, 15, 17,
     26, 29, 92, 158, 169, 190,
     196, 197, 199, 200
Boutall, Kathleen 68
Bredin, Patricia 201
*Bridal Path, The* 20, 25, 190, 194,
     201–5
*Brigadoon* 29
British International Pictures 4
British Lion Films 3, 5, 17
Brown, Geoffrey 9, 10, 12, 13, 20,
     24, 27, 52, 103, 176, 209
Brown, Janet 198
Buchanan, Jack 4
Buñuel, Luis 142
Burton, Alan, Paul O'Sullivan
     and Tim Wells 26

Calvert, Phyllis 11, 24, 40, 67, 75
Campbell, Judy 180
*Captain Boycott* 20, 119–20, 138
*Captive Heart, The* 66–7
Carey, Joyce 46

Carmichael, Ian 92, 200
Castaway (Roeg) 139, 140, 141, 142, 152
'Celtic Fringe' films 9, 19, 201–5
*Champagne* 4
Cineguild 94
Christie, Agatha 185, 186
*Chu Chin Chow* 11
*Colditz Story, The* 66
Cole, George 24, 111, 136, 185, 200
*Constant Husband, The* 9, 11, 20, 23, 99, 113, 190–3, 194
Conway, Jack 5, 44
Cooper, Wilkie 11
Corbett, Harry H. 92
*Cottage To Let* 157
Coward, Noel 46, 59, 99, 162
Crabtree, Arthur 11, 66
Crawford, Anne 10, *39*, 52, 63–4, 67
*Crazy Gang, The* 5
Cryne, Fiona 202
Cummings, Constance 6
Culver, Roland 198
Cusak, Cyril 139

Dahl, Arlene 183
*Das Testament des Doctor Mabuse* 34
Davies, John Howard 154
Davies, Terence 2, 134
Day, Robert 26
Dearden, Basil 19, 26, 66, 67
De Cartier, Iris 2
de Courville, Albert 5, 20
*Demi-Paradise, The* 158
*Diary For Timothy, A* 85, 89
Dighton, John 154, 155, 160, 164
Donat, Robert 20, 24, 119
Dors, Diana 24, 199
Durgnat, Raymond 9, 15, 120, 157

Donohoe, Amanda 139, 140
Dudley Ward, Penelope 158

Ealing 26, 153, 190, 196, 197, 199, 200
*Edge of the World, The* 205
Ekland, Britt 185
*Elizabeth Our Queen* 130
Elvey, Maurice 19, 48
*Endless Night* (film) 10, 11, 16, 22, 25, I24, 175, 178, 185–7
*Endless Night* (novel) 185, 186, 187
Evans, Maurice 13, 24, 37

Fairbanks, Douglas, Jr 18, 24, 181
*Fame is the Spur* 26
female conscription, *National Service Act* (No. 2) 46
Film Society, The 10, 24
Finch, Peter 29
Fleming Report (1944) 159
*Folly To Be Wise* 24, 138, 155, 190, 196–9, 208
Forbes, Bryan 8, 196
Forde, Walter 5, 20, 44, 176
*Fortune is a Woman* 177, 178, 179, 183–5
*49th Parallel* 121
*French Mistress, A* 169
Frend, Charles 29
*Frenzy* 177
Freud, Sigmund (*Totem and Taboo*) 142
*From the Four Corners* 45
Fyffe, Will 44

Gainsborough 1, 5, 11, 51, 85, 94, 209
Genn, Leo 24, 179
*Gentle Sex, The* 19, 48, 74, 163
*Geordie* 9, 18, 20, 190, 194, 201–5
Gilliat, Leslie 11
*Girl in the News* 6, 44

*Girl Must Live, A* 6
Goddard, Doris 202
Gordon, Colin 20, 198
Gorsen, Norah 202
*Grande Illusion, La* 66
Grainger, Percy 85
Granger, Stewart 24, 40, 84, 85, 86, 87, 119
Gray, Sally 24, 179
*Great Expectations* (Lean) 94, 132
Green, Danny 183
*Green for Danger* 11, 14, 25, 175, 177, 178, 179–81, 185
*Green Man, The* 11, 20, 26, 111, 158
Griffiths, Kenneth 194
*Guinea Pig, The* 159
Gurney, Claud 7
Gynt, Greta 184

Haffenden, Elizabeth 27
Hamer, Robert 157
Hamilton, Guy 157
*Hamlet* (1948) 134
Havelock Allan, Anthony 45, 94
*Happiest Days of Your Life, The* (film) 2, 4, 9, 10, 11, 16, 43, 72, 113, 134–5, 148, 152–71, 173, 190, 208
*Happiest Days of Your Life, The* (play) 154, 155, 160, 164
Harrison, Rex 10, 23, 41, 45, 97, 99–101, 190–2
Havelock Allan, Anthony 45, 94
Hawkins, Jack 24, 181, 182, 183
Hay, Will 5
Hayter, James 138
*Heart of Britain, The* 46
*Heavens Above!* 15, 197, 199
Heckroth, Hein 27
Henson, Gladys 160, 200
Herrmann, Bernard 25, 177
Higson, Andrew 50
Hill, John 119

Hird, Thora 68
Hitchcock, Alfred 4, 5, 9, 10, 17, 20, 22, 23, 175–6, 209
Holloway, Stanley 200
Housman, A. E. 152
Houston, Donald 42, 134, 135, 143, 144
Houston, Renée 24, 40, 67, 68, 82
Hulbert, Claude 5
Hulbert, Jack 5
Hunt, Martita 198
Huntley, Raymond 23, 116, 193, 203
Hyde-White, Wilfred 1

*I'm All Right Jack* 15, 197, 199, 200
*I Know where I'm Going* 205
Independent Frame 13
Independent Producers Ltd 94
Individual Pictures 3, 9, 94
*Inspector Calls, An* 157
*Inspector Hornleigh* films 158
*Inspector Hornleigh Goes To It* 44, 165
*In Which We Serve* 46
*I See A Dark Stranger* 3, 7, 9, 10, 14, 15, 18, 20, 23, 24, 25, 41, 94–6, 115–32

Jackson, Gordon 38, 60, 63
Jaffe, Carl 80
*Jamaica Inn* 6
*Jean Simmons's Blue Lagoon Diary* 134
Jenkins, Megs 24, 180
Jennings, Humphrey 51, 85, 89
*Joey Boy* 92, 190
John, Rosamond 24, 179
Johns, Glynis 24, 182
Johnson, Celia 46
Johnson, Katy 122

Johnston, Margaret 101
Jones, Griffith 101

Kendall, Kay 24, 191, 199, 200
Kent, Jean 24, 75, 77, 78, 86, 101
Kerr, Deborah 24, 41, 94, 96,
    116, 121
*Kind Hearts and Coronets* 146, 190
*Kipps* (film) 6, 21, 44, 110
*Kipps* (novel) 21, 22
Korda, Alexander 2, 21, 26, 27,
    45, 94, 132
Korda, Vincent 26
Kossoff, David 188

*Lady Godiva Rides Again* 13, 19,
    175, 190, 196, 199, 201
*Lady in the Lake, The* 18
*Lady Vanishes, The* 5, 6, 46, 124,
    175–6, 179, 181
*La Grande Illusion* 66
*Lamp Still Burns, The* 19, 48, 68
Landy, Marcia 97, 98, 192, 208
Lang, Fritz 24, 30
*La Sortie des usines Lumière* 51
Lean, David 15, 17, 22, 46, 59,
    132, 154, 209
Lee, Belinda 171
Lee, Bernard 187
*Left, Right and Centre* 190, 196,
    199, 200–1
Leigh, Mike 27, 207, 208
Leigh, Vivien 99
Leighton, Margaret 192, 193
Lejeune, C. A. 59, 65, 97
Levy, Louis 11
Lewis, Roger 11
*Life and Death of Colonel Blimp,
    The* 163
*Listen To Britain* 51
Lockwood, Margaret 6, 44, 99,
    136
Lom, Herbert 24, 182

*London Belongs To Me* 13, 18, 157,
    177
London Films 1, 3, 94
*Long Day Closes, The* 2, 134
Losey, Joseph 23
*Love Story* (1945) 88
Lowe, Edmund 6
Lukas, Paul 181

*M* 34
McCallum, John 200
MacDonald, Kevin 8, 10, 12, 13,
    14, 22, 24, 96, 110, 114,
    176–7
McKechnie, James 70, 80
McKendrick, Alexander 205
*Madonna of the Seven Moons* 87
*Magic Box, The* 29
Malleson, Miles 198
*Manxman, The* 4, 6
Marriott, Moore 57
Maskell, Virginia 196
Masters, John 106
Mathieson, Muir 11
Maurey, Nicole 23
Mayer, J. P. 87
Meyer, Leonard 19
Middleton, Guy 24, 101, 113, 135,
    152, 156
Miller, Max 5
*Millions Like Us* 3, 6, 8, 9, 10, 11,
    16, 18, 30, *38*, 44, 45, 47,
    48, 67, 72, 83, 91, 92, 124,
    164, 180, 189, 201, 207
Mills, Hayley 24, 185
Mills, John 40, 84, 85
Ministry of Information (MOI)
    6–7, 45, 50, 51
*Miranda* 158
*Modesty Blaise* 23
Montgomery, Robert 18, 19
Morley, Robert 13, 24, 28, *37*
*Mr Proudfoot Shows a Light* 45

*Murder Ahoy!* 157
*Murder on the Orient Express* 186
*My Fair Lady* 100
*My Heart is Calling* 11
Myers (Connell), Thelma 11

Naismith, Lawrence 156
Neame, Ronald 94
Neill, William Roy 6
*Newcomes, The* (Thackeray) 114
Newton, Robert 159
Nicholson, Nicky 66
*Night Train to Munich* 45, 56,
    99, 175–6, 179, 189

O'Brien, Geoffrey 27–8, 32–3,
    208
O'Gorman, W. 115
O'Rorke, Brefni 116
*O-Kay for Sound* 11
*Oliver Twist* (Lean) 94, 154
Olivier, Lawrence 114
*Only Two Can Play* 8, 9, 11, 16,
    20, 176, 190–1, 193–6
*Open Window, The* 9
Orwell, George ('Decline of the
    English Murder') 86
*Our Man in Havana* 9

Palmer, Lilli *41*, 102
Parker, Cecil 119, 136, 191
*Partners in Crime* 6, 45
*Passport to Pimlico* 156
Pascal, Gabriel 94
*Perfect Strangers* 132, 163
Portman, Eric 51, 52, 64–5, 121
Powell, Michael 15, 22
Powell, Michael and
    Pressburger, Emeric 17,
    25, 32, 94, 121, 205, 209
Price, Dennis 182
*Private's Progress* 92, 137
Purcell, Noel 137

*Pure Hell of St Trinian's, The* 135,
    172, 193
Purdell, Reginald 70, 80

*Queen is Crowned, A* 30

Radford, Basil 24, 56
*Rake's Progress, The* 7, 11, 12, 18,
    22, 41, 94–115, 132, 146,
    179, 190, 191, 192, 208
Randall, Terry 14
Rank, J. Arthur 1, 2, 13, 96, 134,
    154
*Rebecca* (stage version) 5, 158
*Rebel, The* 26
Redgrave, Michael 6, 22, 136
*Red Prophet* 15
Reed, Carol 5, 15, 20, 21, 44, 45,
    154, 175–6
Reed, Oliver 139, 140
Riefenstahl, Leni 53
Rigby, Edward 166
*Ring of Spies* 8, 16, 177, 178, 179,
    185, 187–9
*Robinson Crusoe* (Buñuel) 142
Robson, Flora 24, 67, 76
Roc, Patricia 24, *38*, *39*, 40, 49,
    51, 52, 63, 67, 69, 73, 75
Roeg, Nicholas 139, 141
*Rome Express* 5–6, 10, 177
Rutherford, Margaret 2, 5, *43*,
    135, 154, 156–9

Sabrina 171
*St Trinian's* cycle 4, 9, 10, 17, 19,
    171–3, 190
Sanders, George 185
Saville, Victor 5
*School for Scoundrels* 157
*Scott of the Antarctic* 29
Sellers, Peter 24, 190–1, 193–6
*Seven Sinners* 5, 10, 177
Shaw, George Bernard 21

Shelton, Joy 82
Sheridan, Dinah 30
Sim, Alastair 5, 10, 24, 43, 85, 88,
        119, 135, 138, 152, 156–9,
        171, 179, 185, 197, 201, 202
Simmons, Jean 24, 42, 134, 135,
        143, 144, 146
Sirk, Douglas 17
*Sleeping Sword* 16
*Soldier, Sailor* 45
*Spitfire* 45
Stacpoole, H. De Vere 13, 135,
        142, 147
*Stalag 17* 66
Stark, Graham 194
*State Secret* 14, 18, 177, 178, 181–3
Stevenson, Robert 5
*Storm in a Teacup* 100
*Story of Gilbert and Sullivan, The*
        8, 9, 11, 13, 18, 27–34, 37,
        67, 207
Stroud, Pauline 199

Tavernier, Bernard 97
Tearle, Geoffrey 98
Thomas, Terry 24
*That Hamilton Woman* 45
*That Uncertain Feeling* (Amis)
        194, 196
*They Came By Night* 44
*They Were Sisters* 63
*Third Man, The* 154
*Thirty-nine Steps, The* (Hitch-
        cock) 177
Thomas, Howard 197
*Tom Brown's Schooldays* (Parry)
        159–60
*Toni* 4
*Topsy Turvy* 27, 208

Travers, Bill 24, 202
Tronson, Robert 8, 177
*Two Thousand Women* 7, 9, 10,
        14, 19, 34, 40, 45, 47, 48,
        49, 58, 60, 63, 66, 85, 92,
        164, 208
*Two Way Stretch* 26
Tyzack, Margaret 187

UFA 10, 20
*Under the Greenwood Tree* 4

Valentine, Val 11, 23
Veidt, Conrad 181
*VIPs, The* 158

*Walkabout* 139, 141
Walker, Alexander 99
Walsh, Kay 46
*Waterloo Road* 7, 8, 11, 23, 40,
        48, 49, 60, 84–92, 157
Wattis, Richard 135, 166
Wayne, Naunton 3, 24, 56
Wells, H. G. 21
*Wildcats of St Trinian's, The* 172
*Whiskey Galore* 205
Wilhelm, Wolfgang 7
Williamson, Malcolm 9
Wolfenstein, Martha and Leites,
        Nathan 157
*Wooden Horse, The* 66
Wynter, Dagmar (Dana) 199

*Yank at Oxford, A* 5
*Young Mr Pitt, The* 6, 20, 45

Zanuck, Darryl F. 44
Zetterling, Mai 191, 194